WHAT THEY'RE SAYING *About Essential Eating, A Cookbook . . .*

"Listening and responding to your body's needs can be the most rewarding experience. *Essential Eating, A Cookbook* shows you how to harvest health and happiness through the application of nutritional intelligence. The recipes are easy to follow and the food tastes great."

—GERALD REISINGER, N.D.
Specializing in Preventative Medicine
Kingston, PA

"*Essential Eating, A Cookbook* offers both a nutritious and delicious core diet that provides our bodies with what is essential to function in the realm of health and well-being. Time and again I encourage our customers to explore its potential."

—LEIGH DUFFY
Manager
Everything Natural Health Food Store
Clarks Summit, PA

"In the attempt to locate a common sense approach to nutrition, *Essential Eating, A Cookbook* provides a detailed road map. It addresses how to reverse our deteriorating national health on a personal level. I highly recommend it!"

—MARY ELAINE SOUTHARD, R.N., M.S.N.
Mercy Health Partners
Scranton, PA

"*Essential Eating* is a practical and highly recommended compendium for the health conscious kitchen cook."

—*Midwest Book Review*

"There is an exceptional radiance about Janie. *Essential Eating, A Cookbook* reveals the secret to her sparkle. For two years this program and its recipes have been my eating companions and today I feel better than ever. *Essential Eating, A Cookbook* curbed my sugar cravings, put a glow in my complexion and increased my energy level. This is the cookbook her friends have been waiting for."

—PENNY LINDGREN
TV News Anchor/Medical Reporter
Wilkes Barre, PA

"I became a believer of this eating program after open heart surgery. What a great source for whole foods recipes that taste great and are heart-healthy. With 500,000 open heart surgeries being performed each year, *Essential Eating, A Cookbook* is an essential read!"

—CHARLES R. WERTZ
Wertz Enterprises, Inc.
Clayton, OH

"Within a month of following *Essential Eating,* I've seen a dramatic increase in my energy level and ability to concentrate. I have also seen a dramatic decrease in my allergic reactions and my weight."

—BARBARA COSTNER
New York, NY

"*Essential Eating* is a life-tested plan that incorporates whole and organic foods for promoting better health without the difficulty of calorie counting or extreme food choices."

—*Bloomsbury Review*

"A weight-loss guide that teaches people to eat real foods that are easy-to-digest."

—*Vegetarian Times*

"A wonderful guide to permanent weight loss with no gimmicks."

—DEEPAK CHOPRA
Author, Grow Younger Live Longer
La Jolla, CA

Essential Eating™

A Cookbook

Discover How to Eat, Not Diet

Janie Quinn

AZURE MOON PUBLISHING
Waverly, Pennsylvania
www.essentialeating.com

Essential Eating™, A Cookbook
Discover How To Eat, Not Diet

Copyright © 2000 and 2003 by Janie Quinn

First Printing 2000
Second Printing 2002
Third Printing 2003

Published by Azure Moon Publishing
Post Office Box 771, Waverly, PA 18471
(570) 586-1557
For information or additional books:
www.essentialeating.com

Editor: Lee Ann Cavanaugh
Recipe Editor: Judy Thomas
Food Photography: Rob Lettieri
Book Design: North Market Street Graphics

The food photographed in this book has not been altered in any way. No waxes, dyes, glues or other substances have been added to embellish the recipes. It was our intention to have the food look just as you would *essentially* cook it at home.

Publisher's Cataloging-in-Publication Data
Quinn, Janie
Essential eating : a cookbook : discover how to
eat, not diet / Janie Quinn. — 1st ed.
p.   cm.
Includes bibliographical references and index.
LCCN: 00-101942
ISBN: 0-9679843-5-1
1. Cookery. 2. Nutrition—Popular works.   I. Title
TX652.Q56 2000   641.5
QB100-348

Printed in the United States of America on acid-free paper.

To The Cook Group
and to the special people they brought to my table,
especially my favorite recipe tasters, Tony, Jenifer, Moriah,
Matthew and Erin.

Contents

Chapter 6

Chapter 7

Appendix

Bibliography

Glossary

Epilogue

Index

Above all else, love yourself. Only by loving yourself first, can you give love to others. The foundation for loving yourself is caring for the incredible vessel we have been given to live in during this lifetime. The way we eat is all about love.

Acknowledgments

I do not know the exact moment I decided to follow this path, but I am certain that I was directed by some power outside of myself. Since I began the journey of writing this book I have been amazed, time after time, with the people who have entered my life at just the right moment when I needed them. They came to me unexplained, bearing invaluable gifts.

I must take a moment to thank just a few—my family, my friend and teacher Shelley Summers, Phillip Abdalla, Tony Acquaviva, Jeannette Barnes, Joseph Burinsky, Lee Ann Cavanaugh, James Dillehay, Julie Ehlers, Barry Friedland, Valerie Kiser, Jeff Kluck, June Letteri, Rob Letteri, Jami Lin, Penny Lindgren, Helen Mallon, Bill Milan, Tracy Pitz, Dr. Gerald Reisinger, Jean Rosenkrans, Nancy Rosolino, Tom

Sack, Beth Schulefand-Cheng, Mary Elaine Southard, Dick Stipe, Cindy Szili, Judy Thomas, Angela Thompson, Tina Ward, Oprah Winfrey, and to all the recipe testers and tasters that lovingly prepared and sampled these recipes until they were fine tuned.

I sincerely thank all of these talented people for their contributions to *Essential Eating, A Cookbook*. I deeply respect their talents and welcome their continued support of this book and its concept of well-being through self-love.

Introduction

My path was not through the structured environment of a classroom; it was, instead shaped in everyday living. Through the intense study of nutrition, seasoned with life experience, my passion became healing the body through cooking and eating good food—food that is nutritious, easy-to-digest, great tasting and chemical-free.

I wrote *Essential Eating, A Cookbook* to share this path with you. It is a life-tested way of cooking and eating that promotes health and enables the body to be at ease, not disease. For most of our society, eating remains shrouded in confusion. Our culture continues to propagate the myth that solving the dieting dilemma remains an unsolvable mystery. This is not true! It's easy and you can do it. Eating essentially is a joyful activity that promotes health and prevents dis-ease. This simple way of eating explains how to eat, not diet.

Essential Eating is based on the premise that digestion is the key to restoring and maintaining your health. It has the well-earned distinction of being the only book that outlines a realistic eating lifestyle to restore your health with great tasting, nutritious foods that are easy-to-digest. A half a century ago, the average grocery store stocked an inventory of about a hundred different food items. Today that number has risen to over 20,000 food items. The majority of these new food selections are comprised of ingredients the body doesn't recognize or know how to digest. Ingredients that cannot be digested or broken down by the body are often the cause of dis-ease. Making better food choices could eliminate indigestion, the symptom that leads to the use of the two most prescribed drugs.

Once you read about the digestive and nutritious benefits of sprouted flour in Chapter 4, you will be delighted to learn that Shelley Summers, author of *Creating Heaven Through Your Plate* (Warm Snow Publishers), has opened the first certified organic, sprouted flourmill. It's called the Essential Eating Sprouted Flour Company and it currently produces Sprouted Spelt Flour and Sprouted Cream of Spelt Cereal (absolutely a dream). Organic, sprouted rye flour, sprouted wheat flour and quinoa flour are also available. See Sources under Sprouted Bread, Flour and Pasta.

In the past Americans instinctively knew what to eat. The obesity and dis-ease epidemic that we see today in adults and children did not exist fifty years ago. We have unconsciously forgotten that our bodies require good food to heal properly. Good food is nutritious, easy-to-digest, free of pesticides, preservatives, additives, coloring, and flavorings—and best of all, it's not processed. The foundation for a healthy, prosperous, balanced life is an essential eating lifestyle—good food for a good life.

Those that have embraced *Essential Eating* are experiencing the joy of living in a healthy body. A few of the reported results are improved digestion, weight-loss, lower blood pressure and cholesterol, arthritic and allergy relief, restored energy, a better sense of taste and smell, healthier skin, and bowel regularity. *Essential Eating* has helped those with auto-immune disorders to improve their health. Celiac suffers have overcome their food intolerances. Generally, Essential Eaters feel improved performance, less stress and more enjoyment out of life.

It is empowering to take that first step towards doing something positive. For each individual, taking that first step towards eating essentially means renewed health. From experience and observation, I have found that most people start their essential eating adventure by taking one step. We are creatures of habit, sometimes eating the same foods each week. Take a look at the foods you are currently eating. Then exchange one of the unessential foods with one from *Essential Eating*. Go at your own pace; gradually replacing fake foods for nutritious foods. The path to becoming an Essential Eater starts with just one step! It's easy and you can do it.

You may find that making a change in something as personal as eating could invite opposition from others. Just relax, everyone is at a different place on the path and it's O.K. As you incorporate essential eating into your life, SAVE YOURSELF! Self-preservation is not a trespass against anyone else—it's a way of becoming strong enough to serve as a healthy example for your family, friends, and others. I improved my eating routine under the surveillance of a husband and four children. As I introduced good food into my diet, lost weight, and became healthier, they began to take notice. My desire to save myself improved the lives of my family, friends, and thousands of others that have embraced *Essential Eating*. The best gift I ever gave my family was the knowledge of how to eat, a gift made possible because I saved myself first!

Reflect for a moment about where you spend or expend your time in the course of a day—your office or car, institutions such as schools and hospitals, entertainment centers such as sports arenas and movie theaters, malls, and airports, to name a few. The one commonality of these places is that usually their collective fare does not include nutritious food. Since the first printing of this book, we have seen progress. The power we have as consumers is immeasurable when it comes to making better food choices available.

Finding good food *is* getting easier. We now have thousands of Essential Eaters around the country that are becoming better-informed food consumers, causing the demand and supply of essential food to increase. Some restaurants are preparing *Essential Eating* recipes, a few bakeries are using sprouted flour exclusively, and grocery stores are beginning to respond to the consumers desire for organic food. Cooking, an activity that fell out of vogue is returning to our culture as an activity that is social, sensual, simple, and smart.

I used to think that I could change the world, but I have come to know that I can only change my world. When I began embracing an essential eating lifestyle it became apparent that the environment where I lived, cooked and ate wasn't essential. In addition to eating good food, it became my priority to create an earth-friendly living space that supported the restoration of my health. Just as our bodies have a level of optimum balance, so do our environments. Removing the toxicity from my living and working spaces was the prefect compliment to an essential eating lifestyle. Presently, I am writing a book titled *Essential Environments* to again share with you the essentials of being healthy—it doesn't end at the dinner table.

With much joy I continue to live the essential eating lifestyle. I remain grateful of my restored health and have managed to effortlessly maintain my ideal weight at a size six, not my previous sixteen, in a satisfying, joyful way. The interest *Essential Eating* has generated across America demonstrates that our society is ready, if not overdue, to embrace this intelligent eating lifestyle. It begins with considering that it is possible for you to experience the joy of living in a healthy body. I invite you to use this book to nourish your body, mind and spirit. Start with the first step and save yourself. Try it— you're worth it.

Janie Quinn

Essential Eating

A Cookbook

Chapter 1

The Essential Eating Philosophy

For me, essential eating, nourishing the whole body, mind, and spirit, began when I was introduced to Shelley Summers, one of America's most respected *wholistic* (as in whole food) nutritional counselors. Her answer to the "what do I eat to feel good and be healthy question" changed my life forever. This book is based on her philosophy. To cook and eat food that is easy for the body to digest, promotes health and enables your body to be at ease, not dis-ease. Unburdening the body from indigestion allows it to heal. I have lived this philosophy for years, personally experiencing its rewards. The great thing about essential eating is that it has been life tested and works! My body has proved it, my friends' and families' bodies have proved it and thousands of other bodies around the country have proved it. I now eat more food and weigh less than I ever have as an adult. But more importantly, I can eat as much as I want, whenever I am hungry, as long as it is within the perimeters of this personal eating plan!

My Dance with Food

There was a time in my life when I would comfort myself with food. When upset, I would eat to "stuff" my feelings. I would even eat when I wasn't hungry. Over-eating made me feel shameful and guilty. It was a destructive cycle.

I never was a "dieter." When my body heard the word "diet" it went into the "eat" mode. Every time I tried "dieting," my body, afraid it was going to starve, wanted to eat even more. This destructive eating cycle was my "dance" with food and I was a very bad "dancer." The essential eating plan outlined in this book became my "dance" teacher. And I am happy to share with you the wonderful "dancer" I have become.

For more than twenty years I struggled with my relationship with food. Seeing people getting older and wider, (not wiser), I reluctantly resigned myself to that fate. One day I heard Oprah say "face the fear . . . end the struggle . . . and resolve to change." I did and came up with a plan . . . a plan that worked and continues to work.

What's the Plan?

Essential eating is accomplished through essential cooking. There are three basic diets and each is supported with a weekly menu, shopping list, and a simple, once a week cooking session. It is an easy plan to follow, allowing you to experience the joys of living in a healthy body. One of the many benefits of nourishing your body correctly is that you feel better. Your whole "beingness" is better.

Essential Eating, A Cookbook is informative, uplifting, and illuminating. It teaches you how to fuel your whole body, mind, and spirit. Essential eating is a wholistic approach to cooking and eating food, "wholistic" meaning food that is whole and in its original state, without additives, adulteration, or preservatives. The food *really does* taste great and your body *will* love it. Whenever I cook an essential recipe for my friends and family they know it's "wholesome" and their bodies will feel good after eating it. When first introduced to essential eating, some bodies are surprised at how wonderful "wholesome" food can taste and feel.

A Well Tested "Diet"

The word "diet" is used throughout this book in terms of what we eat as a way of life. This "diet" or "way of eating" is not about counting calories or weighing in. Think of the word diet as broadening, not limiting. This diet is about abundance, not deprivation. In a world full of stress it is comforting to know we can eat in a way that nourishes our bodies and helps us to feel good.

Someone very close to me struggled with a serious eating disorder. She had all the obvious symptoms, but mainly she had a fear of eating because she equated it with getting "fat." The diet in this book saved her life. She now eats almost four times the amount of food she was previously consuming and weighs less! But most importantly, she feels great and her health has been restored.

The path to nourishing your body with healthy food is an exciting one. Possessing the answer to "what food should I eat?" is pure deliverance. It gives the body peace of mind, clarity of thought and more time to experience the joy of life.

Although I am a proponent of a good diet as a way to heal your body, it is only one part of a healthy lifestyle. Medical checkups, herbal supplements, exercise, mental integrity and body work are all part of having balanced health.

Food for Thought

Essential Eating, A Cookbook is a user friendly guide that instructs you how to fuel your body for better health and well-being. Finding, cooking, and eating healthy foods can be a challenge today. We have gone from fifty varieties of food to over five hundred since the founding of our country. This variety can make nutritional decisions difficult at times. Our society used to eat mostly fruits and vegetables, but over time meat and processed foods have become increasingly prominent in our diets. Our "food environment" has become so noisy that our taste buds have become desensitized, craving incredible amounts of spices, sauces, and chemicals to enable us to "feel" our food. Many bodies have forgotten what a plain vegetable tastes like. This book is about providing a plan that enables you to feel your body's responses so it can support you in life.

Essential cooking and eating is an easy way to balance out the ever increasing demands of everyday life. The technology revolution has created an excessively busy and preoccupied culture leaving us with less time to prepare healthy meals. Our bodies are constantly trying to "digest" the pace and the information at an ever escalating rate. Overeating is an attempt to "weigh" your body down so it doesn't get swept away in the current. Even the person who is genetically equipped to "digest" almost anything is not immune to the effects of a poor diet. Essential cooking and eating to the rescue! The easy to follow weekly menus and cooking sessions outlined in Chapter Five enable you to arrive home and have a healthy meal prepared within minutes.

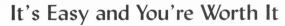

It's Easy and You're Worth It

You can do it and the rewards are worth it. Most likely, essential cooking and eating will be a great departure from your current habits. This "diet" is not about deprivation, it is about nourishment. This book is intended to share with you a way of eating and cooking that will awaken and unburden your body. Behavioral changes can be difficult, but not impossible. Remember, it has taken many years to develop your current eating habits. Eating unhealthy foods is an acquired behavior that you can change. The path to nourishing your body with healthy food is an exciting and rewarding one. To those friends and family members who have used this plan, I applaud you for your courage and discipline in a culture of fast-food and prepackaged "whatever."

As you progress through *Essential Eating, A Cookbook,* you may notice your weight return to normal, your eyes brighten, your skin clear and your energy level remain constant throughout the day. Eating the right food can bring better health and more joy into your life. I invite you to try it.

Chapter 2

What Is Essential Cooking?

Essential cooking is preparing food that is easy for your body to digest, thereby promoting health and enabling your body to be dis-ease free. Essential cooking is preparing wholesome foods as close to their natural state and source of growth as possible. Essential cooking is preparing food that is unaltered, organically grown, and chemical free or at least the purest quality that is available to you. It is NOT about counting calories or fat grams, weighing in, or deprivation. Essential cooking is about using the freshest "in-season" ingredients available. Quality ingredients might be a bit more expensive, but you're worth the investment.

What Is Organic?

Organic means grown without synthetic fertilizers and pesticides. It does not mean the fruits and vegetables are pesticide free as some natural pesticides may be used to enhance growth. Generally, organic foods are more earth friendly, more flavorful and easier to digest than foods treated with synthetic chemicals. Organic food labeling is now regulated making it easier to recognize. Look for the words "certified organic" on the label.

Who, Me Cook?

The rewards of good health are "well" worth incorporating cooking into your schedule. Luckily, we have more modern conveniences, cooking gadgets and equipment to make cooking easier. In order to eat a healthy diet and feel good you simply *have* to prepare food, but it need not be a time consuming or difficult chore. This book teaches you step-by-step how to do it with easy to follow, once a week cooking sessions. (See Chapter Five)

If the thought of cooking and eating differently is overwhelming to you, then perhaps you are not ready to make a change. That is another issue. Those of you who are ready for a change are probably saying that you just mastered low-fat cooking and now here's another program. But this is not a program, this is a way of life. Don't despair—the good news is that all of the information you have accrued over the years about food will help you to make better nutritional decisions from now on.

The only way to get beyond feeling overwhelmed is to work through it. You may have to begin by cooking one recipe. Incorporate that recipe into your current diet and then try another recipe. Before you realize it you will have five or ten recipes that you know how to cook. Encourage yourself to think of cooking as preventative medicine with the recipes serving as your personal prescriptions for good health.

Essential cooking is about knowing what you are eating. When eating out or buying prepackaged foods it is often difficult to know exactly what you are eating or where the ingredients came from. One way to know exactly what you are eating is to prepare it yourself. To heal your body, toxic foods have to be removed from your diet. So you have to cook a little bit. Big deal!

Hopefully, essential cooking and eating will become a healthy addiction—the more you do it, the more you *want* to do it. To eat healthy, you have to make time for cooking in your schedule. Making time in your schedule may mean you have to give up something else—like being sick to your stomach! Our "fast-food" environment has given cooking a bad name. Who "cooks" anymore? Be careful, you might be caught "cooking." Oh my!

The Cooking Learning Curve

Everyone has a different level of cooking ability, based on their experience and exposure, or lack of exposure, to the kitchen, different cooks, and different ingredients.

This book is directed at the novice cook, but keep in mind that it is not a complete "how-to" cookbook. Some of you may need more detailed information concerning definitions, instructions, and/or techniques. To acquire these skills you could invest in a basic cooking reference book or cooking classes. Perhaps you are fortunate enough to know someone who will share their expertise with you. The rewards of good health require time and effort—remember, you did not become ill overnight.

Cooking is one thing, but cooking with the specific ingredients outlined in the various levels of this diet is quite another. Discovering new ingredients and putting them together in an appetizing way is a challenge that requires a certain amount of adjustment. This book will make that transition easier.

This is a learning process and like many other lessons, it has a learning curve. At first there is a lot of information. As the information slowly starts to make sense, your knowledge grows and the application becomes easier. Absorbing information about nourishing your body is like watching a movie. The first time you see it, a few lines are missed, but after repeated viewing, you begin to memorize the lines. Just remember, it is a process. The journey is worth it. You are worth it!

The Continuous Kitchen

The concept of a continuous kitchen is simple. It is preparing ingredients in advance and expanding the available supply of basics, making it easy to assemble healthy meals and snacks in minutes. Think about cooking as an ongoing process. Every time you cook you add to your prepared food supply. For example, if you start to make a vegetable recipe and your vegetables need to be cleaned, peeled and chopped, it will take longer than if you had cleaned, peeled and chopped *extra* vegetables the night before when you made another vegetable dish. In the Weekly Menu section outlined in Chapter Six, recipes are organized in such a manner as to minimize your preparation time. Food preparation, with some advanced planning, makes this way of cooking much easier.

Cook Conventionally, Not Microwave

Essential eating is about preparing fresh, quality food as close to its original state as possible. The intensity of microwave cooking negates this concept. Think of microwaved meals as food that has run a marathon in seconds. How does your body feel after running a marathon—tired, breathless, overextended, spent? Food that has been microwaved doesn't seem to provide the same energy, taste, or consistency of food prepared conventionally. With just a little advanced planning, conventional cooking can be almost as fast. Freezer to microwave to table is not the path to feeling good. Switching from home cooked meals to frozen and fast-food was easy. Going back to freshly cooked food may be more of a challenge. Give it a try. You can do it!

Cooking Equipment

A large percent of the recipes in this book can be prepared using the basic kitchen appliances and utensils. Of course, as with any endeavor that we embrace, it is helpful and economical to have certain tools or resources at our service. Some of these items are essentials and others are luxuries—classify them according to your needs and/or wants. Refer to the Sources Section to obtain information and availability of the equipment mentioned in this chapter.

A blender or food processor, vegetable steamer, a sharp knife, and mesh strainer are all required equipment and usually available in an everyday kitchen. These items will be routinely used in preparing the recipes for each diet.

Acquiring extra conveniences such as a yogurt strainer, juicer, frozen dessert maker, bread machine, food dehydrator, and/or sprouter will depend largely on your budget and resourcefulness. Once you have become familiar with your cooking personality, you will know what equipment and appliances are vital for your exploration of healthy cooking.

Two of my favorite luxuries are a bread machine and a food dehydrator. The money and time they conserve surpasses the initial investment.

A bread machine makes bread baking an effortless and speedy task. It takes about 5–10 minutes to combine the ingredients and the machine does the rest. Frozen 100% sprouted bread can be purchased but remember one of the basic premises of this book is eating the freshest foods available. The warm aroma of fresh baked bread is a great fringe benefit.

A food dehydrator is a great item to help you preserve fresh food. It removes the water from food by continuous circulation of thermostatically-controlled warm air. A variety of foods, from fruits to vegetables to yogurt can be dehydrated. Carrots, celery, onions, peppers and herbs can be dried and used for soups. The operating cost of a food dehydrator is only a few cents per hour and in contrast to traditional canning or freezing methods, it proves to be well worth the purchase. In the middle of the winter, dried apricots from your local farmers' market can be a real treat. Dehydration not only preserves food, but it maintains its nutritional value without compromising the taste.

A food dehydrator is a great way to create foods for "the road." They don't need refrigeration and are great for snacks. Yogurt can be dehydrated into taffy. Homemade tomato sauce can be dehydrated, easily packed, and re-hydrated on your next camping trip!

Dehydrating is also a way to control the quality of the dried foods you are eating and offers a wider selection than is available for purchase. It's convenient, extremely palatable, and economical, saving both time and money.

Dehydrate fruits and vegetables that haven't been cooked and would otherwise spoil. For more information, see Dehydrating Foods in Chapter Six.

Carefully look around your kitchen, taking a mental inventory of your utensils and work space. Remove the pans, platters, bowls, plastic ware, etc. that you do not use on a regular basis. The collections of plastic ware that clog up American kitchens is suffocating! Place kitchen equipment and cooking tools where they are easy to reach, easy to use and easy to clean up. By simplifying your kitchen you will waste less time and energy when cooking. Unclog your kitchen for efficiency.

Chapter 3

Your Health Assessment

Our bodies are truly miraculous! The amount of stress they can deal with, separately or sometimes simultaneously, on an emotional, mental, spiritual, and physical level is amazing. Unfortunately, trying to process all this stress takes its toll on our health. Stress decreases our nutrient levels inviting the development of deficiencies.

Listed below are four groups of symptoms—signals of dis-ease. The first group lists 'simple deficiency' dis-comforts and dis-eases and the last group lists problems associated with 'deep level deficiencies'. Look over these four groups and honestly assess any maladies you may be experiencing presently or intermittently. Identifying with any of the symptoms in the last group usually indicates that you will also share some of the symptoms in the other groups.

FIRST GROUP

Start with Phase One Basic Diet #3 The Basic Balancer, Page 21.
Follow each consecutive Phase 2 months.

acne, occasional

afternoon fatigue, scattered,
  or sleepiness

backaches

bleeding gums

bloodshot eyes

bruising easily

canker sores

cracks at corner of mouth

cold hands/feet

colds/flus, one-two yearly

craving sweets

dandruff, itchy scalp

dull or dry hair

digestion tract irritation, gaseous
  or constipated

5–15 extra pounds

hangnails, finger ridges, spots
  or moons

mucus in back of throat

nervous or anxious

PMS—slight swelling of breasts or abdomen,
  acne, vulnerability, emotional

sensitivity to sunlight

skin 'goose bumps'

vulnerable feeling

self-judging

SECOND GROUP

Start with Phase One Basic Diet #2 The Deep Cleanser, Page 20.
Follow each consecutive Phase 2 months.

acne

allergies to foods, pollens, and molds

bad breath regularly

bed wetting, incontinence, bladder infections

blood pressure imbalance

body odors, sour skin smell, vaginal odors, B.O.

cholesterol imbalance

colds/flu frequently

cramps in muscles, night cramps

edema

hair loss

hay fever

headaches, minor and/or occasional

hives

hot flashes

insomnia

irritability

kidney pain

kidney infections

lung mucus

mood swings

PMS—cramps, retaining fluids, acne, cravings

self-judging

sexual problems

sleep without being rested

swollen glands

urination, frequent and/or up throughout
  the night

vision problems,
bad night vision

yeast infections

THIRD GROUP

Start with Phase One Basic Diet #1 Super Cleanser, Page 19.
Follow each consecutive Phase 2 months.

alcohol cravings	gallstones
anemia	goiters
appetite loss	headaches, migraines
asthma	hemorrhoids
atherosclerosis	herpes
blister-type bumps especially on fingers	hormone imbalances
blood chemistry imbalance	impotence
cataracts	joint pains, problems
diarrhea	lactose intolerant
depression	psoriasis
dizziness	skin rashes
eczema	sterility
fainting	thyroid imbalance
infertility	varicose veins

FOURTH GROUP

Start with Phase One Basic Diet #1 Super Cleanser, Page 19.
Follow each consecutive Phase 2–3 months.

AIDS	Epstein-Barr Virus (EBV)
arthritis	Chronic Fatigue Syndrome
birth defects	epilepsy
cancer	heart disease
candida	lupus
diabetes	multiple sclerosis

The Essential Diet

This diet is simple. It begins with the foods that are easiest for the body to digest, gradually adding back harder to digest foods as you feel better. Each of the seven phases has a detailed YES/NO food list which is presented in Chapter 4. Each subsequent phase simply adds more foods to the "YES" column.

Selecting a Basic Diet

After completing the Health Assessment on page 10–13, select a Basic Diet group based on your symptoms. Trust your body. After all, you live in it. If you are really sick and have a lot of dis-ease symptoms, start with the SUPER CLEANSER. If you are experiencing some dis-ease symptoms but don't actually consider yourself healthy, then start with the DEEP CLEANSER diet. If you think you are fairly healthy, but have a few dis-ease symptoms, then start with the BASIC BAL-ANCER diet. Most bodies begin at the Basic Balancer level.

If you are not sure where to start, try the SUPER CLEANSER for a week and then move up to the DEEP CLEANSER. Usually when your body craves a certain food, it is a sign of readiness to add it back into your diet. Try the next level of the Basic Diet and see how you feel. If a particular food causes problems, stop eating it. Once you determine which one of the three Basic Diets best corresponds to your current health, follow it for two to three months before you move onto the next phase.

Vitamins and Minerals Boost Healing

It is recommended that each phase be followed for two to three months before moving on to the next phase. In my experience vitamin, mineral, and enzyme supplements greatly increase the body's ability to release toxins and break down hard-to-digest foods. Herbal supplements, such as kelp and alfalfa, play a vital role in helping to heal the body's digestive system, enabling you to spend less time on each phase of the diet. For further clarification about supplements, refer to *Creating Heaven Through Your Plate* by Shelley Summers, Warm Snow Publisher.

Mucus Reaction Test

Use this Mucus Reaction Test, developed by Shelley Summers to help you determine if a particular food is a problem. Listen to your body and respond with love to its needs. Relax, your body is ready and willing to help you.

Whenever you eat something your body cannot easily digest, you will get a rather immediate reaction. Once you have eaten something and your body realizes it can't digest that food, it will go into a defense mode creating mucus. Mucus will surround the offending particles to protect the body from them, to ease their movement through the intestines and to stop your body from trying to absorb them.

After a couple of weeks on the appropriate diet, you can use this reaction to aid in determining whether a food you are considering eating is digestible. Take a small bite and wait. Mucus reactions will appear within a few seconds and up to twenty minutes. If you sneeze, get a runny nose, find yourself clearing your throat, or get a coating of white film covering the back of your throat or tongue, you are having a mucus reaction.

These body indications say, *'Don't eat that!' 'I can't digest that!'* I'd suggest you don't eat it. Usually it's just not worth the discomfort.

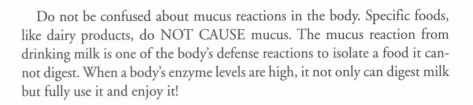

Do not be confused about mucus reactions in the body. Specific foods, like dairy products, do NOT CAUSE mucus. The mucus reaction from drinking milk is one of the body's defense reactions to isolate a food it cannot digest. When a body's enzyme levels are high, it not only can digest milk but fully use it and enjoy it!

Getting Started

Begin by analyzing your diet. You will probably see that you eat the same things again and again every week. Let's call that your existing diet. If some of your existing diet is within the parameters of the new diet, that's great. But if it isn't, then don't be overwhelmed. Simply pick a few recipes for the first week that you think you can repeat in the weeks to follow and work on them. For example, if you eat hamburgers for lunch once a week, substitute one of the sandwiches listed in the Recipe Section instead. It is through small increments like this that progress is made.

The hardest part of embarking on a different way of eating is the beginning of the journey. Remember, changing your eating habits is a process and it will take awhile to assimilate or digest this new information. Proceed slowly and don't get discouraged. Optimally, starting with the Weekly Menu and omitting all of the "NO" foods from your diet is the best way to see results and feel better. But realistically, you may not have the time and/or the energy to convert your eating habits all at once.

Prepare some Staple Recipes, adding a couple of new recipes each week until you have a new "basic" diet. Start with five new recipes and keep them simple. Make a copy of the recipes for easy reference and keep the ingredients on hand. Select a variety of recipes from different food categories, such as Breakfast And Brunch, Sandwiches, Vegetables, Fish, and Cakes And Sweets. Refer to the Weekly Menu section for ideas. It is suggested that each diet be followed for two months before additional "YES" foods are added back into the diet. Remember, each phase is an eight week course designed to add easy-to-digest foods to your diet, allowing the body to heal and feel better.

Eating Out

Of course you can dine out on the essential eating plan. Don't be shy about asking the waiter questions about the ingredients and how they are prepared. Most waiters are more than happy to assist in your quest to eat healthy. When I was on the Basic Diets, I took a couple slices of sprouted bread in a baggie when I went out to eat so I didn't feel deprived as others

TEN STEPS TO ESSENTIAL EATING

The Metamorphosis

1. Read and digest the narrative sections of this book. It will save you time in the long run. Take the Health Assessment, pages 10–13.

2. Select a BASIC DIET: *Super Cleanser, Page 19*
   Deep Cleanser, Page 20
   Basic Balancer, Page 21

3. Make two copies of the YES/NO food list for the BASIC DIET you select. Post one in your kitchen and keep one in your car or wallet for grocery shopping.

4. Copy the Weekly Menu and Cooking Schedule for the BASIC DIET you choose and keep them handy for easy reference. The Weekly Menu will include Basic Recipes that you will have to make first and have on hand or incorporate in a few recipes to begin with.

5. Make a copy of the Staples and Shopping List for the Weekly Menu. This is your shopping list.

6. Shop for the ingredients utilizing the Sources guide for the unavailable or special items.

7. Make Basic Recipes, freezing extra when possible.

8. Set aside the allotted time for weekly food preparation and most importantly *prepare* the food.

9. Keep experimenting and adding new recipes as you work through the BASIC DIETS and PHASES to GRADUATION.

10. Have fun healing.

ate from the bread basket. I also took an herbal tea bag just in case it was not available and for dessert I would take a maple candy and melt it into my cup of tea.

Depending on the Basic Diet you are following, here are some menu suggestions for ordering out: broiled or baked fish with butter or olive oil, roasted chicken, steamed vegetables, most vegetable dishes (without cheese or cream), baked potatoes, chicken frittatas, broth-based vegetable soups, omelets, polenta with vegetables, green salad drizzled with olive oil, eggs, and potatoes. Some Chinese and Southwestern menu items are "safe." Make sure to ask how the food is prepared and what ingredients are used. Ask and ensure the safety of the foods you order instead of assuming and suffering.

Patronize "safe" restaurants, where the food is fresh and the preparation methods are clean and simple. Hang in there. In our lifetime we *will* see restaurants convert to wholistic cuisine. It is the wave of the future. Imagine eating out and ordering sprouted grain breads and cold-pressed coffee!

Chapter 4

Yes/No Foods

The YES/NO food list for each phase is outlined here. PHASE ONE: Basic Diets starts with the easiest to digest foods. (See the Food Digestion Chart in the Appendix) Subsequent phases gradually add back harder to digest foods as your body heals. It's simple. Follow each diet for two to three months or until your body is ready to reintroduce more foods. All the "YES" foods listed are optional in the sense that you do not have to eat them all. If there is something on the list you do not care for, you do not have to eat it. Have fun healing.

BASIC DIET #1: SUPER CLEANSER

FOOD CATEGORY	YES FOODS	NO FOODS
FRUITS:	dates, apricots, and avocados	all other fruits
VEGETABLES:	arrowroot, artichokes, asparagus, beets, carrots, celeriac, celery, Chard, chives, cranberries, cucumbers, endive, fennel, garlic, greens: arugula, beet greens, chicory, corn salad, dandelion, escarole, radicchio, watercress, and mustard greens, Jerusalem artichoke, jicama, lettuce, okra, black olives, green peas, snap peas, snow peas, peppers, poppy seeds, pumpkins, radishes, sorrel, spinach, squash, tapioca, wild rice	all other vegetables
DAIRY PRODUCTS:	eggs and yogurt only	all other dairy products
MEATS:	fish only	all other meats and shellfish
NUTS AND SEEDS:	none	all nuts and seeds
GRAINS:	quinoa, quinoa flour, quinoa flakes, and 100% sprouted sourdough bread	amaranth, barley, buckwheat, couscous, kamut, millet, oats, rice, rye, spelt, teff, triticale, wheat, and their flours and pastas
SWEETENERS:	100% maple syrup, maple sugar, maple cream, stevia	all other sweeteners
OILS:	butter, ghee	all other oils, including margarine and vegetable shortening
SOY PRODUCTS:	none	all soy products
BEANS AND LEGUMES:	none	all beans and legumes
HERBS AND SPICES:	cooking herbs, spices, extracts	goldenseal
SPECIAL ITEMS:	baking powder, baking soda, carob powder	coffee, chocolate, alcohol, brewer's and nutritional yeast, vinegar and all condiments (catsup, mustard, horseradish, pickles, mayonnaise, anything with vinegar)

SUPER CLEANSER NUTRITIONAL RULES

1. Eat something as soon as you get up in the morning and then eat a little something every two hours.
2. Fruits can be eaten with anything except other fruits. Leave a half hour between different fruits.

SUPER CLEANSER FOOD PERCENTAGES

70–80% VEGETABLES (no raw vegetables, except in juice form/sprouted sourdough flour digests like a vegetable)
10–20% FRUITS (quinoa digests like a fruit)
10%   EVERYTHING ELSE (all other YES foods listed above)

BASIC DIET #2: DEEP CLEANSER

FOOD CATEGORY	YES FOODS	NO FOODS
FRUITS:	dates, apricots, avocados, bananas, and figs	all other fruits
VEGETABLES:	all vegetables including potatoes (except those in NO column)	the cabbage family, corn, and cornmeal
DAIRY PRODUCTS:	eggs, yogurt, kefir, and kefir cheese	all other dairy products
MEATS:	fish only	all other meats and shellfish
NUTS AND SEEDS:	none	all nuts and seeds
GRAINS:	100% sprouted grains, quinoa, and their flours, and quinoa flakes	amaranth, barley, buckwheat, couscous, kamut, millet, oats, rice, rye, spelt, teff, triticale, wheat, and their flours and pastas
SWEETENERS:	100% maple syrup, maple sugar, maple cream, stevia	all other sweeteners
OILS:	butter, ghee	all other oils, including margarine and vegetable shortening
SOY PRODUCTS:	miso and tamari	all other soy products
BEANS AND LEGUMES:	SPROUTED beans and legumes	all regular beans and legumes
HERBS AND SPICES:	cooking herbs, spices, extracts, medicinal herbs, herbal teas	goldenseal
SPECIAL ITEMS:	baking powder, baking soda, carob powder	coffee, chocolate, alcohol, brewer's and nutritional yeast, vinegar and all condiments (catsup, mustard, horse-radish, pickles, mayonnaise, anything with vinegar)

DEEP CLEANSER NUTRITIONAL RULES

1. Eat something as soon as you get up in the morning and then eat a little something every two hours.
2. For Everyone: Fruits can be eaten with anything except other fruits. Leave a half hour between different fruits. For Children under 3, keep fruit and vegetables separate.
3. Sprout all beans and legumes.
4. Avoid shellfish.

DEEP CLEANSER FOOD PERCENTAGES

FOR ADULTS:
- 70%   VEGETABLES (no raw vegetables, except in juice form/sprouted grains and flours digest like vegetables)
- 20%   FRUITS (quinoa digests like a fruit)
- 10%   EVERYTHING ELSE (all other YES foods listed above)

FOR PREGNANT WOMEN:
- 60%   VEGETABLES (no raw vegetables, except in juice form/sprouted grains and flours digest like vegetables)
- 20%   FRUITS (quinoa digests like a fruit)
- 20%   EVERYTHING ELSE (all other YES foods listed above)

FOR CHILDREN UNDER 12:
- 20%   FRUITS AND VEGETABLES (no raw vegetables, except in juice form)
- 80%   EVERYTHING ELSE (all other YES foods listed above)

BASIC DIET #3: BASIC BALANCER

FOOD CATEGORY	YES FOODS	NO FOODS
FRUITS:	dates, apricots, avocados, bananas, figs, and coconut	all other fruits
VEGETABLES:	all vegetables including potatoes, corn, and cornmeal	the cabbage family: broccoli, cauliflower, cabbages, Brussel sprouts, kale, collard greens, and kohlrabi
DAIRY PRODUCTS:	eggs, yogurt, kefir, kefir cheese, and sour cream	all other dairy products
MEATS:	fish and chicken	all other meats and shellfish
NUTS AND SEEDS:	none	all nuts and seeds
GRAINS:	100% sprouted grains and quinoa, their flours and pastas, quinoa flakes	amaranth, barley, buckwheat, couscous, kamut, millet, oats, rice, rye, spelt, teff, triticale, wheat, and their flours and pastas
SWEETENERS:	100% maple syrup, maple sugar, maple cream, stevia	all other sweeteners
OILS:	butter, ghee, olive oil	all other oils including margarine and vegetable shortening
SOY PRODUCTS:	miso and tamari	all other soy products
BEANS AND LEGUMES:	SPROUTED beans and legumes	all regular beans and legumes
HERBS AND SPICES:	all cooking herbs and spices, extracts, medicinal herbs,and all teas including black and green tea	goldenseal
SPECIAL ITEMS:	baking powder, baking soda, carob powder	coffee, chocolate, alcohol, brewer's and nutritional yeast, vinegar and all condiments (catsup, mustard, horseradish, pickles, mayonnaise, anything with vinegar)

BASIC BALANCER NUTRITIONAL RULES

1. Eat something as soon as you get up in the morning and then eat a little something every two hours.
2. For Everyone: Fruits can be eaten with anything except other fruits. Leave a half hour between different fruits. For Children under 3, keep fruit and vegetables separate.
3. Sprout all beans and legumes.
4. Avoid shellfish.

BASIC BALANCER FOOD PERCENTAGES

Remember, sprouted grains, flours, and pastas digest like vegetables.

FOR ADULTS:
60%	VEGETABLES (20% of your vegetables can be raw, excluding raw juices)
20%	FRUITS (quinoa digests like a fruit)
20%	EVERYTHING ELSE (all other YES foods listed above)

FOR PREGNANT WOMEN:
50%	VEGETABLES (20% of your vegetables can be raw, excluding raw juices)
20%	FRUITS (quinoa digests like a fruit)
30%	EVERYTHING ELSE (all other YES foods listed above)

FOR CHILDREN UNDER 12:
20%	FRUITS AND VEGETABLES (20% of your vegetables can be raw, excluding raw juices)
80%	EVERYTHING ELSE (all other YES foods listed above)

PHASE TWO DIET

FOOD CATEGORY	YES FOODS	NO FOODS
FRUITS:	all fruits (except those in NO column)	citrus (oranges, lemons, limes, tangerines, tangelos, pineapples, grapefruits), pears, apples, kiwi, papaya, guava, and mangos
VEGETABLES:	all vegetables	
DAIRY PRODUCTS:	eggs, yogurt, kefir, kefir cheese, sour cream, cream cheese, and cottage cheese	all other dairy products including buttermilk, cheese, and milk
MEATS:	fish, chicken, and turkey	all other meats and shellfish
NUTS AND SEEDS:	hazelnuts only	all other nuts and seeds
GRAINS:	100% sprouted grains and quinoa, their flours and pastas, quinoa flakes	amaranth, barley, buckwheat, couscous, kamut, millet, oats, rice, rye, spelt, teff, triticale, wheat, and their flours and pastas
SWEETENERS:	100% maple syrup, maple sugar, maple cream, stevia, malt syrups, rice and rice bran syrups	all other sweeteners
OILS:	butter, ghee and olive oil	all other oils including margarine and vegetable shortening
SOY PRODUCTS:	miso and tamari	all other soy products
BEANS AND LEGUMES:	SPROUTED beans and legumes	all regular beans and legumes
HERBS AND SPICES:	cooking herbs and spices, extracts, medicinal herbs, and all teas including black and green tea	goldenseal
SPECIAL ITEMS:	baking power, baking soda, carob powder, vinegar and most condiments (catsup, mustard, horseradish, and pickles)	coffee, chocolate, alcohol, brewer's and nutritional yeast, and mayonnaise

PHASE TWO NUTRITIONAL RULES

1. Eat something as soon as you get up in the morning and then eat a little something every two hours.
2. Fruits can be eaten with anything except other fruits. Leave a half hour between different fruits.
3. Sprout all beans and legumes.
4. Avoid shellfish.

PHASE TWO FOOD PERCENTAGES

FOR ADULTS:
- 50%   VEGETABLES (20% of your vegetables can be raw, excluding raw juices)
- 20%   FRUITS
- 30%   EVERYTHING ELSE (all other YES foods listed above)

FOR PREGNANT WOMEN:
- 40%   VEGETABLES (20% of your vegetables can be raw, excluding raw juices)
- 20%   FRUITS
- 40%   EVERYTHING ELSE (all other YES foods listed above)

FOR CHILDREN UNDER 12:
- 10–20%   FRUITS AND VEGETABLES (all can be raw, if desired)
- 80–90%   EVERYTHING ELSE (all other YES foods listed above)

PHASE THREE DIET

The Phase Three foods are listed below. There are a lot of additions in this phase, so add foods back carefully now. Congratulations for reaching this point! Again, follow this diet for two months or until you feel like adding more foods to your diet. Keep up the good work!

FOOD CATEGORY	YES FOODS	NO FOODS
FRUITS:	all fruits (except those in NO column)	apples and pears
VEGETABLES:	all vegetables	
DAIRY PRODUCTS:	eggs, yogurt, kefir, kefir cheese, sour cream, cream cheese, and cottage cheese	all other dairy products
MEATS:	fish, poultry, rabbit, and lamb	all other meats and shellfish
NUTS AND SEEDS:	hazelnuts and almonds	all other nuts and seeds
GRAINS:	100% sprouted grains and quinoa, millet, oats, and their flours and pastas, quinoa flakes	amaranth, barley, buckwheat, couscous, kamut, rice, rye, spelt, teff, triticale, wheat, and their flours and pastas
SWEETENERS:	100% maple syrup, maple sugar, maple cream, stevia, malt syrups, rice and rice bran syrups, and blackstrap molasses	all other sweeteners
OILS:	butter, ghee, olive oil, and grape seed oil	all other oils including margarine and vegetable shortening
SOY PRODUCTS:	miso and tamari	all other soy products
BEANS AND LEGUMES:	SPROUTED beans and legumes	all regular beans and legumes
HERBS AND SPICES:	herbs, spices, extracts and teas	goldenseal
SPECIAL ITEMS:	baking powder, baking soda, carob powder, vinegar, most condiments (catsup, mustard, horseradish, and pickles), and occasional tequila	coffee, chocolate, alcohol, brewer's and nutritional yeast, and mayonnaise

PHASE THREE NUTRITIONAL RULES

1. Eat something as soon as you get up in the morning and then eat a little something every two hours.
2. Fruits can be eaten with anything except other fruits. Leave a half hour between different fruits.
3. Sprout all beans and legumes.
4. Avoid shellfish.
5. Do NOT eat starches (grains and soy products) with proteins (dairy, eggs, fish, meats, nuts, and seeds.)

PHASE THREE FOOD PERCENTAGES

FOR ADULTS:
- 50%   VEGETABLES (20% of your vegetables can be raw, excluding raw juices)
- 20%   FRUITS
- 30%   EVERYTHING ELSE (all other YES foods listed above)

FOR PREGNANT WOMEN:
- 40%   VEGETABLES (20% of your vegetables can be raw, excluding raw juices)
- 20%   FRUITS
- 40%   EVERYTHING ELSE (all other YES foods listed above)

FOR CHILDREN UNDER 12:
- 10–20%   FRUITS AND VEGETABLES (all can be raw, if desired)
- 80–90%   EVERYTHING ELSE (all other YES foods listed above)

PHASE FOUR DIET

FOOD CATEGORY	YES FOODS	NO FOODS
FRUITS:	all fruits (except those in NO column)	apples and pears
VEGETABLES:	all vegetables	
DAIRY PRODUCTS:	eggs, yogurt, kefir, kefir cheese, sour cream, cottage cheese, cream cheese, and buttermilk	all other dairy products
MEATS:	fish, poultry, lamb, and rabbit	all other meats
NUTS AND SEEDS:	hazelnuts, almonds, cashews, and pecans	all other nuts and seeds
GRAINS:	100% sprouted grains and quinoa, quinoa flakes, couscous, millet, oats, rice, rye, teff, and their flours and pastas	amaranth, barley, buckwheat, kamut, spelt, triticale, wheat, and their flours and pastas
SWEETENERS:	100% maple syrup, maple sugar, maple cream, stevia, malt syrups, rice and rice bran syrups, blackstrap and sorghum molasses, cane and date sugar, fructose, and honey	
OILS:	butter, ghee, olive oil, and grape seed oil	all other oils including margarine and vegetable shortening
SOY PRODUCTS:	miso, tamari, and tempeh	all other soy products
BEANS AND LEGUMES:	SPROUTED beans and legumes	all regular beans and legumes
HERBS AND SPICES:	herbs, spices, extracts and teas	goldenseal
SPECIAL ITEMS:	baking powder, baking soda, carob powder, vinegar, condiments, occasional coffee, and tequila	other alcohol, mayonnaise, chocolate, brewer's and nutritional yeast

PHASE FOUR NUTRITIONAL RULES

1. Eat something as soon as you get up in the morning and then eat a little something every two hours.
2. Fruits can be eaten with anything except other fruits. Leave a half hour between different fruits.
3. Sprout all beans and legumes.
4. Avoid shellfish.
5. Do NOT eat starches (grains and soy products) with proteins (dairy, eggs, fish, meats, nuts, and seeds.)

PHASE FOUR FOOD PERCENTAGES

FOR ADULTS:
- 50%   VEGETABLES (20% can be raw)
- 20%   FRUITS
- 30%   EVERYTHING ELSE (all other YES foods listed above)

FOR PREGNANT WOMEN:
- 40%   VEGETABLES (20% can be raw)
- 20%   FRUITS
- 40%   EVERYTHING ELSE (all other YES foods listed above)

FOR CHILDREN UNDER 12:
- 10–20%   FRUITS AND VEGETABLES (all of the vegetables can be raw)
- 80–90%   EVERYTHING ELSE (all other YES foods listed above)

SEMI-FINAL PHASE DIET

FOOD CATEGORY	YES FOODS	NO FOODS
FRUITS:	all fruits	
VEGETABLES:	all vegetables	
DAIRY PRODUCTS:	all except . . .	milk
MEATS:	all except . . .	shellfish
NUTS AND SEEDS:	all except . . .	macadamia, Brazil nuts and pistachios
GRAINS:	all except . . .	kamut, spelt, wheat, their flours
SWEETENERS:	all natural sweeteners	
OILS:	butter, ghee, olive, grape seed, corn, safflower, and soybean oils	all other oils including margarine and vegetable shortening
SOY PRODUCTS:	all soy products except . . .	soy powder
BEANS AND LEGUMES:	SPROUTED beans and legumes	all regular beans and legumes
HERBS AND SPICES:	herbs, spices, extracts and teas	goldenseal
SPECIAL ITEMS:	baking powder, baking soda, carob powder, vinegar and most condiments, occasional coffee and tequila, other alcohol, mayonnaise, chocolate, brewer's and nutritional yeast	beer and wine

SEMI-FINAL PHASE NUTRITIONAL RULES

1. Eat something as soon as you get up in the morning and then eat a little something every two hours.
2. Fruits can be eaten with anything except other fruits. Leave a half hour between different fruits.
3. Sprout all beans and legumes.
4. Avoid shellfish.
5. Do NOT eat starches (grains and soy products) with proteins (dairy, eggs, fish, meats, nuts, and seeds.)

SEMI-FINAL PHASE FOOD PERCENTAGES

FOR ADULTS:
    70%   VEGETABLES AND FRUITS (0–50% can be raw foods)
    30%   EVERYTHING ELSE

FOR PREGNANT WOMEN:
    50%   FRUITS AND VEGETABLES (0–50% can be raw vegetables)
    50%   EVERYTHING ELSE

FOR CHILDREN UNDER 12:
    10–30%   FRUITS AND VEGETABLES (0–30% can be raw vegetables)
    70–90%   EVERYTHING ELSE

FINAL PHASE DIET

Although all foods are added back into the diet at this time, continue to select most of your food choices from The Core Diet on the next page. Milk, cheese, nuts, unsprouted grains and beans, chocolate and alcohol may always be difficult for your body to digest. All of the NO foods from Phase Four (page 20) and the Semi-Final Phase (page 21) are embellishments to the Core Diet. Meaning they can be eaten occasionally, not regularly.

FINAL PHASE NUTRITIONAL RULES

1. Eat something as soon as you get up in the morning and then eat a little something every two hours.
2. Fruits can be eaten with anything except other fruits. Leave a half hour between different fruits.
3. Sprout all beans and legumes.
4. Avoid shellfish.
5. Do NOT eat starches (grains and soy products) with proteins (dairy, eggs, fish, meats, nuts, and seeds.)

FINAL PHASE FOOD PERCENTAGES

FOR ADULTS:
70%	VEGETABLES AND FRUITS (0–50% can be raw foods)
30%	EVERYTHING ELSE

FOR PREGNANT WOMEN:
50%	FRUITS AND VEGETABLES (0–50% can be raw vegetables)
50%	EVERYTHING ELSE

FOR CHILDREN UNDER 12:
10–30%	FRUITS AND VEGETABLES (0–30% can be raw vegetables)
70–90%	EVERYTHING ELSE

THE CORE DIET

FOOD CATEGORY	CORE DIET	EMBELLISHMENTS
FRUITS:	all fruits	
VEGETABLES:	all vegetables	
DAIRY PRODUCTS:	eggs, yogurt, kefir, kefir cheese, and sour cream	all other dairy products
MEATS:	fish and chicken	all other meats
NUTS AND SEEDS:	none	all nuts and seeds
GRAINS:	100% sprouted grains and quinoa, their flours and pastas, quinoa flakes	all regular grains
SWEETENERS:	all natural sweeteners: 100% maple syrup, maple sugar, maple cream, rice and rice bran syrups, blackstrap and sorghum molasses, cane and date sugars, fructose, and honey	
OILS:	butter, ghee, olive oil, and grape seed oil	all other oils including margarine and vegetable shortening
SOY PRODUCTS:	miso and tamari	all other soy products
BEANS AND LEGUMES:	SPROUTED beans and legumes	all regular beans and legumes
HERBS AND SPICES:	all herbs, spices, extracts and teas	
SPECIAL ITEMS:	baking powder, baking soda, carob powder, vinegar, condiments, occasional coffee and tequila	other alcohol, mayonnaise, chocolate, brewer's, and nutritional yeast

CORE DIET NUTRITIONAL RULES

1. Eat something as soon as you get up in the morning and then eat a little something every two hours.
2. Fruits can be eaten with anything except other fruits. Leave a half hour between different fruits.
3. Sprout all beans and legumes.
4. Avoid shellfish.
5. Do NOT eat starches (grains and soy products) with proteins (dairy, eggs, fish, meats, nuts, and seeds.)

CORE DIET FOOD PERCENTAGES

FOR ADULTS:
    70%   FRUITS AND VEGETABLES (0–70% of the vegetables can be raw)
    30%   EVERYTHING ELSE

FOR PREGNANT WOMEN:
    50%   FRUITS AND VEGETABLES (0–50% of the vegetables can be raw)
    50%   EVERYTHING ELSE

FOR CHILDREN UNDER 12:
    10–30%   FRUITS AND VEGETABLES (0–30% of the vegetables can be raw)
    70–90%   EVERYTHING ELSE

IMPORTANT NUTRITIONAL RULES!

*Before getting acquainted with the foods in the Basic Diet you have selected, there are some **nutritional rules** and **food explanations** that need to be clarified.*

1. **Eat something when you first get up in the morning and then eat something every two hours after that, until retiring.**

    Eating every two hours keeps your body's blood sugar level balanced and discourages hypoglycemic reactions. When your body is healed, it compensates for the differences in blood sugar levels, allowing longer times between eating. But in the beginning phases, you need to eat every two hours to lessen the stress on your system.

    Eating every two hours doesn't have to be a meal. A few dried dates, a slice of sprouted bread, a maple candy, or a glass of juice will do just fine. Don't worry, you really have to work hard at putting on weight from eating too many fruits and vegetables. Many people's weight problems have to do with eating foods that they can't properly digest. High calorie foods, such as butter and maple syrup, can only be 20% of your diet.

    In Phase Three of the diet, the time between snacking and meals can increase to two and one half to three hours. If this longer interval stresses you, go back to every two hours.

2. **Eat fruits with anything *except* other fruits.** Separate eating different fruits by a half hour. Mixed fruits confuse the pancreas and cause hypoglycemic reactions in the body. Quinoa digests like a fruit but doesn't have fructose so it can be eaten with fruit.

3. **Sprout all beans and legumes.** Unsprouted beans and legumes are indigestible. Beans, legumes, lentils and dried peas are notorious gas producers because the human body simply does not have the enzymes needed to digest them.

4. **Avoid shellfish.** Shellfish always presents a problem for the digestive system.

5. **Do not eat starches with proteins.** Combining starches, (grains and soy products) and proteins, (dairy, eggs, fish, meats, nuts, and seeds) together creates major digestive problems. This rule comes into play when starches are added back in the Semi-Final Phase of the diet.

    Whenever starches and proteins are mixed, many toxins are created in the system because one of the foods does not break down. This situation creates digestive discomfort.

    Eat proteins with other proteins, fruits, vegetables, sweeteners and oils. Eat starches with other starches, fruits, vegetables, sweeteners and oils. (See the Appendix for a list of proteins and starches)

Yes/No Food Explanations

This section will help you understand why eliminating certain foods from the diet is critical for the healing process to take place. Refer to the YES/NO food list from the diet you have selected as you go through these explanations. These explanations guide you through each food category outlined in the diet.

Fruits

Eat fresh, cooked, dried or juiced fruits. Bodies with sugar imbalances may experience difficulty with fruit sugars. These sugars digest too quickly and raise the blood sugar level, causing a hypoglycemic reaction.

The fruits listed for each of the Basic Diets digest slowly, and for most people, do not cause sugar reactions, even though some of them, like dates, are very sweet to the taste. In the beginning, all other fruits are forbidden because they tend to cause hypoglycemic/sugar level reactions. Apples and pears are the last fruits to come back into the diet. They have high, quick sugar levels and eating them will raise your blood sugar level as much as several spoonfuls of sugar.

Check the labels on store-bought juice. One hundred percent juice doesn't always mean one hundred percent of the same juice. Most juices available on the market shelves today are blends of several fruits. Since the body cannot digest multiple fruits, juice blends need to be removed from the diet.

Coconut is often a new and unfamiliar item in the diet. Coconut is actually a dried fruit. It can be purchased shredded and dried from a health food store or fresh from a grocery or produce store. Many grocers will split the coconut for you or you can do it yourself by striking a hammer on its shell. The trick is to hold the coconut in your hand, not on a hard surface while cracking the shell. Tap lightly until the shell cracks. Remove the white meat from the brown shell, cut in chunks and refrigerate. Raw coconut can be shredded for recipes. Dried coconut freezes better than fresh coconut.

Vegetables

Of all the foods we eat, vegetables have the most variety of tastes and textures. Vegetables, unlike fruits, can be combined. Try to eat only vegetables that are in season. Herbs and spices actually fall into this digestive category and lend themselves very well to their vegetable cousins.

Potatoes and corn are digested by the same enzymes that digest other vegetables. Although categorized as starchy vegetables, they are different from starches such as grains which are digested by different pancreatic enzymes.

The entire cabbage family needs to be avoided in the beginning phases of the diet. They all can be difficult to digest, causing gas and bloating. (Refer to the Food Categories in the Appendix for a complete list of vegetables)

You may be wondering what the difference is between cornmeal, polenta and grits? These are all names for corn that is ground to different consistencies. Cornmeal is usually ground finer than polenta or grits. Read the label on your corn flakes to make sure they contain just corn or corn meal; salt is okay. Corn grits and hominy grits are other names for ground corn. As a general rule,

use a finer grind for baking and a coarser grind for cereal and entree dishes. The most common color is yellow, but there is also a white variety.

The terms "broth" and "stock" are interchangeable in the recipes. Home-made stock is preferred but canned is permissible.

Fresh pumpkin is great in the recipes when possible, but canned is acceptable. Make sure it is solid-packed, one hundred percent pumpkin.

Cranberries are in the vegetable category. Grocery stores usually carry fresh cranberries from October through January. After that, some stores carry them in the frozen foods section. Frozen, sliced cranberries may also be available from the bakery department of a large grocery store. Dried cranberries may be substituted in most recipes but they tend to be more expensive and take longer to cook. Plan ahead and make the Cranberry Spread when fresh cranberries are in season and freeze a years supply! One hundred percent unsweetened cranberry juice from concentrate can be purchased in most health food stores and is great for making Cranberry Juice and Cranberry Salad Dressing.

Black olives, tapioca, and wild rice, based on their digestive characteristics, are three other foods in the vegetable category that are not often considered vegetables. Wild rice is not a rice at all, but the seed from a grass. Tapioca is extracted and dried from the root of the cavassa plant in South America. Tapioca flour is a powdered form usually used in dessert recipes. These are all welcome additions to the diet when trying to increase your vegetable intake.

Arame, hijiki, and nori are three sea vegetables high in vitamins and minerals. A great addition to any diet, arame has a sweet and mild sun-dried flavor. Hijiki is a black seaweed with a strong flavor and firm texture. Hijiki is tough in its raw state, but softens when cooked. Nori grows wild off the coast of Maine and California. It is a good source of protein, B vitamins, vitamin C and E. Nori is a thin, purplish-black sheet of pressed seaweed, most commonly used in sushi rolls.

Raw vegetables are very difficult to digest, unless, of course, they are juiced. The cell walls of vegetables are made of cellulose and there is nothing in the human body that will break down cellulose except chewing. Externally, juicing or cooking breaks down cellulose. In the Super Cleanser and Deep Cleanser Diets, raw vegetables are out, but they will be added back in the Basic Balancer.

Dairy Products

Eggs are in the dairy category because they are a protein that needs hydrochloric acid (HCL) to digest, as do other dairy products. Eggs have taken a beating over the last few years. They seem to be the scapegoat for high-cholesterol diets. Granted, egg yolks are one of the most concentrated sources of cholesterol in the diet. Yet recent research suggests that for most people, dietary cholesterol is not the primary reason for high blood cholesterol. Rather, saturated fats and an unbalanced diet are the main culprits. Eggs are one of the easiest proteins to digest. When taking proper levels of vitamins and minerals, rarely do people have a problem with eggs.

Milk takes large amounts of both hydrochloric acid and lactose enzymes to properly break it down so that it is usable by the body. Most people lacking high levels of HCL and lactose enzymes have allergic reactions to dairy products.

In the Graduation Phase, milk is added back as an embellishment. Remember, milk takes an enormous amount of energy and nutrients to break down. Sometimes the body will be able to do this and sometimes it won't. Use the mucus reaction as a guide.

In the process of making soured and cultured dairy products such as yogurt, kefir, cottage cheese, cream cheese, sour cream, buttermilk, and cheeses, the milk molecule is broken down. Yogurt is called "predigested" because the milk molecule is so thoroughly broken down that low levels of HCL and lactose enzymes easily complete the process. Kefir and kefir cheese are also acidophilus cultures like yogurt.

Kefir, which has the consistency of eggnog, is available in health food stores. Kefir cheese is similar to cream cheese in texture with more of a "tangy" taste.

Sour cream is mostly the fat of milk, which, like butter, seems to digest easily. The souring process breaks down the milk molecule.

Yogurt is a great staple because it is one of the easiest foods to digest. Plain yogurt can be used as a milk substitute in many recipes by diluting it to the consistency of milk. To make one cup, spoon three or four tablespoons (depending on the desired thickness) of yogurt into a measuring container and add water to make one cup.

Optimally, making homemade yogurt is the best way to know the ingredients of your yogurt. But realistically, most of us buy it from the store. Most of the store brands have sugar (fructose) and starch emulsifiers added. Again, be sure to read the label.

To reduce the yogurt taste so it doesn't overpower a recipe, many times Yogurt Cheese is called for in a recipe. Yogurt Cheese is yogurt that has been drained of most of its liquid. It is great for making dips and sauces. (Refer to Recipes in Chapter 6)

All of these dairy products can be used as a substitute for milk by diluting them with water and sweetening them with maple syrup. A little maple syrup whipped into some sour cream makes a great whipping cream; kefir cheese, yogurt, sour cream and eggs can be used to make cheesecakes.

In Phase Four of the diet buttermilk is added back. Drink it straight, bake with it or use it in salad dressings. Check for mucus reactions when you reintroduce it.

Meat and Fish

Meat and fish, like dairy products, require hydrochloric acid in the stomach to break down their molecular structures. High levels of HCL are needed to digest most meat, but fish and chicken are

two of the easiest meat proteins to break down. All other meat, including turkey, need higher amounts of HCL to properly digest.

Shellfish are out of the diet. There are two main problems with it. One, the water in which they are grown may be toxic. Two, the protein structure in shellfish is very hard for the body to break down—hence the many allergies to shellfish.

During the Super Cleanser Diet, it is very important to eat digestible proteins. Eating only fruits and vegetables is a severe cleanse to begin with and may cause you to feel ill. The addition of simple proteins helps keep the pace of the cleanse at a positive level. You don't have to eat fish if you don't want to. Try eggs and dairy instead, but get some high quality, easy-to-digest proteins into your body.

Knowing the source and distributor of your fish and poultry is the best way to ensure you are buying healthy and fresh food. To find out, ask questions like, "Where was it grown or caught?" "How long since it was caught?" "What was it fed?" and "Was it ever frozen?" Stay away from buying "seasoned" fish and meats, as you have no way of knowing what has been added or when. Seasonings added at the store or fish market often mask a lack of freshness.

To cut down on the chance of bacteria growth on poultry, do not wash it prior to freezing. Instead, make sure the chicken is wrapped airtight and freeze it in the store packaging. Thaw chicken carefully and always clean thoroughly before cooking.

Hopefully, you have access to a local fish market. Find out what day they receive fresh fish and buy only fish that has arrived that day. You can buy fish and freeze it, but stay away from frozen or fresh-frozen-defrosted fish if possible since you have no way of knowing how long it has been frozen.

Do the smell test when buying fish. Fresh fish does not smell "fishy." Fresh fish is firm and not "mushy" or "slimy." Never buy fish that is displayed in plastic wrap. Plastic holds the bacteria in and prevents you from smelling or being able to feel the texture of the fish.

Nuts and Seeds

Take a break from these wonderful snacks. Nuts and seeds are great sources of proteins, oils, and nutrients but very difficult to digest; that is, they take large amounts of HCL and bile (the soap-like substance from the liver and gallbladder that breaks down fats) to break them down.

Even when nuts and seeds are added back into the diet, go easy on them. Use them to complement foods. Remember, sprouted seeds are much easier to digest and sprouting increases their nutritional value, providing a good source of vitamins. Macadamia, Brazil, and pistachio nuts contain fats that are especially hard to digest, so use them sparingly.

Grains

Grains or starches are digested by a number of enzymes with the major one coming from the pancreas. These foods are quickly transformed into sugars and give us energy and nutrients. They do, that is, if we can digest them properly. Most people can't. The pancreas needs huge amounts of B vitamins to digest grains. Stress depletes B vitamins so it's not surprising that most people are deficient in them.

Inability to digest starches is a major problem even though it is easily corrected given the proper diet, nutrient intake, and time. Pancreatic stress can lead to problems. When the pancreas is stressed it loses its ability to release appropriate amounts of insulin into the bloodstream. Removing starches from the diet relieves the stressed pancreas and symptoms begin to clear. Be patient. Although symptoms can clear quickly, it may take a year or more to fully heal the pancreas.

Once a grain has been sprouted, most bodies recognize it as a vegetable rather than a starch which requires pancreatic enzymes. Therefore, eating sprouted grains and sprouted grain products *does not* stress the pancreas.

Spelt contains more B vitamins than any other of the wheat grains. Sprouted spelt flour is used in many recipes in place of regular flour. Spelt used to be called the "bread makers" flour in Europe before it fell out of favor due to the need for more preparation than regular wheat flour. Sprouted wheat flour is called "panocha" flour. Bread dough enhancer, which is primarily gluten, digests as a vegetable protein and is acceptable to use in bread recipes.

Quinoa (keen-wa) is small grain that resembles millet (or bird seed) but comes from an herb similar to lambs quarters. It behaves like a grain but it digests like a fruit. You can cook it just like rice in about 15 minutes. Quinoa also comes in flour and flake form.

Quinoa is a food that can fill the space in your diet created by the absence of starches. Since most pastas are made with wheat they are out of the diet in the beginning phases. Instead, try quinoa and corn pastas found in most health food stores.

If quinoa causes you indigestion, it is probably too alkaline and needs to be more acidic. To raise the acidity level, cook it in water with a grated lemon rind or a teaspoon of lemon extract. This helps to balance the pH which makes quinoa easily digestible for everyone.

The grains of amaranth, barley, buckwheat, couscous, millet, oats, rice, rye, teff, and triticale are reintroduced in the Semi-Final Phase of the diet. Millet is the easiest grain to digest followed by oats. Rice, in all its types and forms, is also reinstated in the diet. Remember, don't use rice products with protein foods, use them with other starches.

Amaranth is a good source of iron and calcium. It's sweet and peppery in flavor and crunchy in texture. Amaranth grains can be sprouted. Teff dates back over 3,000 years to Egyptian civilization. Teff and amaranth are now being cultivated in the Western mountain states. Teff is minuscule in size and is best used as a cereal or mixed with other grains.

The Graduation Phase adds three varieties of wheat to the diet: spelt, kamut, and whole wheat. These grains and their flours are the hardest grains to digest. Use them as embellishments in your diet. For example, once a month try a recipe using spinach pasta made with wheat flour.

Sweeteners

Maple syrup is digested very slowly so it doesn't cause a sugar rush in the bloodstream. Because many of these recipes use maple syrup, you don't have to deny those cravings for something sweet. The four forms of 100% maple syrup that you can use are: maple syrup, maple sugar (syrup boiled down to a sugar consistency), maple cream (syrup cooked into a thick spread that needs to be refrigerated to keep its consistency), and maple candy (syrup cooked and formed into hard candy). Always use 100% maple syrup and maple products. (See Sources under Sweeteners)

Other types of sugars are absorbed too quickly into the bloodstream during the initial stages of the diet. Add natural sweeteners back into the diet as noted in the different levels.

Stevia is an herb that grows in Peru, China, and Brazil. It can be purchased in most health food stores as an extract or in a white powder form. Considered a food additive by the FDA, stevia extract is extremely sweet and tastes a little like molasses. A drop or two in a cup of tea is equal to a spoonful of other sweeteners, yet it will not cause sugar reactions in the bloodstream.

In Phase Two of the diet, malt syrups, rice and rice bran syrups are returned to the diet. The words 'malt' or 'malted' indicate a grain that has been sprouted! Malt, short for maltose, is the sugar in grains. Barley malt is boiled until it achieves a dark color and a strong sweet flavor. Malt syrups vary in color and sweetness.

Phase Three of the diet reintroduces blackstrap molasses, which comes from sugar cane. The use of a sugar cane product signals the incorporation of cane juice and its various derivatives into the diet. Sucanat is a popular brand of granulated cane juice. Sucanat may be used in recipes, in equal measurements, for white refined or brown sugar.

Phase Four through Graduation Phases adds all of the concentrated natural sweeteners including sorghum molasses, honey, and date sugar. Date sugar made from granulated, dehydrated dates, is sweeter than white sugar and contains more nutrients, especially iron. Two-thirds cup of date sugar can be substituted for one cup of white sugar.

There are 300 varieties of honey available in the United States alone. Buy locally harvested honey. As with vegetables and fruits, honey that has been produced in your area is easier for the body to assimilate and digest. The floral source determines a honey's taste, which can range from very mild to intense. As a general rule, clover, or a blend of mild varieties is the best choice for recipes.

Oils

One hundred percent real butter is the easiest fat for the body to digest. Yes, I said fat. Our fat-free culture has given fat a bad name. Right here and now, we have to adjust our negative thinking about fats and acknowledge the vital role they play in a healthy diet. The reality is that the right kind of fat can be good, eaten in moderation. Our bodies need a certain amount of oils in the diet to supply, digest, and utilize fat-soluble vitamins and minerals. Fats need to be healthy and useable. So enjoy using a little butter (1–2 sticks a week!).

Liquid lecithin is a thick and sticky oil extracted from soybeans. It is known for its excellent ability to emulsify oils. Lecithin adds the thickness and creaminess to recipes usually provided by an egg. Lecithin based butters and oil alternatives can be used in all of the basic diets.

After butter, olive oil seems to be the easiest concentrated oil to digest. Because bottled oils require a lot of digestive processing, it usually takes several months for any of the other oils to come back into the diet. The more processed a food is, the more difficult it becomes to digest and utilize. Eventually all oils will return to the diet. Until then, patience is recommended.

Grape seed oil, a flavorful oil made from grape seeds, is next on the list of easily digested oils. This oil has a pale, leafy color and a slightly nutty flavor. Two benefits of using grape seed oil are that it contains a substantial amount of vitamin E and it doesn't burn when cooking at high temperatures. It's also great to use in stir-fry cooking.

Remember, concentrated oils are not natural and they are very difficult to digest. At one point some varieties of nuts are added back into the diet, but their oils are not. There are natural enzymes in the nuts that help your body break down the oils, but those enzymes are not present in the oil.

Eventually more oils, such as corn, safflower, and soybean are added back into the diet. Use only "cold-pressed" oils, those that are not subjected to temperatures higher than 110 degrees. Most oils are extracted from foods using high heat which destroys most of the nutrients in them. Along with these oils, you can also add mayonnaise, made from these "cold-pressed" oils, back into the diet. Since all concentrated oils are hard to digest, always go easy on them. (Refer to Sources)

When all oils are finally added back into the diet, periods of difficulty in digesting them may still surface. If you find yourself experiencing indigestion with fats, just back off from eating them for a few weeks.

Soy Products

All soy products originate from soybeans. Beans digest as starches and use pancreatic enzymes. Since most people initially have difficulty producing enough enzymes, soy products may present some problems. For this reason, people with more serious health problems, such as cancer or diabetes, need to avoid soy products and fermented foods like tofu, soy cheese, tempeh, soy powders, soy milk, miso, and tamari.

Miso and tamari (natural soy sauce) are fermented to the point where most bodies do not recognize them as starches any longer. They are the easiest soy products to digest. When soy products are added back into the diet remember, they digest as starches. Do not mix starches and proteins. Eat them with other starches, fruits, vegetables, sweeteners, and oils. For example, use soy sauce with vegetables but not with fish.

Miso is a fermented soybean paste. The mashed soybeans are aged and cured like cheese. It is used primarily as a seasoning and in the preparation of sauces. Miso paste comes in a variety of flavors and colors, from Blonde to Hatcho. Barley miso is also a wonderful addition to many recipes.

Beans and Legumes

Regular beans and legumes (lentils and dried peas) are notorious gas producers. When a food causes gas, it is rotting and putrefying in the intestines and not digesting properly. This happens with unsprouted beans because the body *does not* have the enzymes needed to digest them.

When beans are growing they are full of vegetable sugars but when they're dried, the sugars are converted into a starch. Our bodies do not possess the enzymes necessary to break down that starch or, it seems, the ability to develop these enzymes.

There is a simple way to remedy this problem, making beans and legumes not only digestible but delicious. When you sprout beans and legumes, you reverse the vegetable sugars-to-starch process. As the sprouts grow, the starches are converted back into vegetable sugars. Once this process is complete, the body can digest them as a vegetable.

You can cook sprouted beans and use them just as you would normally. Beans and legumes are easy to sprout as outlined in the Sprouting Beans Recipe in the Recipe Section. As they sprout, the vitamin and mineral levels skyrocket. For that reason, bodies crave sprouted beans.

When the body is functioning with serious problems, the overall digestive level usually can't handle even sprouted beans and legumes. During the Super Cleanser Diet, stay away from sprouted beans and legumes for a month or so and then try introducing them into your diet. Watch for mucus reactions. Try a variety of sprouted beans and legumes to see which ones your body prefers.

Herbs, Spices, and Seasonings

Herbs are treated as vegetables by the body and most people don't have any problems with them. When a body has trouble in this area, it usually has to do with blood chemistry problems. If you have chosen the Super Cleanser Diet to start, don't use herbs or spices for a month or more. Slowly start reintroducing them back into your diet, one at a time.

If a recipe calls for fresh herbs and you only have dried available, substitute one third of the required amount of fresh herbs with dried herbs. One teaspoon of dried herbs equals one tablespoon of fresh herbs. Tailor the amount of herbs required in a recipe to suit your palate or sensitivity. Do not wash fresh herbs until ready to use in a recipe. Fresh herbs can be stored in a cup with an inch of water in the refrigerator.

A few words about salt. Salt is essential to life and our bodies crave it. But like all out-of-balance cravings, the desire for too much salt indicates an imbalance in the body sometimes linked to mineral deficiencies.

The body needs a balance of minerals, including sodium. Bodies prefer having these nutrients delivered in natural forms from food as opposed to adding it. On a weekly basis, a quarter teaspoon to a half teaspoon of salt per person is a general rule. Your taste buds will adapt as your body comes into balance.

Try dulse. Dulse is a red colored sea vegetable that grows off the coast of Maine, Canada, Oregon and Alaska. It is soft and chewy in texture with a salty seafood taste. It can be eaten out of the bag or soaked in water for a few minutes to soften. Use in sandwiches, salads or stir-fry recipes. Dulse is high in iron, protein, A and B vitamins. Dulse can also be dried in a dehydrator and crumbled on quinoa, soups, pasta or popcorn.

Specialty Foods

Carob beans come from the pod of an evergreen tree that grows in the Mediterranean. It's often proclaimed as a chocolate substitute, though you won't find many chocolate lovers who will agree. I prefer to think of it as just carob and not compare it to chocolate. It has an entirely different taste. It is sold in a powder form, ground from dried carob bean pods. Carob digests as a protein quite easily. During the Basic Diets, skip the carob chips. The oils in them are too intense at this particular stage.

Arrowroot powder, obtained from the root of a West Indian plant, can be exchanged measure for measure for cornstarch. Kudzu root may be used in recipes requiring a thickener. Agar-Agar is a sea vegetable gel, sold in the form of flakes that can also be used as a thickening agent in recipes. The seaweed is boiled, pressed into a gel and then dried into flakes.

Coffee is a popular beverage but it is hard to digest. Coffee is not included in any of the Basic Diets but it can return later on if you desire. Digesting coffee presents a number of problems. First, it has some very strong, natural chemicals that can upset the blood chemistry and slow down the healing process. Secondly, when you pour hot water on the coffee grounds, it releases the oils and

acids of the bean. These two substances create digestive problems; the oils are indigestible and the acids compete with the natural stomach acids. Lastly, the acids and oils interact with the caffeine, creating most of the negative side effects people experience from coffee and associate with caffeine.

There is a better way to make coffee using a coffee extract. Basically, you make a coffee extract just like you would an herbal extract. It is called cold-pressed coffee. (See the Cold-Pressed Coffee recipe under Beverages in the Recipe Section, Chapter 6) This is the most wonderful coffee I have ever tasted. There is no bitter taste, stomach upset, or caffeine side effects. This coffee is digested as a fruit by the body, since coffee beans are the fruit of a tree!

Like coffee, chocolate has some harsh natural chemicals that can slow down the healing process. Once picked, fermented, and dried, chocolate beans go through a gentle heating and grinding process leaving 70% cocoa butter and 30% chocolate solids. After this step, all kinds of stuff is added to chocolate making it even harder to digest than it already is. Once the chocolate is smooth, it is poured into unsweetened chocolate baking squares. This is the purest form of chocolate and the only one you should use. Cocoa powder is produced by removing the cocoa butter through a chemical residue process—avoid it if possible.

The inherent oil—cocoa butter—demands high levels of bile to break it down, making it a food to avoid while following the Basic Diets. Chocolate can come back into the diet eventually, in moderation.

When I first began this way of eating, the only food I thought I couldn't do without was chocolate. I was a chocoholic. Determined to heal my body, I gave up chocolate. At this point my body doesn't even want it and I don't think about it. Now that's a healed body!!

Alcohol places a lot of stress on your the body. If it's added back into the diet make sure you take extra vitamin and mineral food supplements, like alfalfa and kelp, to compensate for the nutrients required to flush the alcohol from your body. Tequila is the easiest alcohol for the body to digest. The fact that it comes from a cactus is part of what makes it different. Wine and beer contain high levels of impurities that cause more stress on the body than distilled alcohol, so they are added back into the diet after tequila and hard liquors.

Brewer's yeast is the yeast by-product of brewing beer. Nutritional yeast is a yeast grown on molasses. Both are great sources of the B vitamins among other nutrients and are digested as proteins. They require a lot of HCL to digest, more than most bodies have and that causes problems for most people. Mixed with the right foods, yeast can be wonderful but in the beginning phases, leave it out.

Vinegar's acidity level presents a problem, even the small amounts contained in condiments, such as catsup, prepared mustard, horseradish, and pickles. When your system gets out of balance, the pH balance suffers. One of the first things that the proper diet corrects are the acid/alkaline imbalances that affect all other body functions.

Food Percentages

Work out your food percentages "by volume." My diet consists of six to ten cups of food a day based on my level of activity. Using eighty percent fruits and vegetables, that's about five to eight cups of fruits and vegetables and one to two cups of everything else. Measure volume for salad-type vegetables in packed cups.

Sprouted grains, beans, and legumes digest like vegetables so remember to count them in your vegetable percentage. Quinoa digests like a fruit, count it in your fruit percentage.

The Super Cleanser and Deep Cleanser Diets keep the level of fruits and vegetables high to aid in cleansing the toxins from the body and to promote healing. Most adult bodies settle into a maintenance program of seventy percent fruits and vegetables and thirty percent of everything else.

It will probably take you eight to ten months to reach the Core Diet phase. As our environment becomes more stressful, we need to eat more easy-to-digest foods to stay balanced. Hard-to-digest foods should be considered embellishments to the Core Diet. Even though embellishments have been added in the Phase Four Diet through Graduation, eat them sparingly. Make eighty to ninety percent of your food choices from the Core Diet list.

The information in this chapter about what foods to eat, when to eat them, and in what percentages is the foundation for this way of eating. Refer back to this chapter as you work through the levels of the diet. To help you apply this information, the next chapter outlines three weekly menus for the Basic Diets, including shopping lists and cooking schedules. Refer to the Weekly Menus in Chapter 5 for examples of what to eat for the three Basic Diets. Have fun experimenting!

Chapter 5

Weekly Menus

This chapter includes a weekly menu, shopping list, cooking schedule, and cooking session for each of the three Basic Diets. Following the weekly menus will help to organize your "eating week." These menus are intended as guidelines to begin putting meal plans together. The main intention of the weekly menu is to show how to make a variety of dishes after an easy once a week cooking session. In the beginning you may prefer preparing less variety until you build up a personal repertoire of *your* "eating week." Have fun experimenting with new menus.

Easy Once a Week Cooking Sessions

The easy once a week cooking sessions show how to prepare extra ingredients and use them in different recipes throughout the week. If possible, bake a few items once a week and freeze them, thereby expanding your supply of prepared foods. Remember the concept of the continuous kitchen, from Chapter Three, where ingredients have been prepared or partially prepared at an earlier time making it easy to assemble meals when they are needed.

The idea of the continuous kitchen is that when you are hungry or it is time to eat, the food has already been prepared. Get in the habit of cooking while you prepare other foods. For example, baked potatoes take about 45 minutes to cook. During that time you could peel and chop vegetables or cook quinoa. Another example is to prepare an item for baking and put it in the oven when you sit down for dinner. When you're done with dinner, voilà, sweets!

Save Time Cooking

The following examples involve cooking whole foods and using them in a variety of recipes over a few days. These are some suggestions on how to plan ahead and save time in your continuous kitchen.

For a really simple weekly menu, bake several potatoes and cook a pot of quinoa. Steam a variety of vegetables, bake a tray of carob brownies, and a pan of cornbread. Then each day create your own combinations by adding whole foods to make: potatoes and eggs, grilled cornbread with maple syrup, quinoa with steamed vegetables, Carob Brownies with maple cream or Yogurt Cheese Frosting, Herbed Quinoa Salad, baked potatoes with vinegar-free salsa, and Quinoa Stuffed Peppers. Put some cooked vegetables, such as carrots, yams and butternut squash, in a blender or food processor with some broth and herbs, pulse to make a soup.

Bake 6–8 baked potatoes at a time. Serve for dinner, dice and sauté with eggs for breakfast, peel and purée with broth and cooked vegetables, such as carrots, onions, green beans, squash, and some herbs for a soup. Use potatoes in Salmon Cake recipe, reheat with Roasted Root Vegetables and top with vinegar-free salsa, or use in potato salad.

Make a double batch of corn polenta. When polenta is soft, eat as warm cereal topped with butter and maple syrup or serve in a dish with grilled or roasted vegetables. Place half of the recipe in a loaf pan and chill until firm. Slice and grill for breakfast topped with butter and maple syrup. Grill the remainder of the loaf for dinner topped with cooked vegetables or cut polenta into cubes and drop into heated broth for soup.

Make a double or triple batch of quinoa. Eat it hot, cold or with steamed, grilled or roasted vegetables. Use in Quinoa Pilaf, Spinach And Quinoa Salad, Quinoa Stuffed Pepper recipes, or add to heated vegetable soup.

Some vegetables can be cooked in bulk and refrigerated for a few days. Steam red beets. Eat warm, make beet soup, cold beet salad, or mash with potatoes. Roast carrots. Eat warm or cold. Mash with dill, or blend in a food processor with sautéed onions and some broth to make carrot soup. Sauté spinach. Eat warm, sauté with mushrooms and scrambled eggs, or use in spinach

frittata. Roast or bake peppers. Make Quinoa Stuffed Peppers, Veggie Sticks or eat warm as a side dish or chop and add to quinoa.

Cook economically. Make a double batch of waffles and muffins and freeze them. Make and freeze a months supply of cookies. Instead of cooking one thing at a time, look at the recipes you want to cook and do "like" tasks together. For example, if you are preparing three recipes that call for chopped onions, total the chopped onions needed and chop them all at once. Put one item in to bake and prepare another recipe or clean and chop vegetables while the item is baking. Heat the oven or put water on the stove to boil while you clean and measure ingredients.

Hard boil 8–12 eggs. Peel and eat whole, make egg salad or chop on salads. By now I'm sure you are getting the picture. Have fun creating your own menus and keeping a continuous kitchen.

More Tips

Substitute ingredients according to the season, using the freshest ingredients available to you. Chard, kale and spinach can almost always be interchanged. Using red, green, hot or mild peppers is a personal preference. Use these menus as a guide. Make substitutions within the "YES" foods as you prefer, such as apricots instead of dates or snow peas instead of asparagus. With a little practice you will create and convert recipes on your own.

Foods cooked just prior to consumption are best. But if that is not possible then the cooking schedules and sessions that follow will help you to prepare and store foods for a few days. Just remember that the longer the food is stored the less nutritious it becomes.

Adjust the recipe to the number of servings you wish to prepare. Some beverage suggestions to include with your menus are water, cranberry juice, carrot juice, tomato juice, apricot nectar, and herbal iced or hot tea. Have fun cooking and planning new menus.

SUPER CLEANSER SAMPLE WEEKLY MENU

(BASED ON EATING EVERY TWO HOURS)

DAY 1

MORNING	Pumpkin Quinoa Waffles
MID-MORNING	Apricot Nectar/Quinoa Flake Cookies
NOON	Carrot Soup/Sprouted Sourdough Toast
AFTERNOON	Yogurt With Maple Syrup
LATE AFTERNOON	Carrot or Cranberry Juice
EVENING	Spaghetti Squash With Asparagus (freeze half)
LATE EVENING	Dried Dates

DAY 2

MORNING	Quinoa Cereal/Sprouted Sourdough Toast/Cranberry Spread
MID-MORNING	Pumpkin Quinoa Muffins
NOON	Carrot Soup/Sprouted Sourdough Toast
AFTERNOON	Dried Dates
LATE AFTERNOON	Veggie Sticks With Herbed Yogurt Cheese
EVENING	Herbed Baked Fish (Make Half Recipe)/Vegetable Quinoa Pilaf/Sautéed Spinach
LATE EVENING	Quinoa Flake Cookies
	(Prepare Tuna Fish Salad For Tomorrow While You Make Dinner)

DAY 3

MORNING	Cranberry Yogurt Cheese Sandwich
MID-MORNING	Dried Dates
NOON	Tuna Fish Salad On Half Of An Avocado
AFTERNOON	Yogurt With Maple Syrup
LATE AFTERNOON	Veggie Sticks With Herbed Yogurt Cheese
EVENING	Curried Quinoa With Zucchini and Peas
LATE EVENING	Pumpkin Bread

DAY 4

MORNING	Sprouted French Toast
MID-MORNING	Pumpkin Bread
NOON	Tuna Fish Salad On Sprouted Sourdough Toast
AFTERNOON	Carrot or Cranberry Juice
LATE AFTERNOON	Dried Apricots
EVENING	Baked Trout/Vegetable Quinoa Pilaf/Fresh Beets
LATE EVENING	Quinoa Flake Cookies
	(Prepare Green Pea And Quinoa Soup While You Make Dinner)

DAY 5

MORNING	Quinoa Cereal/Sprouted Sourdough Toast/Cranberry Spread
MID-MORNING	Pumpkin Bread
NOON	Green Pea And Quinoa Soup
AFTERNOON	Dried Apricots
LATE AFTERNOON	Cranberry Yogurt Cheese Sandwich
EVENING	Spinach Fritatta (Make Half Recipe)/Vegetable Quinoa Pilaf
LATE EVENING	Yogurt With Maple Syrup

SUPER CLEANSER STAPLES

The shopping list that follows is based on the assumption that certain foods will always be on hand in the pantry; therefore those foods do not appear on the weekly shopping lists.

FRUITS
dried apricots
dried dates
apricot nectar

VEGETABLES
bottled 100% cranberry juice
fresh cranberries (or dried)
canned solid-packed pumpkin
fresh garlic
organic vegetable broth cubes
wild rice

DAIRY PRODUCTS
eggs
yogurt

FISH
canned tuna (packed in water)

GRAINS
quinoa
quinoa flour
quinoa flakes
100% sprouted sourdough bread

OILS
butter
ghee
cooking spray

SWEETENERS
100% maple syrup
maple sugar

SPECIAL ITEMS/HERBS & SPICES
arrowroot
baking powder
baking soda
basil
carob powder
cayenne pepper
cinnamon
curry powder
dill weed
dry mustard
garlic powder
lemon extract
marjoram
mint
onion powder
oregano
paprika
pepper
pumpkin pie spice
salt
vanilla extract

These staples are based on the Super Cleanser Sample Weekly Menu. Some ingredients, because of the volume in which they are purchased, will last more than a week. Hopefully you already have some of the herbs and spices on hand.

SUPER CLEANSER SHOPPING LIST

Based on the Super Cleanser Sample Weekly Menu for two

VEGETABLES

1 lb	asparagus
2–4	fresh beets (about 1 pound)
1 lb	carrots
bunch	celery
bunch	chives
2 whole	sweet red peppers
4½ cups	peas (about 1½ pounds fresh or frozen)
3 bunches	spinach (about 4 pounds)
2 medium	zucchini (about 5 cups)
2 quarts	fresh cranberries
	(or dried: see Cranberry Spread Recipe)
1 quart	carrot juice
bunch	parsley
1	spaghetti squash (about 2½ pounds)
7 cups	vegetable broth

FISH

¾ lb	flounder
2 whole	trout (gutted with heads removed)

SUPER CLEANSER COOKING SCHEDULE

In preparation for this week's menu, stock up on the staples, shop for the ingredients, and prepare the basic recipes. Schedule a few hours (about three depending on expertise) of cooking time the day before you start. By preparing a few foods once a week, meals are easier to assemble each day. Make a copy of the Super Cleanser Sample Weekly Menu recipes for easy reference of ingredients and preparation instructions. Get ready to cook!

The weekly recipes are divided into THREE cooking categories:

1. **Basic recipes to make and have on hand:**

   Cranberry Spread
   Yogurt Cheese
   Herbed Yogurt Cheese
   Yogurt Cheese
   Cranberry Juice
   Quinoa Flake Cookies (freeze extras)

2. **Recipes and recipe items that can be prepared in advance:**

   Pumpkin Bread
   Pumpkin Quinoa Muffins and Waffle batter
   Carrot Soup
   Cook the quinoa and bake spaghetti squash
   Veggie Sticks
   Vegetable Quinoa Pilaf
   Tuna Fish Salad (make Day 2 while you prepare dinner)
   Fresh Beets
   Green Pea and Quinoa Soup (make Day 4 while you prepare dinner)

3. **Recipes made or assembled on the spot:**

   Quinoa Cereal
   Herbed Baked Fish
   Cranberry Yogurt Cheese Sandwich
   Sautéed Spinach
   Baked Trout
   Spinach Fritatta
   Curried Quinoa With Zucchini And Peas
   Spaghetti Squash With Asparagus
   Pumpkin Quinoa Waffles
   Sprouted French Toast
   Tuna Fish Sandwich

SUPER CLEANSER COOKING SESSION

- Preheat oven to 350 degrees.
- In a large saucepan, combine and cook 7 cups of water and 3½ cups of rinsed uncooked quinoa for the following recipes: See Basic Quinoa Recipe for cooking times.
  > *Curried Quinoa With Zucchini And Peas* (requires 1 cup cooked quinoa)
  > *Vegetable Quinoa Pilaf* (requires 6 cups cooked quinoa)
- Set the timer for the quinoa.
- Put an inch of water in a large pot with a strainer insert or vegetable steamer; place beets in steamer. Bring to a boil. Reduce heat to medium and steam beets 45 minutes to an hour until tender when pierced with a fork. Add water as needed so it doesn't evaporate and burn the pan.
- Follow Spaghetti Squash recipe. Clean and bake squash. Set timer.
- While quinoa is cooking, gather, clean and chop all the vegetables for:
  > *Spaghetti Squash With Asparagus (asparagus, red pepper)*
  > *Veggie Sticks (carrots, zucchini, pepper)*
  > *Vegetable Quinoa Pilaf (carrots, spinach)*
  > *Carrot Soup (carrots)*
  > *Spinach Frittata (spinach)*
- Steam the vegetables for the Veggie Sticks recipe in an insert placed in the pot with the boiling water on the stove. See the recipe for steaming time. Remove from pan and cool. Refrigerate. Put asparagus and sliced peppers in separate containers and refrigerate for Spaghetti Squash recipe.
- Remove quinoa from stove when timer rings. Cool.
- Check beets; they should be tender when pierced with a fork. Cool, slip off skins, cut into chunks, and place in a covered bowl. Refrigerate.
- Remove squash from oven when done. Cool. Remove squash from skin (see recipe), refrigerate.
- In a large mixing bowl, prepare Pumpkin Bread batter. Pour into loaf pans and bake for 45 minutes. If a toothpick inserted in the center comes out clean, the bread is done. Cool, slice, wrap airtight, and freeze one of the loaves for later use.
- While the Pumpkin Bread is baking, sauté the vegetables for Vegetable Quinoa Pilaf. Add the cooked quinoa. Cool mixture and place in an airtight container and refrigerate.
- In a large container with a lid, mix a double batch of Pumpkin Quinoa Muffins. When Pumpkin Bread is done turn oven to 400 degrees and cook half of the muffins for 12–15 minutes.
- With the remaining half of the Pumpkin Quinoa Muffin batter, add the additional water and yogurt called for in the Pumpkin Quinoa Waffle recipe. Refrigerate in container until breakfast. At breakfast, bake all the waffles, and freeze what you do not eat.
- Refer to the recipes for more detailed instructions.

DEEP CLEANSER SAMPLE WEEKLY MENU
(BASED ON EATING EVERY TWO HOURS)

DAY 1
MORNING	Pancakes
MID-MORNING	Dried Apricots
NOON	Vegetable Soup
AFTERNOON	Vegetable/Tomato Juice
LATE AFTERNOON	Date Bars
EVENING	Veggie Patties/Baked Potato/Fresh Beets
LATE EVENING	Quinoa Flake Cookies

DAY 2
MORNING	Smoked Salmon On Kefir Cheese Toasts
MID-MORNING	Date Bars
NOON	Baked Potato Topped With Kefir Cheese And Vinegar-Free Salsa
AFTERNOON	Carrot or Cranberry Juice
LATE AFTERNOON	Yogurt With Maple Syrup
EVENING	Vegetable Soup/Grilled Kefir Cheese And Tomato Sandwich
LATE EVENING	Dried Figs

DAY 3
MORNING	Mushroom Scrambled Eggs
MID-MORNING	Date Bars
NOON	Potato/Beet/Quinoa Salad With Yogurt Chive Dressing
AFTERNOON	Carrot or Cranberry Juice
LATE AFTERNOON	Dried Apricots
EVENING	Salmon Burgers/Simply Green Beans
LATE EVENING	Baked Bananas

DAY 4
MORNING	Cranberry Kefir Cheese Sandwich
MID-MORNING	Dried Dates
NOON	Tuna Fish Salad On Sprouted Toast
AFTERNOON	Vegetable/Tomato Juice
LATE AFTERNOON	Quinoa Flake Cookies
EVENING	Potato, Onion And Kefir Cheese Frittata
LATE EVENING	Banana Yogurt Smoothie

DAY 5
MORNING	Sprouted French Toast (or Overnight French Toast)
MID-MORNING	Banana
NOON	Veggie Patties On Sprouted Toast
AFTERNOON	Quinoa Flake Cookies
LATE AFTERNOON	Carrot or Cranberry Juice
EVENING	Veggie Fish Packets
LATE EVENING	Yogurt With Maple Syrup

DEEP CLEANSER STAPLES

The shopping list that follows is based on the assumption that certain foods will always be on hand in the pantry; therefore those foods do not appear on the weekly shopping lists.

FRUITS
dried apricots
dried dates
dried figs

VEGETABLES
bottled 100% cranberry juice
cranberries (fresh or dried)
canned vegetable broth
    (if not homemade)
fresh garlic
organic vegetable broth cubes
vegetable/tomato juice

DAIRY PRODUCTS
eggs
kefir cheese
yogurt

FISH
canned tuna fish (packed in water)

GRAINS
quinoa
quinoa flakes
quinoa flour
100% sprouted bread
100% sprouted spelt flour
100% sprouted seed flour

OILS
butter
ghee
cooking spray

SWEETENERS
100% maple syrup
maple sugar

SOY PRODUCTS
tamari sauce

SPECIAL ITEMS/HERBS & SPICES
arrowroot
baking powder
baking soda
basil
carob powder
cayenne pepper
cinnamon
dill weed
dry mustard
ground ginger
lemon extract
mint
vinegar-free salsa
nutmeg
onion powder
oregano
paprika
pepper
salt
vanilla extract

These staples are based on the Deep Cleanser Sample Weekly Menu. Some ingredients, because of the volume in which they are purchased, will last more than a week. Hopefully you already have some of the herbs and spices on hand.

DEEP CLEANSER SHOPPING LIST

Based on the Deep Cleanser Sample Weekly Menu for two

FRUITS

5 ripe	bananas

VEGETABLES

6 large	baking potatoes
quart	carrot juice
1 lb	bag of carrots
bunch	celery
bunch	chives
1 lb	green beans
½ lb	mushrooms
bunch	green onions
bag	onions
fresh	parsley
5 lb	bag of potatoes
1	red pepper
1	yellow pepper
1 large	sweet potato or yam
bunch	spinach (about 1 pound)
2 medium	tomatoes
1 large	tomato
4	plum tomatoes
28 oz	can cut or diced tomatoes
1 small	zucchini (1 cup)

FISH

6 oz	can salmon (skinless and boneless)
6 slices	smoked salmon or lox, thinly sliced
¾ lb	flounder
¾ lb	white fish fillets (sole, snapper or flounder)

DEEP CLEANSER COOKING SCHEDULE

In preparation for this week's menu, stock up on the staples, shop for the ingredients, and prepare the basic recipes. Schedule a few hours (about three depending on expertise) of cooking time the day before you start. By preparing a few foods once a week, meals are easier to assemble each day. Make a copy of the Deep Cleanser Sample Weekly Menu recipes for easy reference of ingredients and preparation instructions. Get ready to cook!

The weekly recipes are divided into THREE cooking categories:

1. **Basic recipes to make and have on hand:**

   Cranberry Spread
   Cranberry Juice/Ice Tea
   Quinoa Flake Cookies (freeze and use as needed)
   Sprouted Bread Crumbs (freeze and use as needed)
   Yogurt Cheese

2. **Recipes and recipe items that can be prepared in advance:**

   Pancake Mix
   Vegetable Soup
   Date Bars
   Fresh Beets
   Veggie Patties
   Baked Potatoes
   Yogurt Chive Dressing

3. **Recipes made or assembled on the spot:**

   Pancakes
   Smoked Salmon On Kefir Cheese Toasts
   Baked Potatoes Topped With Kefir Cheese And Vinegar-Free Salsa
   Grilled Tomato And Kefir Cheese Sandwiches
   Mushroom Scrambled Eggs
   Potato, Beets, And Quinoa Salad With Yogurt Chive Dressing
   Potato, Onion And Kefir Cheese Frittata
   Salmon Burgers
   Simply Green Beans
   Sprouted French Toast (or Overnight French Toast)
   Veggie Fish Packets
   Banana Yogurt Smoothie
   Yogurt With Maple Syrup

DEEP CLEANSER COOKING SESSION

- Preheat oven to 400 degrees.

- While the oven is heating, put a large covered pot with strainer insert on the stove. Fill with 1-inch of water and bring to a boil.

- While water is heating, clean 6 baking potatoes, place in the oven 30–45 minutes, until cooked through. Set timer.

- Clean beets (skins on) and place in steaming pot, reduce to a simmer and steam according to Fresh Beets Recipe. Set timer. As the beets steam, water may have to be added to the pot.

- While beets and potatoes are cooking, mix ingredients for Date Bars. When potatoes are done, set aside and let cool. (Use 2 potatoes for Day One dinner, 2 for Day Two lunch with topping, 1 in cold salad for Day Three lunch and one in frittata for Day Four.) Reduce oven temperature to 350 degrees and bake Date Bars for 30 minutes. Set Timer.

- When beets are done, remove from heat. Let cool to touch and slip off skins. Refrigerate for Day One dinner and Day Three lunch.

- While Date Bars are baking, put 4 cups of water or vegetable broth and 2 cups rinsed quinoa in a medium sauce pan. Cook as directed in Cooking Quinoa recipe. Note: quinoa recipe is doubled. Set timer for quinoa.

- Remove Date Bars from oven when timer rings. Let cool, cut into squares and store in air-tight container. Freeze extras.

- During the time the quinoa is cooking, mix, in an airtight container, all of the ingredients for the pancake recipe except the baking powder. Refrigerate up to two days. Just before cooking, mix in baking powder.

- Note: Day Three lunch is a salad made up of the already cooked potato, beets and remaining cooked quinoa that was not used in the Veggie Patties. Mix all ingredients together with Yogurt Chive Dressing.

- When quinoa is done, remove from heat. Let cool for later use in Veggie Patties recipe. Refrigerate the rest for Day Three lunch.

- Clean and chop vegetables for Vegetable Soup. Chop enough celery and onions for both soup recipe and Veggie Patties recipe. Make 6 servings recipe, freeze extras. Make soup according to the recipe but eliminate the last step.

- As soup cools and before processing, clean the rest of the vegetables for Veggie Patties and place in food processor. Finish Veggie Patties recipe. Let cool and refrigerate 4 patties for Day One, and freeze the remaining 8 patties for future use.

- Blend cooled soup in food processor. Refrigerate up to three days.

- Continuous kitchen tips: Make a double batch of pancakes. Cook and freeze half. Warm in toaster oven or toaster to reheat. Make a double batch of Date Bars and Quinoa Flake Cookies and freeze half.

BASIC BALANCER SAMPLE WEEKLY MENU
(BASED ON EATING EVERY TWO HOURS)

DAY 1

MORNING	Corn Cereal/Sliced Bananas/Sprouted Toast
MID-MORNING	Carob Brownie
NOON	Cranberry Kefir Cheese Sandwich
AFTERNOON	Dried Dates
LATE AFTERNOON	Carrot or Cranberry Juice
EVENING	Herbed Baked Chicken And Vegetables/Vegetable Quinoa Pilaf
LATE EVENING	Banana Yogurt Smoothie

DAY 2

MORNING	Overnight French Toast
MID-MORNING	Dried Apricots
NOON	Chicken sandwich on sprouted toast with kefir cheese and avocado
AFTERNOON	Popcorn
LATE AFTERNOON	Carob Brownie
EVENING	Spinach Frittata/Roasted Root Vegetables
LATE EVENING	Banana

DAY 3

MORNING	Banana Yogurt Smoothie/Sprouted Toast With Cranberry Spread
MID-MORNING	Carob Brownie
NOON	Avocado/Tomato/Kefir Cheese Sandwich
AFTERNOON	Baked Corn Chips/Vinegar-Free Salsa
LATE AFTERNOON	Cold Vegetable Quinoa Pilaf (as salad)
EVENING	Sweet Root Vegetable Soup/Cornbread
LATE EVENING	Dried Apricots

DAY 4

MORNING	Grilled Or Toasted Cornbread With Maple Syrup
MID-MORNING	One Half Cranberry Kefir Cheese Sandwich
NOON	Chicken Vegetable Soup/Baked Corn Chips
AFTERNOON	Apricot Cheese Stuffed Celery
LATE AFTERNOON	One Half Cranberry Kefir Cheese Sandwich
EVENING	Tuna Pasta Nicoise/Sprouted Bread
LATE EVENING	Popcorn

DAY 5

MORNING	Mushroom Scrambled Eggs/Sprouted Toast With Cranberry Spread
MID-MORNING	Banana Yogurt Smoothie
NOON	Tuna Pasta Nicoise/Sprouted Bread
AFTERNOON	Apricot Cheese Stuffed Celery
LATE AFTERNOON	Baked Corn Chips/Vinegar-Free Salsa
EVENING	Pasta With Quick Red Sauce/Green Salad/ Cranberry Vinaigrette
LATE EVENING	Dried Dates

BASIC BALANCER STAPLES

The shopping list that follows is based on the assumption that certain foods will always be on hand in the pantry; therefore those foods do not appear on the weekly shopping lists.

FRUITS
dried apricots
dried dates

VEGETABLES
baked corn chips
bottled 100% cranberry juice
cranberries (fresh or dried)
canned vegetable broth
fresh garlic
vinegar-free salsa
popcorn

DAIRY PRODUCTS
eggs
kefir cheese
yogurt

MEATS
canned tuna (packed in water)

GRAINS
corn grits
cornmeal
macaroni shaped corn pasta
quinoa
quinoa flour
spelt flour
100% sprouted bread

SWEETENERS
100% maple syrup
maple sugar

OILS
butter
ghee
olive oil
cooking spray

SPECIAL ITEMS/HERBS & SPICES
arrowroot
basil
carob powder
cinnamon
dill weed
dry mustard
marjoram
minced onions
nutmeg
oregano
paprika
parsley
pepper
rosemary
salt
tarragon
vanilla extract

These staples are based on the Basic Balancer Sample Weekly Menu. Some ingredients, because of the volume in which they are purchased, will last more than a week. Hopefully, you already have some of the herbs and spices on hand.

BASIC BALANCER SHOPPING LIST

Based on the Basic Balancer Sample Weekly Menu for two

—ᴍᴍ—

FRUITS

1 ripe	avocado
3 ripe	bananas

VEGETABLES

1 can	black olives
bunch	carrots
bunch	celery
bunch	chives
1 lb	green beans
bunch	green onions
¾ lb	mushrooms
1 bag	onions
bunch	fresh parsley
2	parsnips
1 red	pepper
1 lb	small new potatoes
5 lbs	russet potatoes
1½ lb	rutabaga
2 bunches	spinach
1 large	sweet potato or yam
28 oz	can cut or diced tomatoes
1 can	tomato sauce

MEATS

6 lb	whole chicken

BASIC BALANCER COOKING SCHEDULE

In preparation for this week's menu, stock up on the staples, shop for the ingredients, and prepare the basic recipes. Schedule a few hours (about three, depending on expertise) of cooking time the day before you start. By preparing a few foods once a week, meals are easier to assemble each day. Make a copy of the Basic Balancer Sample Weekly Menu recipes for easy reference of ingredients and preparation instructions. Get ready to cook!

1. **Basic recipes to make and have on hand:**

   Cranberry Spread (extra can be frozen)
   Carob Brownies (can be frozen)
   Cranberry Juice/Ice Tea
   Yogurt Cheese

2. **Recipes and recipe items that can be prepared in advance:**

   Cooked Quinoa For Pilaf
   Overnight French Toast
   Cornbread
   Easy Tomato Sauce (if not store bought)
   Cranberry Vinaigrette
   Apricot Cheese Stuffed Celery

3. **Recipes made or assembled on the spot:**

   Corn Cereal
   Cranberry Kefir Cheese Sandwich
   Herb Roasted Chicken And Vegetables
   Vegetable Quinoa Pilaf
   Banana Yogurt Smoothie
   Chicken sandwich
   Spinach Frittata
   Roasted Root Vegetables
   Avocado/Tomato/Kefir Cheese Sandwich
   Sweet Root Vegetable Soup
   Chicken Vegetable Soup
   Tuna Pasta Nicoise
   Corn Pasta

BASIC BALANCER COOKING SESSION

Preheat oven to 350 degrees. Clean and bake chicken according to Herb Roasted Chicken and Vegetable Recipe. A six pound chicken will take approximately 2 hours to bake.

- While the chicken is baking, combine 1 cup rinsed quinoa and 2 cups water or broth in a medium saucepan. Set timer per directions in Cooking Quinoa recipe.

- If a second oven is available, preheat to 350 degrees. While quinoa is cooking, assemble and begin to mix ingredients for Carob Brownies. Do not combine dry and wet ingredients for brownies until oven is ready. If only one oven is available, wait until chicken is cooked. Bake brownies.

- When timer rings, remove quinoa from stove and let cool. If time allows, make Vegetable Quinoa Pilaf. If not, refrigerate quinoa until ready to use.

- While brownies are baking, mix ingredients for cornbread. When brownies are finished, turn oven to 375 degrees. Bake cornbread.

- As cornbread bakes, begin to clean and cut vegetables for Roasted Root Vegetable recipe. When cornbread is baked, turn oven up to 410 degrees. Roast vegetables per recipe instructions.

- Remove chicken from oven when cooked. Serve for dinner or refrigerate for Day One.

- Tips for the continuous kitchen: save the extra chicken from Day One dinner to make sandwiches for Day Two lunch. After making the sandwiches, remove remaining chicken by tearing or cutting into bite-size pieces. Refrigerate pieces until adding to the soup in Day Four lunch.

- Use the remaining Roasted Root Vegetables from Day Two dinner to make Sweet Root Vegetable Soup for Day Three dinner. Place the vegetables in a sauce pan and add the remaining ingredients as stated in the recipe. (Remember, the veggies are already cooked.) On Day Four just add the chicken pieces to make Chicken Vegetable Soup.

- Double the recipe for Cranberry Vinaigrette. Use in Tuna Pasta Nicoise and toss with greens.

Chapter 6

Recipe Categories

The Recipe Section is categorized in a somewhat traditional manner, but understand that eating every two hours is not conducive to a breakfast, lunch and dinner schedule. As can be seen in the Weekly Menu Section, foods are outlined by every two hours, not just breakfast, lunch and dinner.

Most of the recipes are for the Basic Diets. Once you have followed essential eating for several months, you will begin to make your own food combinations from the YES/NO foods list. You will be able to convert recipes and create recipes of your own. I have a friend who purchased an ice cream maker and has been creating her own sweet concoctions within the parameters of the diet! (See "Frozen Desserts" in the recipe section)

Reading the Recipes

Let me explain the format of the recipes to make them even more user-friendly. Each recipe lists the PHASE of the diet to the side of the recipe name. This makes it easy to select the recipes you can cook based on your YES/NO foods list. This is how it works. If the Super Cleanser is listed then everyone on the Super Cleanser level to Graduation can use this recipe. If the recipe lists Basic Balancer, then only Basic Balancers to Graduation can use this recipe. If the recipe lists Basic Balancer, then there are foods included that the bodies following the Super Cleanser and Deep Cleanser cannot digest yet.

Variations and/or ingredient substitutions are noted in italics at the end of each recipe. Most often, like ingredients can be substituted as you work through the Phases. For example, Phase Two may substitute olive oil instead of butter when sautéing vegetables. Basic Balancers may substitute corn flour for quinoa flour where noted. Look for these substitutions at the end of the recipes.

The TIME noted on each recipe is the time to prepare and cook the foods. This may vary depending on your level of expertise and the type of stove or oven you have.

The number of SERVINGS is based on average portions. Use this as a guide. If you prepare a recipe for a snack it might have a different number of servings than if you prepare it for an entree.

When a recipe is capitalized within a recipe, such as Yogurt Cheese or Cranberry Spread, it can be located in its appropriate recipe category.

In the beginning, you will need to prepare a few basic recipes to have on hand or freeze for future use. If a recipe calls for an ingredient that needs to be previously prepared, such as Yogurt Cheese or Sprouted Beans, refer to the recipe for how-to instructions.

For all recipes, flour does not need to be sifted, but fluff it up before measuring, because it tends to get compacted when shipped. All diets may use extracts (like vanilla or orange), baking soda, baking powder, spray on cooking oils and other lecithin-based butter and oil alternatives.

When cooking different vegetables at the same time, cut them in a uniform size as it helps them to cook more evenly. Cook hard, dense vegetables, such as carrots, potatoes, onions, and celery first and then add soft ones like mushrooms, greens, and sprouts. Use your eyes in cooking. If it doesn't look right, it probably isn't.

It is a good idea to read each recipe completely prior to preparation to make sure you have all the ingredients on hand. This is where the copy of your weekly menu comes in handy.

These recipes are intended to help you introduce new and easy-to-digest ingredients back into your diet. Your body will signal its preferences. It's your job to listen—for example, if garlic doesn't taste good to you, then omit it. If you want more spice, than add it. Use these recipes as inspiration for developing your own creations.

The following is a list of recipes for each of the three Basic Diets.

Super Cleanser Recipe List

Recipe Index Page 327

Basics

Fish Broth, Homemade Ghee, Hard Boiled Eggs, Herbed Yogurt Cheese, Homemade Yogurt, Sprouted Bread Crumbs, Vegetable Broth, Yogurt Cheese, Yogurt Milk

Beverages

Cranberry Juice, Cream Soda and Ginger Ale, Date Shake, Fruit Smoothie, Lassi

Breads and Muffins

Cinnamon Muffins, Cranberry Pumpkin Bread, Pumpkin Bread, Pumpkin Quinoa Muffins, Zucchini Bread and Muffins

Breakfast and Brunch

Cinnamon Toast, Granola, Pancakes, Pumpkin Pancakes, Pumpkin Quinoa Waffles, Quinoa Cereal, Sprouted French Toast, Waffles

Salads

Crab Salad, Green Bean and Olive Salad, Tuna Fish Salad

Sandwiches

Cranberry Yogurt Cheese Sandwich, Fried Egg Sandwich, Smoked Salmon Sandwich

Soups

Green Pea and Quinoa, Green Pea, Pumpkin, Quinoa Vegetable

Sauces, Spreads, and Marinades

Avocado Dressing, Cranberry Spread, Essential Mayonnaise, Fruit Dressing, Fruit Preserves, Guacamole, Roasted Garlic Dressing, White Gravy, Yogurt Chive Dressing

Grains

Cooked Quinoa, Curried Quinoa with Zucchini and Peas, Green Quinoa, Quinoa with Asparagus and Basil, Vegetable Quinoa Pilaf

Vegetable Entrees

Poached Eggs on Wild Rice, Spaghetti Squash with Asparagus, Spinach Frittata, Stir-Fried Carrots, Jicama and Watercress, Vegetable Omelet

Vegetables

Fresh Beets, Herbed Mixed Peas, Maple Acorn Squash, Roasted Garlic, Sautéed Greens, Sautéed Spinach, Veggie Sticks, Vegetable Herb Rice, Zucchini Pancakes

Fish

Baked Trout, Crab Cakes, Fish Florentine, Herbed Baked Fish, Lemon Oregano Sea Bass, Poached Salmon with Dill, Salmon Loaf, Yogurt Baked Halibut

Dehydrated Foods

Fruit Leather, Maple Taffy

Cakes and Sweets

Apricot Yogurt Parfait, Carob Fudge, Carrot Cake, Creamy Maple Yogurt, Fruit Cobbler with Maple Topping, Gingerbread, Pan-fried Apricots, Pumpkin Cake, Vanilla Custard

Frostings and Toppings

Maple Caramel Frosting, Maple Crumb Topping, Maple Frosting, Yogurt Cheese Frosting, Yogurt Cheese Whipping Cream

Frozen Desserts

Apricot Sorbet

Cookies, Crackers, and Bars

Apricot Bars, Carob Brownies, Carob Cake Brownies, Date Bars, Fudgey Carob Brownies, Granola Bars, Maple Cookies, Meringue Cookies, Pumpkin Cookies, Quinoa Flake Cookies, Quinoa "Oatmeal" Cookies, Quinoa Cookies

Deep Cleanser Recipe List
Recipe Index Page 327

In addition to all the Super Cleanser Recipes listed.

Basics

Graham Cracker Crust, Sprouted Pie Crust, Sprouted Soy Milk, Sprouted Wheat Flakes, Sprouted Wheat Flour

Beverages

Banana Yogurt Smoothie

Tea Blends

Ginger Tea Blend, Lemon Tea Blend, Licorice Tea Blend, Mint Tea Blend, Muscle Relaxing Tea Blend, Sun Tea, Super Cleanser Tea Blend

Breads and Muffins

Baking Powder Biscuits, Fig Bread, Sprouted Rye Bread, Olive Rosemary Bread, Spelt Zucchini Bread

Breakfast and Brunch

Chunky Granola, Coffee Cake, Cream of Sprouted Spelt Cereal, Egg Soufflé, Mushroom Scrambled Eggs, Overnight French Toast, Smoked Salmon on Kefir Cheese Toast

Salads

Cooked Carrot Salad, Shredded Carrot Salad

Sandwiches

Portobello Mushroom Sandwich, Sprouted Bean Bruschetta

Soups

Beet Soup, Butternut Squash, Carrot, Carrot Celery Root, Creamy Green Bean, Creamy Mushroom, Fish Stew, Miso, Potato and Greens, Potato Leek, Spicy Pumpkin, Sweet Potato, Sweet Root Vegetable, Tomato Pomodoro, Vegetable Lentil, Vegetable Wild Rice

Sprouted Beans, Legumes, and Seeds

Bean Balls, Cooking Sprouted Beans, Refried Beans, Shelley's Chili, Sprouted Baked Beans, Sprouted Bean Burgers, Sprouted Bean and Tomato Bisque, Sprouted Bean Dip, Sprouted Pea Soup, Sprouted Pea Stew, Sprouted Soyburgers

Sauces, Spreads, and Marinades

Baked Potato Topper, Basil Tomato Sauce, Crabmeat Dip, Creamy French Dressing, Mushroom Gravy, Quick Tomato Sauce, Vinegar-Free Catsup

Pasta and Grains

Cranberry Stuffing, Quinoa Stuffing, Sprouted Grain Stuffing, Tomato and Fennel Quinoa

Vegetable Entrees

Caponata, Hash Brown Omelet, Italian Omelet, Mushroom Curry, Mushroom Crusted Quiche, Portobello Pizzas, Potato, Onion and Kefir Cheese Frittata, Potato Vegetable Patties, Quinoa Stuffed Peppers, Spaghetti Squash with Red Sauce, Vegetable Pizza, Veggie Patties, Winter Squash Burgers

Vegetables

Apricot Cheese Stuffed Celery, Artichokes with Potatoes, Carrots and Leeks, Baked Potato Fries, Butternut Squash, Potato and Tomato Gratin, Carrot Loaf, Celery Root Mashed Potatoes, Chard with New Potatoes, Cottage Potatoes, Curried Sweet Potatoes, Eggplant, Tomato and Onion Gratin, Fried Wild Rice, Italian Green Beans, Mashed Potatoes, Mediterranean Mushrooms, Oven Fried Potatoes, Potato Pancakes, Roasted Celery Root, Onions and Mushrooms, Roasted Root Vegetables, Simply Steamed Beans, Spanish Wild Rice, Sweet Potato Casserole, Vegetable Mashed Potatoes, Vegetable Stuffed Squash, Wild Rice with Apricots

Fish

Fish Burgers, Mediterranean Fish, Oriental Salmon Fillets, Salmon Burgers, Salmon Potato Cakes, Salmon with Vegetables, Striped Bass with Tomato Sauce, Stuffed Fish Rolls, Tuna Burger, Tuna Casserole, Veggie Fish Packets

Dehydrated Foods

Banana Chips, Beet Chips, Dehydrated Tomato Sauce, Tomato Leather, Zucchini Chips

Cakes and Sweets

Apricot Cake, Angel Food Cake, Baked Bananas, Banana Cheesecake, Banana Cream Parfait, Carob Pound Cake, Maple Bundt Cake, Maple Layer Cake, Poppy Seed Cake, Brownie Sheet Cake, Pumpkin Chiffon Pie, Pumpkin Spice Cake, Upside-Down Apricot Cake, Yogurt Sundae

Frozen Desserts

Cranberry Frozen Yogurt, French Vanilla Frozen Yogurt

Cookies, Crackers, and Bars

Butterscotch Brownies, Cranberry Cookies, Date Squares, Poppy Seed Crackers, Sprouted Graham Crackers, Wheat Thin Crackers

Basic Balancer Recipe List
Recipe Index Page 327

In addition to the Super Cleanser and Deep Cleanser recipes listed.

Basics

Basic Polenta, Chicken Broth, Coconut Milk, Corn Flake Crust, Raw Coconut

Beverages

Coconut Carob Drink

Tea Blends

Black Tea Blend

Breads and Muffins

Banana Bread, Breadsticks, Cornbread, Quinoa Cornbread, Sprouted Spelt Bread

Breakfast and Brunch

Banana Flats, Breakfast Burrito, Corn Cakes, Corn Cereal, Corn Flake Cereal, Cornmeal Pancakes, Grilled Polenta

Salads

Cucumber Carrot Salad, Egg Salad, Herbed Quinoa Salad, Marinated Mushroom Salad, Marinated Tomato and Potato Salad, Potato, Beet and Cucumber Salad, Roasted Corn Salad, Slivered Endive Salad, Spinach and Quinoa Salad, Spinach Avocado Salad, Tuna and Potato Salad, Wild Rice Salad

Sandwiches

ALT, Grilled Kefir Cheese and Tomato, Salmon Spread, Veggie Sandwich Spread

Soups

Avocado Cucumber, Chicken Avocado, Polenta Stew, Quick Chicken Noodle, Quick Gazpacho, Roasted Squash and Tomato, Spinach Corn, Sweet Potato, Tomato Florentine, Tortilla, Vegetable, Wholesome Chicken

Sprouted Beans, Legumes, and Seeds

Kidney Bean Salad

Sauces, Spreads, and Marinades

Asparagus Guacamole, Basil Dressing, Cranberry Vinaigrette, Cucumber Dill Dressing, Gazpacho Dressing, Miso Dressing, Roasted Tomato Basil Pesto

Grains and Pasta

Buttered Noodles, Pasta with Olive Mushroom Sauce, Pasta with Quick Red Sauce, Pasta Primavera, Confetti Rice with Corn Tortillas

Vegetable Entrees

Quesadilla, Roasted Sweet Potato Tortillas, Soft Polenta with Mushrooms, Vegetable Enchiladas

Vegetables

Mashed Yams, Polenta Bites, Sweet Potato Fries

Fish and Chicken

Crab Quiche, Salmon Appetizer Roll, Sushi Rolls, Tuna Pasta Nicoise, Tuna Quiche, Chicken Burgers, Chicken Cacciatore, Chicken Hash, Chicken Paella, Chicken Spinach Loaf, Chicken Vegetable Loaf, Chicken with Herb Sauce, Herb Roasted Chicken and Vegetables, Marinated Chicken, Meatballs, One Pan Chicken and Vegetables, Oven Fried Chicken, Quick Italian Chicken, Rosemary Lemon Chicken, Stir-Fry Chicken, Tandoori Chicken, Tandoori Chicken Shish-ka-bob

Cakes and Sweets

Caramel Corn, Carob Sour Cream Cake, Crunch Parfait, Layered Cheesecake

Frostings and Toppings

Maple Sugar Icing

Cookies, Crackers, and Bars

Carob Cookies, Cheese Crackers, Coconut Icebox Cookies, Coconut Macaroons

Recipes

Basics

The basic recipes are food items that need to be prepared prior to making other recipes, such as Fish Broth, Sprouted Bread Crumbs, and Yogurt Cheese. Also included here are "how to" instructions on basic foods, such as Almond Milk, Hard-boiled Eggs, and Vegetable Broth.

Almond Milk

1 cup almonds
1 ½ cups water

PHASE THREE
4 servings
6 hours

Soak almonds in water to soften, about 6 hours or overnight. Totally blend nuts and water in a blender. Strain through a fine sieve. Adjust consistency with more or less water. Add maple syrup if a sweeter milk is desired. Store refrigerated in an airtight container. Yields about 2 cups.

Nut milks are a great way to get protein into your diet. They are easier to digest than oat or rice milk.

Basic Polenta

2 cups yellow or white corn grits
6 cups water
1 teaspoon sea salt (optional)

BASIC BALANCER
6 servings
15 minutes

In large sauce pan bring water to a boil. Slowly whisk in corn grits and simmer, stirring frequently for 10 minutes, until thickened and grits are soft. Serve hot with maple syrup and butter or in desired recipe.

For grilled polenta, pour cooked polenta into greased loaf pan and chill overnight. Slice and fry in buttered skillet about 8 minutes on each side until crisp on the outside. For variation, make polenta with vegetable or chicken broth instead of water and serve topped with sautéd or grilled vegetables.

Cashew Milk

1 cup raw cashews
3 cups water
2 tablespoons maple syrup

PHASE FOUR
6 servings
10 minutes

Purée all ingredients in a blender until smooth. Add syrup to sweeten. Store in an airtight container in the refrigerator.

Try over a bowl of organic corn flakes!

Chicken Broth

2 pounds chicken, pieces or bones
8 cups water
1 large onion, quartered
2 large carrots or parsnips, cut in 2-inch pieces
3 celery stalks, cut in 3-inch pieces
4 fresh parsley sprigs
2 bay leaves
½ teaspoon ground pepper
1 teaspoon dried thyme
1 teaspoon dried marjoram
1 teaspoon dried oregano
salt to taste

BASIC BALANCER
8 servings
1 hour 45 minutes

Place the washed chicken parts or bones in a large stock pot. Add the water and all remaining ingredients, except salt. Bring to a boil, reduce heat, and simmer partially covered for 1–1½ hours or up to 4 hours. Skim off the film during the first 30 minutes. Salt to taste, strain, and cool uncovered. Chill and skim off congealed fat.

Do not use the liver or heart of the chicken as it clouds the broth. Broth may be stored in the refrigerator for up to three days or frozen in pre-measured amounts for soups and sauces. Also, the broth can be frozen in ice cube trays and then stored in plastic bags for easy use.

Coconut Milk

1 cup shredded, dried coconut
1 teaspoon sweetener
3 cups water
pinch of salt

BASIC BALANCER
4 servings
5 minutes

Blend ingredients in a blender for 3 minutes. Strain. Makes about 2 cups. Servings depend on recipe usage.

✐ *This is a rich milk that can be used for sauces, puddings, or a super rich drink.*

Corn Flake Crust

5 cups corn flakes
1 tablespoon maple syrup
2 tablespoons softened butter
¼ teaspoon cinnamon

BASIC BALANCER
8 servings
10 minutes

Preheat oven to 350 degrees. Put corn flakes in a plastic bag and crush into fine crumbs with a rolling pin; makes about 2 cups of crumbs. Place crumbs in a medium bowl and mix in syrup, butter, and cinnamon. Press crumbs in the bottom and up the sides of an 8 or 9-inch pie plate, baking dish, or spring form pan. If the pie or cheesecake is to be baked, add the filling and bake according to the recipe. If the filling is already cooked, bake the crust for 6–8 minutes, or until lightly browned. Cool before filling.

Graham Cracker Crust

1⅔ cups Sprouted Graham Cracker Crumbs
¼ cup maple sugar
⅓ cup softened butter

DEEP CLEANSER
8 servings
15 minutes

Preheat oven to 375. In a medium bowl, blend ingredients with a fork. Using the back of a large spoon, press crumbs evenly into a 9-inch pie plate or spring form pan. Bake 6 minutes. Set on wire rack to cool.

✐ *For a no-bake crust, chill in refrigerator for 30 minutes. Fill with chilled yogurt filling or freeze for frozen yogurt filling.*

Fish Broth

1 ½ pounds white fish and bones
1 large carrot, sliced
1 cup chives, cut in 2-inch lengths
2 stalks celery, chopped
2 cloves
1 bay leaf
¼ teaspoon ground pepper
8 cups cold water
salt to taste

SUPER CLEANSER
7 servings
45 minutes

Chop vegetables. In a large stock pot, combine all the ingredients except salt and bring to a boil. Reduce heat and simmer, uncovered, for 30 minutes, skimming any foam off the surface. Season to taste with salt. Cool uncovered. Strain.

౸ *Deep Cleansers and beyond may use 1 large onion instead of chives.*

Homemade Ghee

2 cups butter (4 sticks)

SUPER CLEANSER
servings based
on usage
45 minutes

In a medium saucepan, melt butter over low heat. Simmer 30 minutes. Cool until bubbles stop and solids sink to the bottom of the pan. When cool enough, pour only the top oil into an airtight container and discard solids. Refrigerate up to one month.

౸ *For a version that does not store as long, melt two sticks of butter, skim the whey particles off the top and discard. Pour cooled oil in airtight container and refrigerate up to two weeks. Ghee can also be purchased.*
Ghee (or clarified butter) is butter with the excess water and a few protein molecules skimmed off or cooked out of the oil. One of the advantages of ghee is that it can be heated to high temperatures without burning, since the excess water and proteins are what makes butter burn easily.

Hard-Boiled Eggs

6 large eggs

SUPER CLEANSER

6 servings

25 minutes

In a medium sauce pan, place eggs and enough water to cover them by 1-inch. Bring water to boil over medium-high heat. Boil for 3 minutes and remove from heat. Cover and let sit for 10 minutes. Fill a medium bowl with 1 quart cold water and 2 cups of ice cubes. Transfer eggs to ice water with slotted spoon and let sit 5 minutes. To shell hard-boiled eggs, crack the shell on the counter and roll between the palms of the hands. This will make shelling easier.

Herbed Yogurt Cheese

2 cups Yogurt Cheese
½ teaspoon dried oregano
½ teaspoon dried basil
½ teaspoon dried marjoram
2 tablespoons chopped parsley
1 clove garlic, minced (optional)

SUPER CLEANSER

8 servings

10 minutes

Blend all ingredients together and chill.

   Other fresh or dried herbs to use in combination or alone: tarragon, cilantro, chervil, or watercress. Create other variations using any of the following: cayenne, sage, marjoram, thyme, onion powder, chives, curry powder, or savory. Or: chopped dates or ground apricots, nutmeg, allspice, ginger, cloves and cinnamon.

Homemade Yogurt

1 quart skim or whole milk (see note below)
½ cup low fat yogurt
¼ cup powdered milk

SUPER CLEANSER
6 servings
4 hours

Place milk in a saucepan and warm on medium heat until almost boiling, 185–190 degrees. Cool milk to 115 degrees and add yogurt and powdered milk. Keep warm, no less than 105 degrees, for 3–4 hours or until firm.

ᴄ⁓ *Container can be wrapped in down blanket or jacket to keep warm or use an electric yogurt maker. Although milk is used in this recipe, it turns into yogurt which is a YES food.*

Raw Coconut

1 whole coconut

BASIC BALANCER
8 servings
10 minutes

With the coconut in one hand and a hammer in the other, strike the center of the coconut with the hammer. Most coconuts are already scored in the middle. Do not put the coconut on a hard surface to strike. It should crack easily while holding it over a sink. Coconut milk will leak out once the shell is cracked. Once the coconut is broken into pieces, carefully separate the shell from the raw coconut using a knife. Grate or shred for recipes. Refrigerate, as it is perishable. Shredded coconut can be dehydrated. Chunks of coconut can also be frozen; shred or grate when ready to use.

Sprouted Bread Crumbs

4 slices sprouted sourdough bread

SUPER CLEANSER
servings based
on usage
10 minutes

Toast bread slices until crisp but not burnt. Let cool. Tear into chunks and place in food processor. Pulse until bread turns into crumbs. Yields 2 cups.

❧ *Sprouted sourdough bread may be purchased at a health food store. Other diets can use sprouted grain bread. Crumbs can be wrapped tightly and frozen for future use.*

Sprouted Pie Crust

1 cup sprouted flour
¼ teaspoon salt
⅓ cup butter
1 tablespoon kefir cheese
2 tablespoons water

DEEP CLEANSER
1 pie crust
15 minutes

In a medium bowl, mix flour and salt. Using a pastry knife or fork, cut butter into flour and blend until mixture resembles coarse crumbs. In a small bowl, mix kefir cheese and water. Add liquid to crumb mixture. Dough will still be crumbly. On a lightly floured surface, knead until dough is smooth, adding a little flour if needed to prevent sticking. Roll out to 12-inch diameter. Using an 8-inch pie pan, lay crust over and flute edges.

❧ *Double recipe for two pie crusts. Dough can be stored in the refrigerator for three days.*

Fresh Arugula

OPPOSITE PAGE:
Sprouted Pea Soup

Grilled Kefir Cheese
& Tomato Sandwich

Quinoa Stuffed Peppers

OPPOSITE PAGE:
Maple Acorn Squash

Vegetable Quinoa Pilaf

ABOVE:
Fresh Bell Peppers

OPPOSITE PAGE:
Carrot Cucumber Salad
Roasted Corn Salad

Fresh Chili Peppers

RIGHT:
Potato Leek Soup
Tomato Florentine Soup

OPPOSITE PAGE:
Roasted Garlic

ABOVE:
Eggplant, Tomato
and Onion Gratin

OPPOSITE PAGE:
Baked Trout
Oven Fried Potatoes

Sprouted Soy Milk

1 cup sprouted soybeans
1 tablespoon melted butter
2 tablespoons honey or maple syrup
10 cups boiling water
¼ teaspoon salt

DEEP CLEANSER
8 servings
13 hours

This is a "hot water method" of making soy milk developed by Cornell University. It produces a nutritious and good tasting milk. Using boiling water prevents activation of the enzyme lipoxidase which tends to make soy milk bitter tasting. When sprouted soybeans are used, the resulting product is digested like a vegetable in the body.

Check soybeans over, discarding any broken beans. Soak in 3 cups water for 12 hours. Rinse and drain. Bring the 10 cups of water to a rolling boil and keep boiling. Put two cups of the boiling water into the blender and run for one minute. This will preheat blender. Wrap blender top with a towel to protect yourself from getting burned. Empty blender. Now blend ⅓ of the soaked beans with 1⅓ cup boiling water for 3 minutes. Strain through a cheesecloth. Repeat process. Add the butter, honey and salt to the strained milk. Add extra water to make 1 quart of milk. Heat strained milk in double boiler for 30 minutes. Refrigerate. Servings depend on recipe usage.

Sprouted Wheat Flakes

1 pound wheat berries

DEEP CLEANSER
8 servings
40 minutes

Soak wheat berries in water for at least 36 hours, changing the water once or twice. A small tip should emerge at the pointed end of the grain. Spread the soaked berries out on a hard, flat surface. Pound them flat with a rolling pin. Spread them on a screen to dry. A cool dehydrator or a 100 degree oven will speed up the process. Servings depend on recipe usage.

Wheat flakes may be used in hot cereal, granola, cookies, and meat loaf recipes as a rolled oats substitute.

Sprouted Wheat Flour

1 pound wheat berries

DEEP CLEANSER
8 servings
40 minutes

Soak a pound of wheat berries in water for at least 36 hours, changing the water once or twice. A small tip should emerge at the pointed end of the grain. Drain. Spread the berries to dry on screens, using a cool dehydrator or dry on cookie sheets in a 100 degree oven. When thoroughly dry, grind the berries in a regular flour mill.

℮ *Sprouted wheat flour is called PANOCHA flour.*

Vegetable Broth

1 cup chives, cut in 2-inch lengths
1 cup coarsely chopped celery with leaves
1 cup coarsely chopped carrot
4 sprigs parsley, with stems
1 teaspoon dried thyme
1 bay leaf
1 teaspoon salt
1 teaspoon pepper
½ teaspoon onion powder
8 cups water

SUPER CLEANSER
7 servings
40 minutes

Place all ingredients in a large stock pot. Bring to a boil. Reduce heat and simmer, uncovered, for 45 minutes. Cooking broth longer makes it bitter. Strain through a sieve or a colander lined with cheesecloth. Cool broth uncovered. Yields about 7 cups.

℮ *Deep Cleansers and beyond may substitute 2 large leeks, sliced, for chives and add 2 large potatoes, chopped. Vegetable broth is the liquid in which vegetables have been cooked. It is fine to vary this recipe. Try adding garlic or beet greens. Use broth immediately or refrigerate in a tightly covered container for 3 to 4 days. Broth may be frozen for up to 1 month. Freeze in 1 to 2 cup containers for easy use.*
   Broth can be as simple as saving your cleaned vegetable scraps and simmering in water.

Yogurt Cheese

32 ounces yogurt (2 pounds)

SUPER CLEANSER
4 servings
2–12 hours

Put yogurt into a yogurt strainer. A regular strainer lined with cheesecloth or a cheesecloth bag, suspended over a bowl, will also work. Cover and leave in refrigerator for at least 2 hours. Yogurt Cheese becomes thicker the longer it is allowed to drain. Its thickest point should be reached in 24 hours. Discard whey and store airtight up to 9 days in the refrigerator. Yields 2 cups.

Yogurt is composed of coagulated particles that are suspended in a watery liquid. Yogurt Cheese is made by draining off the liquid, while retaining the curds. The Yogurt Cheese will keep up to two weeks in an airtight container. Yogurt Cheese can be used as a substitute for cream cheese and sour cream. It also makes delicious dips, salad dressings, spreads, and cheese cakes. Mix more vanilla, maple syrup, or fruit purées into yogurt for a sweeter result. (For yogurt strainer, see Sources)

Yogurt Milk

3 tablespoons Yogurt Cheese
1 cup water
1 teaspoon maple syrup

SUPER CLEANSER
2 servings
2 minutes

In a small bowl, whisk the ingredients together. The mixture should have the consistency of milk. Adjust consistency with more or less water or Yogurt Cheese. Add more syrup to make milk sweeter. Yogurt Milk is used in many recipes as a substitution for milk. Servings depend on recipe usage.

⅓ cup of yogurt may be substituted for Yogurt Cheese. Depending on the type of yogurt used, there may be harmless tiny white specks remaining in the milk.

Beverages

Many types of easy-to-digest beverages are included here. Try both hot and cold selections from Hot Herbal Cranberry Drink to Banana Yogurt Smoothies. Make Cranberry Juice and keep it in the refrigerator for an easy snack.

Don't forget about plain, fresh water. Water is the body's most essential nutrient and should be the primary beverage in the essential eating diet.

Banana Yogurt Smoothie

2 cups yogurt
2 overripe bananas
4 teaspoons maple syrup (or to taste)
¾ teaspoon cinnamon
2 pinches nutmeg
¼ teaspoon vanilla

DEEP CLEANSER
4 servings
5 minutes

Blend all ingredients until smooth.

Phase Two Diet may add 4 tablespoons hazelnut butter.

Coconut Carob Drink

1 quart coconut milk
4 tablespoons maple syrup
4 teaspoons carob powder
3 teaspoons melted butter
1 ½ teaspoons vanilla
pinch of salt

BASIC BALANCER
4 servings
10 minutes

Blend all ingredients. See how to make Coconut Milk under Basics.

Cream Soda and Ginger Ale

1 tablespoon maple syrup
3 drops vanilla (or to taste)
sparkling water
fresh ginger slices for ginger ale

SUPER CLEANSER
1 serving
2 minutes

Combine maple syrup and vanilla in a glass and add sparkling water. For ginger ale, add slices of fresh ginger.

Cold-Pressed Coffee

1 pound regular grind, organic coffee
12 cups cold water

PHASE FOUR
72 servings
36 hours

Mix coffee and water in a large bowl or jar. Let sit, without refrigerating, for 36 hours. Strain the grounds using a 3 quart strainer lined with moist coffee filters. Scoop grounds onto filters to hold them in place. Run the remaining liquid through the grounds, saving the strained liquid in a jar or jars. The strained liquid is the coffee extract. Pour 1–2 cups of plain cold water over the grounds and add this diluted coffee extract to the stronger extract. This way you get the most for your money. A fine sieve may also be used to strain the coffee grounds from the liquid. A few of the finer grounds will fall through, but they will settle to the bottom of the extract. Remember, coffee made this way digests like a fruit!

To make one cup of coffee, taking into consideration cup size, extract strength, and personal taste, place 1–4 tablespoons of extract into a cup and add boiling water. To store, refrigerate the extract in a jar or freeze in ice cube trays. Servings depend on usage per cup.

℮ *Making coffee using boiling water to "extract" the coffee flavor from the coffee bean, releases the coffee's oil and acids into the water causing digestive problems. Using the cold-pressed method does not cause this release and makes the most wonderful cup of coffee without stomach upset.*

Cranberry Juice

4 cups 100% pure cranberry juice
4 cups water
1 cup maple syrup

SUPER CLEANSER
8 servings
5 minutes

Pour a 32 ounce jar of cranberry juice into a large pitcher. Fill empty juice jar with water and add to pitcher. Add maple syrup and stir. Chill and serve. Additional maple syrup can be added for a sweeter taste. Because cranberries digest like a vegetable, this is a vegetable drink!

℮ *Just Cranberry is made by R. W. Knudsen Family and comes in 32 fluid ounce jars. Most health food stores and some grocery stores stock this product. It is 100% pure cranberry juice made from concentrate. Other brands will work if they are 100% pure cranberry juice. The juice is a little pricey, but remember it is doubled in volume by water in this recipe.*

Date Shake

½ cup pitted, chopped dates
2–3 teaspoons water
1 cup yogurt
1 cup crushed ice

SUPER CLEANSER
2 servings
5 minutes

Pit and chop dates. Mix with 2–3 teaspoons of water. Put dates and yogurt in a blender, pulse on and off to make a paste mixture. Put ice cubes in a plastic bag and hammer into small pieces before adding to the blender. Blend until foamy.

℮ *Add 1 teaspoon of carob powder for variation.*

Fruit Smoothie

1 cup fruit (only one kind, not mixed)
⅔ cup yogurt
½ teaspoon vanilla extract
½ cup 100% pure cranberry juice
¼ cup maple syrup
4 ice cubes
¼ cup water

SUPER CLEANSER
2 servings
5 minutes

Combine all ingredients in a blender and purée until smooth. Serve.

Ginger Cranberry Tea

6 cups water
1 cup 100% pure cranberry juice
½ cup maple syrup (or to taste)
1 3-inch piece fresh ginger, peeled and thinly sliced
4 herbal tea bags

DEEP CLEANSER
8 servings
40 minutes

In a saucepan, combine all the ingredients, except the tea bags. Bring to a simmer over medium heat, stirring to mix. Remove from heat, add tea bags and let steep for 5 minutes. Remove tea bags and continue to steep for up to 30 minutes. Strain and serve hot or cold.

Hot Herbal Cranberry Drink

16 fluid ounces 100% pure cranberry
juice (½ quart)
16 ounces water
2 herbal orange or spice teas bags
dash of ground cloves
½ cup maple syrup (or to taste)
6 cinnamon sticks (optional)

DEEP CLEANSER
6 servings
10 minutes

In a medium saucepan, combine ingredients and heat. Remove tea bags from the pan and serve beverage in mugs with cinnamon sticks.

Lassi

1 cup yogurt
6 tablespoons maple syrup
8 drops rose water
¾ cup water
¼ teaspoon ground cardamom

SUPER CLEANSER
1 serving
1 minute

Blend until smooth. Serve cold.

Peach Juice

6 ripe pitted peaches
4 tablespoons maple syrup (or to taste)

PHASE TWO
4 servings
20 minutes

Juice the peaches in a juicer. Add maple syrup for a sweeter taste. If a juicer is not available, purée peaches and maple syrup in a blender. Thin with water to desired consistency.

   Pour undiluted peach juice on nonstick plastic sheets and dehydrate for fruit roll-ups. Freeze juice in plastic water bottles for an on-the-go snack. Take out of the freezer in the morning and by lunch it will be thawed. Meanwhile it has a built-in ice cube.

Sunrise Shake

1 cup fresh squeezed orange juice
¼ cup 100% pure cranberry juice
¼ cup water
1 cup yogurt
1 tablespoon maple syrup (or to taste)

PHASE THREE

2 servings

3 minutes

In a blender or a bowl using a whisk, blend all ingredients until well combined. Pour shake into two glasses. Serve.

Tea Blends

Again, I am immensely beholden to Shelley Summers for her endless reserve of tried and true recipes. Her tea combinations are both appealing and healing. Comfrey, uva ursi, and rose petals form the basis of most of the blends. These herbs are cleansing without the harshness that often accompanies detoxification. Although mild, they assist in keeping toxins out of the blood, toning the kidneys and bladder, and supplying vitamin C.

To brew, simply stir the dried herbs (one rounded teaspoon per each cup) into a pot of simmering water. Herbs may be loose, tied in cheesecloth, or placed in a tea ball (one cup of herbs makes 32–36 cups of tea). Remove pot from heat and let stand, no longer than 5 minutes. After 5 minutes the tannins make the tea bitter. Other medicinal herbs for specific healing can be added. Strain tea and serve hot or cold, sweetened to taste or not at all.

Sun tea is another way to enjoy your favorite herbal tea. For an easy on-the-go beverage, freeze tea in water bottles. As the tea melts, it is kept cold by the frozen center.

Herbal tea blends can be stored for up to six months in airtight containers. The simple act of preparing tea enhances the ritual of drinking tea for pleasure and health. A tea break is replenishing and renewing in more ways than one.

Black Tea Blend

1 rounded teaspoon black tea, flavored
   or unflavored
1 rounded teaspoon comfrey
1 rounded teaspoon rose petals
1 rounded teaspoon uva ursi
1 rounded teaspoon corn silk
5 cups pure water

BASIC BALANCER
4 servings
10 minutes

Bring water to a simmer and stir in herbs, either loose, in a tea ball, or in a piece of cheese cloth tied with a string. Remove pan from the heat and let stand, no longer than 5 minutes. After 5 minutes the tannins make the tea bitter. Strain and serve hot or cold, sweetened or unsweetened.

Ginger Tea Blend

1 rounded teaspoon comfrey
1 rounded teaspoon rose petals
1 rounded teaspoon corn silk
1 rounded teaspoon uva ursi
1 rounded teaspoon ground ginger
5 cups pure water

DEEP CLEANSER
4 servings
10 minutes

Bring water to a simmer and stir in herbs, either loose, in a tea ball, or in a piece of cheese cloth tied with a cotton string. Remove pan from the heat and let stand, no longer than 5 minutes. After 5 minutes the tannins make the tea bitter. Strain and serve hot or cold, sweetened or unsweetened.

Lemon Tea Blend

1 rounded teaspoon comfrey
1 rounded teaspoon rose petals
1 rounded teaspoon uva ursi
1 rounded teaspoon lemon balm
pinch or two of lemon basil
4 cups pure water

DEEP CLEANSER
4 servings
10 minutes

Bring water to a simmer and stir in herbs, either loose, in a tea ball, or in a piece of cheese cloth tied with a string. Remove pan from the heat and let stand, no longer than 5 minutes. After 5 minutes the tannins make the tea bitter. Strain and serve hot or cold, sweetened or unsweetened.

Licorice Tea Blend

1 rounded teaspoon comfrey
1 rounded teaspoon rose petals
1 rounded teaspoon uva ursi
1 rounded teaspoon corn silk
1 rounded teaspoon hyssop, anise seed,
   or licorice root
5 cups pure water

DEEP CLEANSER
4 servings
10 minutes

Bring water to a simmer and stir in herbs, either loose, in a tea ball, or in a piece of cheese cloth tied with a string. Remove pan from the heat and let stand, no longer than 5 minutes. After 5 minutes the tannins make the tea bitter. Strain and serve hot or cold, sweetened or unsweetened.

Mint Tea Blend

1 rounded teaspoon comfrey
1 rounded teaspoon rose petals
1 rounded teaspoon uva ursi
1 rounded teaspoon spearmint
1 rounded teaspoon peppermint
pinch of cat mint
5 cups pure water

DEEP CLEANSER
4 servings
10 minutes

Bring water to a simmer and stir in herbs, either loose, in a tea ball, or in a piece of cheese cloth tied with a string. Remove pan from the heat and let stand, no longer than 5 minutes. After 5 minutes the tannins make the tea bitter. Strain and serve hot or cold, sweetened or unsweetened.

Muscle Relaxing Tea Blend

1 rounded teaspoon comfrey
1 rounded teaspoon rose petals
1 rounded teaspoon uva ursi
1 rounded teaspoon red clover
1 rounded teaspoon wood betony
5 cups pure water

DEEP CLEANSER
4 servings
10 minutes

Bring water to a simmer and stir in herbs, either loose, in a tea ball, or in a piece of cheese cloth tied with a string. Remove pan from the heat and let stand, no longer than 5 minutes. After 5 minutes the tannins make the tea bitter. Strain and serve hot or cold, sweetened or unsweetened.

Sun Tea

8 herbal tea bags
8 cups water

DEEP CLEANSER
8 servings
35 minutes

Put tea bags in a half gallon glass jar or pitcher. Fill with cold water and let sit for 30 minutes to one hour or until desired strength. It will brew faster if you put the jar in the sun, but it is not necessary. Chill and serve with sprig of mint if desired.

Try different combinations of your favorite herbal teas.

Deep Cleanser Tea Blend

1 rounded teaspoon comfrey
1 rounded teaspoon rose petals
1 rounded teaspoon uva ursi
1 rounded teaspoon red clover
1 rounded teaspoon chamomile
pinch of ground ginger
5 cups pure water

DEEP CLEANSER
4 servings
10 minutes

Bring water to a simmer and stir in herbs, either loose, in a tea ball, or in a piece of cheese cloth tied with a string. Remove pan from the heat and let stand, no longer than 5 minutes. After 5 minutes the tannins make the tea bitter. Strain and serve hot or cold, sweetened or unsweetened.

Breads and Muffins

Baking with flours, such as quinoa, corn and sprouted spelt flour presents an entirely new baking experience for most. These vegetable and sprouted flours are easy to digest and a welcome addition to the diet. By substituting these flours, favorite recipes like Banana Bread, Cornbread, and Zucchini Muffins can be prepared in a healthy way.

Baking Powder Biscuits

4 teaspoons maple sugar
2 cups sprouted spelt flour
3 teaspoons baking powder
½ teaspoon salt
⅓ cup cold butter (5⅓ tablespoons)
⅞ cup diluted kefir cheese or kefir milk
    (2 tablespoons less than 1 cup)

DEEP CLEANSER
4 servings
30 minutes

In large bowl, whisk dry ingredients until fluffy. Cut butter into dry ingredients with a knife or pastry blender. With a fork, mix in diluted kefir cheese (or kefir milk) and make into sticky dough. Knead 6–8 times on lightly floured surface. Pat or roll out dough to ¾-inch thickness. Cut out 12 biscuits with round cookie cutter, glass, or canning jar lid. Combine trimmings, knead, and cut. Place on ungreased cookie sheet and bake at 400 degrees for 8–12 minutes. Serve hot.

To dilute the kefir cheese, place 2 tablespoons of cheese in a measuring cup. Add cold water to equal 1 cup, then remove 2 tablespoons of water to make ⅞ cup. Stir remaining water and kefir until blended. It will be the consistency of milk.

Fig Bread

½ cup figs, thickly sliced
2 cups sprouted spelt flour
1 teaspoon baking soda
1½ teaspoons baking powder
1 teaspoon cinnamon
⅛ teaspoon ground cloves
¼ teaspoon nutmeg
2 large eggs
¾ cup maple syrup
2 tablespoons melted butter
2 tablespoons water

DEEP CLEANSER
8 servings
55 minutes

Heat oven to 350 degrees. In a large bowl, mix flour, baking soda, baking powder, cinnamon, cloves, and nutmeg. In a food processor, blend the eggs, maple syrup, butter and water. Turn the processor off and add the dry ingredients and the figs; pulse until smooth. Bake in a loaf pan (4½ × 8-inch) coated with cooking spray for 30–40 minutes or until done in the center. Let cool 10 minutes in pan before turning out on rack to cool.

Breadsticks

½ teaspoon maple sugar
1 tablespoon active dry yeast
6 cups sprouted spelt flour
½ teaspoon salt
3 tablespoons poppy seeds (divided)
2 tablespoons olive oil

BASIC BALANCER
30 sticks
1 hour 45 minutes

In a small bowl, dissolve the sugar and the yeast in ¼ cup warm (105 degree) water. Set aside for 5–6 minutes until creamy. Place 5½ cups flour, salt and 1 tablespoon poppy seeds in the bowl of an electric mixer, mix with the paddle attachment. Make a well in the center of the flour mixture and add the yeast mixture, oil, and 2 cups of lukewarm water. Stir until the dough forms a ball. Turn the dough out onto a lightly floured surface, and knead until smooth and elastic, about 5 minutes, adding up to ½ cup flour if dough is too sticky. Place dough is a large oiled bowl, and allow to rest in a warm place about 1 hour.

Preheat oven to 375 degrees. Punch down dough, transfer to a lightly floured surface, and divide dough in half, keeping one half covered while working. Press each half into a ½-inch thick, 6 × 12-inch rectangle. Sprinkle each half with 1 tablespoon poppy seeds, gently press into dough. Cut rectangle lengthwise into 12 strips. Lightly oil four baking sheets. (Or use two sheets, and keep half of dough covered while proceeding.) Pick up each piece of dough and stretch the width of the baking sheet. Place sticks 1½-inches apart on the baking sheets. Bake 20 minutes or until light brown. Bread sticks will keep for several days stored in an airtight container. Sticks may be frozen.

ᕔ *Remember poppy seeds digest like a vegetable. Other seeds, such as sesame or flax may be substituted for poppy seeds when they come back into the diet.*

Sprouted Rye Bread

1¼ cup room temperature water
2½ tablespoons room temperature butter
2 tablespoons maple syrup
1½ teaspoons salt
1½ cups sprouted spelt flour
¾ cup sprouted wheat flour
¾ cup sprouted rye flour
1 tablespoon carob powder
3 teaspoons gluten
1¼ teaspoons yeast

DEEP CLEANSER
1 loaf
2 hours

Place all the ingredients in a bread maker in the above order or according to the directions for the machine, program for a 1½ pound loaf and press start.

ᕔ *Sprouted rye and sprouted wheat flour may be ordered from the Essential Eating Sprouted Flour Company. See Sources under Sprouted Bread, Flour and Pasta. Phase Two may substitute barley malt syrup for maple syrup and Phase Three may substitute with blackstrap molasses.*

Cinnamon Muffins

2 cups quinoa flour
1½ teaspoons baking powder
1 teaspoon baking soda
2 teaspoons cinnamon
⅛ teaspoon salt
½ cup yogurt
1 large egg
½ cup maple syrup
2 tablespoons melted butter
1½ teaspoons vanilla extract

SUPER CLEANSER

8 servings

20 minutes

Preheat oven to 350 degrees. In a medium bowl, mix flour, baking powder, baking soda, cinnamon and salt. In a large bowl, combine remaining ingredients. Using an electric mixer, beat on low speed until blended. Stir in dry ingredients. Mix by hand until all ingredients are moistened. Batter will be stiff. Divide batter into 12 muffin cups. Bake 12 minutes, until light brown. Remove and cool slightly on a wire rack. Serve warm.

↬ *Deep Cleansers and beyond may use 2¼ cups sprouted spelt flour instead of quinoa flour.*

Cornbread

1 cup sprouted spelt flour
1 cup yellow cornmeal
1 tablespoon baking powder
½ teaspoon salt
½ cup maple syrup
¼ cup Yogurt Cheese
1 cup water
1 large egg, lightly beaten
4 tablespoons melted butter

BASIC BALANCER

8 servings

35 minutes

Preheat oven to 375 degrees. In a large bowl, mix flour, cornmeal, baking powder, and salt. In a small bowl, combine syrup, Yogurt Cheese, water, eggs, and butter; add to flour mixture and mix just until blended. Pour into a buttered 8-inch square pan. Bake until bread springs back when gently pressed in the center, about 18 minutes.

↬ *1¼ cup corn flour may be substituted for sprouted spelt flour. For variation, add 4 ounce can of chopped green chilies and/or ½ cup corn kernels to batter.*

Banana Bread

6 tablespoons melted butter
½ cup maple syrup
2 large eggs, lightly beaten
4 ripe mashed bananas
1 cup quinoa flour
1 cup cornmeal
1 teaspoon baking soda
1 teaspoon baking powder
½ teaspoon salt

BASIC BALANCER

12 servings

55 minutes

Preheat oven to 375 degrees. In a large mixing bowl, blend butter and syrup. Add eggs and bananas. Mix in rest of ingredients. Pour into greased loaf. Bake for 35–45 minutes until it tests done. Or use muffin tins and bake 16–18 minutes.

3 egg whites may be substituted for whole eggs.

Cranberry Pumpkin Bread

1 cup canned or fresh pumpkin
1 cup maple sugar
¼ cup water
2 large eggs
¼ cup butter
2 cups quinoa flour
3 teaspoons baking powder
½ teaspoon salt
¼ teaspoon baking soda
¼ teaspoon ground cinnamon
¼ teaspoon ground ginger
⅛ teaspoon ground cloves
1 cup fresh or frozen cranberries, rinsed
  and picked through

SUPER CLEANSER

8 servings

45 minutes

Heat oven to 350 degrees and butter a loaf pan. In a large bowl, using an electric mixer, beat together pumpkin, sugar, water, eggs, and butter. Add flour, baking powder, salt, baking soda, and spices, stirring just until batter is smooth. Mix in cranberries and spoon batter into loaf pan, spreading evenly. Bake in middle of oven 1 hour and 15 minutes, or until tester in center comes out clean. Cool in pan on rack 10 minutes. Turn bread out onto rack and cool completely. Makes 1 loaf.

Deep cleansers may substitute sprouted spelt flour for quinoa flour.
Bread may be stored covered in refrigerator up to 4 days.

Olive Rosemary Bread

2½ teaspoons active dry yeast (1 package)
2 cups warm water (110 degrees)
½ cup coarsely chopped black olives
6 cups sprouted spelt flour
3 teaspoons gluten
1 tablespoon chopped fresh rosemary
2½ teaspoons salt

DEEP CLEANSER
12 servings
3 hours

Put warm water in a bowl and sprinkle with the yeast. Let mixture stand 5 minutes; it will look bubbly. Using an electric mixer, combine olives, flour, gluten, rosemary, and salt in a bowl. Make a well in the middle and pour in yeast mixture. Knead dough on medium speed until soft and smooth, 10–12 minutes. Transfer dough to a lightly floured surface and shape into a ball. Return bread dough to the bowl, cover and let rise in warm place until doubled, about 1 hour. On a lightly floured surface, knead dough 10–15 times. Shape into a tight, round loaf. Dough can be divided into two small round loaves at this point, if desired. Place dough on a baking sheet dusted with cornmeal. Cover and let rise in a warm place for 40 minutes. Preheat oven to 400 degrees. Using a serrated knife, cut a large, shallow X on the top of the loaf. Bake until the loaf is golden and sounds hollow when tapped on the bottom, 40–50 minutes. Bake 30–40 minutes for smaller loaves.

↪ *This bread may also be made by kneading the dough by hand, if desired. Lora Brody's Bread Dough Enhancer may be substituted for gluten.*

Maple Buttermilk Bread

2 cups sprouted wheat flour
1 cup sprouted spelt flour
4 tablespoons powdered buttermilk
1 teaspoon salt
1 tablespoon room temperature butter
3 tablespoons maple syrup
1 cup water
2½ teaspoons yeast
3 teaspoons gluten

PHASE FOUR
8 servings
4 hours

Place the ingredients in a bread maker according to the directions for the machine. Program for basic bread and press start.

This recipe makes about a 1½–2 pound loaf of bread. Laura Body's Bread Dough Enhancer may be substituted for gluten.

Pumpkin Bread

4 large eggs
¼ cup melted butter
½ cup yogurt
2 teaspoons vanilla extract
¾ cup water
1 15 ounce can solid-pack pumpkin
   (or 2 cups fresh)
3⅔ cups quinoa flour
1½ teaspoons salt
2 teaspoons cinnamon
1 teaspoon pumpkin pie spice
2 teaspoons baking soda
4 teaspoons baking powder
2½ cups maple sugar

SUPER CLEANSER
16 servings
1 hour 15 minutes

Preheat oven to 350 degrees. Combine first six ingredients in a large mixing bowl and stir until smooth. Add the rest of the ingredients and stir until combined. Coat 2 loaf pans with cooking spray and divide batter between them. Bake for 45–55 minutes or until toothpick in center comes out clean. Let cool on rack for 10 minutes and turn loaves out onto plate. Loaves can be frozen.

This recipe may be used in muffin pans or mini loaf pans. Just remember to decrease the baking time accordingly. Basic Balancers can substitute sprouted spelt flour for quinoa and serve with Cream Cheese Frosting.

Pumpkin Quinoa Muffins

1 cup quinoa flour
1 cup quinoa flakes
2 teaspoons baking powder
2 teaspoons baking soda
2 teaspoons cinnamon
½ teaspoon salt
½ teaspoon nutmeg or pumpkin pie spice
½ cup maple syrup
¾ cup canned pumpkin
2 large eggs
3 tablespoons melted butter
¼ cup Yogurt Cheese
1¼ cups water

SUPER CLEANSER
12 servings
30 minutes

Preheat oven to 400 degrees. Mix flour and flakes with powder, soda and salt and spices. In a separate bowl, mix together syrup, pumpkin, eggs, butter, Yogurt Cheese and water. Add to dry ingredients. Spray muffin tins with cooking spray and fill cups ¾ full with batter. Bake 12–15 minutes.

Recipe can be doubled and divided. Make muffins with half and waffle batter with the remaining half by adding an additional 3 tablespoons Yogurt Cheese and ½ cup water or until desired consistency. Three egg whites may be substituted for whole eggs.

Sprouted Spelt Bread

⅓ cup cornmeal
3 cups sprouted spelt flour
1 teaspoon salt
2½ tablespoons room temperature butter
¼ cup maple syrup
1 cup room temperature water
1½ teaspoons yeast
3 teaspoons gluten

BASIC BALANCER
8 servings
4 hours

Place all the ingredients in a bread maker according to the directions for the machine. Program for Basic Bread and press start.

This recipe makes about a 1½–2 pound loaf of bread. Lora Brody's Bread Dough Enhancer may be substituted for gluten.

Quinoa Cornbread

1½ cups cornmeal
½ cup quinoa flour
1½ teaspoons baking powder
1½ teaspoons baking soda
1 teaspoon salt, optional
2 egg whites
¼ cup Yogurt Cheese
¾ cup water
4 tablespoons melted butter
½ cup maple syrup
1 teaspoon vanilla extract

BASIC BALANCER
9 servings
35 minutes

Preheat oven to 350 degrees. Mix dry ingredients in bowl. In separate bowl, beat together egg, Yogurt Cheese, water, butter, syrup, and vanilla. Add flour mixture to liquids. Blend ingredients and pour batter into greased muffin tins, or 8-inch square baking pan. Bake for 18–20 minutes or until center is done.

> *1 cup yogurt may be substituted for the Yogurt Cheese and water.*

Zucchini Bread and Muffins

3 cups quinoa flour
1 teaspoon baking soda
2 teaspoons cinnamon
½ teaspoon salt
½ teaspoon baking powder
1 cup maple syrup
½ cup melted butter
3 large eggs
1 cup grated zucchini
¼ cup water
¼ cup carob powder (optional)

SUPER CLEANSER
12 servings
1 hour 15 minutes

Preheat oven to 350 degrees. In a large bowl, add flour, baking soda, cinnamon, salt, and baking powder. In a separate bowl, whisk together syrup, eggs, butter, and water. Add zucchini to egg mixture and mix. Pour wet ingredients into flour mixture and stir just until mixed. Pour batter into 2 greased loaf pans. Bake for 1 hour, until tester in middle comes out clean. Or fill 24 muffin cups ¾ full and bake 10–15 minutes. Test for doneness.

> *Deep Cleansers and beyond may substitute 1½ cups corn flour for 1½ cups quinoa flour. For carob muffins, add ¼ cup carob powder to dry ingredients and 3 tablespoons water to egg mixture.*

Spelt Zucchini Bread

3 cups sprouted spelt flour
2 teaspoons baking powder
1 teaspoon baking soda
½ teaspoon salt
1 teaspoon cinnamon
1 large egg white
1 cup maple syrup
2 tablespoons melted butter
¾ cup water
¼ cup yogurt
2 teaspoons vanilla extract
2 cups grated, zucchini, with skin left on
(about ¾ pounds)

DEEP CLEANSER
8 servings
50 minutes

Preheat oven to 350 degrees. Grease a 9 × 5-inch loaf pan with cooking spray. In a large bowl, mix flour, baking powder, baking soda, salt and cinnamon. In a small bowl, lightly beat egg white. Whisk in syrup, butter, water, yogurt, and vanilla until blended.

Stir in zucchini. Add zucchini mixture to bowl of dry ingredients and mix until just blended. Pour batter into loaf pan. Bake 30–40 minutes or until tester inserted into center comes out clean. Set pan on wire rack and cool for 10 minutes. Turn out onto wire rack and let cool completely.

> *For Carrot Bread, substitute 2 cups grated carrots for zucchini. For Carrot-Zucchini Bread, use 1 cup grated carrot and 1 cup grated zucchini. Feel adventurous? Add ½ cup carob powder to dry ingredients! Mini muffin tins may also be used. Bake 12–18 minutes. Yields 4½ dozen.*

Breakfast and Brunch

Experience the pleasures of breakfast with these recipes. It's as easy as a bowl of cereal or a plate of pancakes.

If time is a consideration, make Overnight French Toast or prepare the pancake batter the night before. Coffeecake, Granola Bars, or Banana Bread can be baked and frozen for easy travel or an early morning rush.

Banana Flats

1 cup corn flour
½ teaspoon baking soda
pinch of salt
2 large eggs
½ cup water
½ cup yogurt
3 ripe bananas
2 teaspoons ghee or butter

BASIC BALANCER

4 servings

20 minutes

In a medium bowl, mix flour, soda, and salt. In a separate bowl, mix eggs, water and yogurt. Add to dry ingredients. Peel bananas, cut in half, and then cut lengthwise in thirds. Dip banana pieces in batter and fry on hot griddle, greased with melted butter or ghee.

Breakfast Burrito

1 large potato, grated
4 large eggs
1 tablespoon butter
4 corn tortillas
¼ cup kefir cheese
4 tablespoons vinegar-free salsa

BASIC BALANCER

2 servings

25 minutes

Preheat oven to 350 degrees. In a small pan, sauté grated potato in 1 tablespoon butter over medium heat until browned. Remove potatoes to a plate. In the same pan, melt remaining butter and scramble eggs. On a separate ungreased griddle or pan, heated to low, place the tortillas in a stack. As the bottom tortilla warms, after a few seconds, flip the stack and warm the second one. Continue to flip and turn the stack until all sides of each tortilla are warmed. Tortillas can also be warmed individually. Divide and layer potatoes, eggs, kefir cheese, and salsa between tortillas. Roll tortillas and wrap in foil. Heat until warmed through, about 6–8 minutes. Serve.

⌐ *For variation, sauté a serrano chili and/or green onion with eggs.*

Buttermilk Waffles

1 large egg
2⅔ cups buttermilk
1⅓ cups sprouted spelt flour
1⅓ cups cornmeal
2 teaspoons baking soda
1 teaspoon baking powder
1 teaspoon salt
⅓ cup maple sugar
¼ cup melted butter

PHASE FOUR

4 servings

20 minutes

Heat waffle iron. In a large bowl, beat egg until blended and stir in buttermilk. In another bowl, stir together flour, cornmeal, baking soda, baking powder, salt, and sugar. Add flour mixture and melted butter to the buttermilk mixture. Stir until batter is evenly moistened. Cook according to waffle iron directions. Serve hot with butter and maple syrup.

Chunky Granola

2 large eggs at room temperature
3 large egg whites at room temperature
2 teaspoons vanilla extract
2 teaspoons cinnamon
½ teaspoon salt
1 teaspoon baking powder
1 cup maple sugar
2¾ cups quinoa flakes
⅓ cup sprouted spelt flour

DEEP CLEANSER

8 servings

30 minutes

Preheat oven to 350 degrees. Coat a baking sheet with cooking spray. In the bowl of an electric mixer, beat eggs, egg whites, vanilla, cinnamon, salt, baking powder, and sugar. Using a rubber spatula, fold in the quinoa flakes and flour. Spread mixture evenly on the baking sheet in a thin layer. Bake 15–20 minutes, until lightly browned. With a spoon or spatula, break up granola into small chunks. Return pan to oven and bake 10–15 minutes longer, until granola is dry and crisp. Remove pan from oven and let cool. Makes about 4 cups.

Serve over yogurt or eat plain as a snack. Granola can be frozen.

Cinnamon Toast

2 teaspoons maple sugar
1 teaspoon cinnamon
1 tablespoon butter
4 slices 100% sprouted sourdough bread

SUPER CLEANSER

2 servings

5 minutes

In a small bowl, mix sugar and cinnamon. Toast bread, divide and spread butter on toast slices. Sprinkle with cinnamon sugar.

Coffee Cake

FOR CAKE:
   1½ cups sprouted spelt flour
   2 teaspoons baking powder
   ½ teaspoon salt
   ¾ cup maple sugar
   3 tablespoons butter
   1 large egg
   3 tablespoons Yogurt Cheese
   ⅓ cup water
   1 teaspoon vanilla

FOR TOPPING:
   2 teaspoons cinnamon
   ½ cup maple sugar
   2 tablespoons sprouted spelt flour
   2 tablespoons melted butter

DEEP CLEANSER

8 servings

45 minutes

Preheat oven to 350 degrees. In a medium bowl, mix flour, baking powder, salt and sugar. With a pastry cutter, cut butter into flour mixture. In a small bowl, lightly beat egg, add Yogurt Cheese, water and vanilla. Add to flour mixture. In a small bowl, mix the first three topping ingredients and blend in melted butter. Mix until crumbly. In a 9-inch square or spring form pan, greased with cooking spray, spread batter on the bottom and sprinkle with topping. Bake for 25–30 minutes or until a toothpick in the center comes out clean.

ᕤ *Recipe can be doubled and baked in 9 × 13-inch pan.*

Corn Cakes

1 cup corn flour (yellow, white or combination)
¼ teaspoon baking soda
pinch of salt
½ cup yogurt
½ cup water
1 large egg
1 tablespoon maple syrup

BASIC BALANCER
4 servings
15 minutes

In a medium bowl, mix flour, soda, and salt. In a separate bowl, blend yogurt, water, egg, and syrup. Add to dry ingredients and mix. Drop batter in ¼ cupfuls onto heated nonstick pan or greased griddle and cook until bottoms are golden, and small bubbles start to form on top, 3–4 minutes. Flip and cook until the other side is browned, 1–2 minutes longer. Serve topped with butter and maple syrup.

Corn Cereal

⅓ cup yellow corn grits
1 cup water
2 tablespoons maple syrup
pinch of salt

BASIC BALANCER
1 serving
10 minutes

In a small pan, bring water to boil. Add grits and salt, stirring frequently to avoid lumps. Reduce heat and cook 10–15 minutes, until grits are soft. Transfer cereal to a bowl and drizzle with syrup. Add more syrup if a sweeter taste is desired.

ℰ *Butter may be added if desired.*

Cream of Sprouted Spelt Cereal

1 cup water
2 tablespoons Essential Eating Cream of Sprouted
   Spelt Cereal
dash of salt (optional)
maple syrup
butter (optional)

DEEP CLEANSER
1 serving
8 minutes

Place water in a small saucepan. Whisk in cereal and salt. Bring to a rapid boil; reduce heat. Simmer, stirring frequently to avoid lumps, 8–10 minutes. Add more water or cereal to make desired consistency. Transfer cereal into bowl and drizzle with maple syrup and add butter if desired.

ℰ *Essential Eating Sprouted Spelt Cereal may be ordered from the Essential Eating Sprouted Flour Company. See Sources under Sprouted Bread, Flour and Pasta.*

Corn Flake Cereal

1 bowl 100% corn flakes
1 tablespoon sour cream or Yogurt Cheese
½ cup water
maple sugar or syrup to taste

BASIC BALANCER

1 serving

5 minutes

Pour corn flakes into a cereal bowl. In a separate bowl, dilute 1 tablespoon sour cream with ½ cup water and pour over cereal.

༆ *Phase Two Diet can substitute cream cheese for sour cream.*

Cornmeal Pancakes

1 cup yellow cornmeal
1 teaspoon salt
2 tablespoons maple syrup
1 cup boiling water
1 egg or two egg whites
½ cup water
2 tablespoons yogurt or Yogurt Cheese
2 tablespoons melted butter
½ cup quinoa flour or corn flour
2 teaspoons baking powder

BASIC BALANCER

4 servings

20 minutes

Combine cornmeal, salt, and syrup in a bowl. Stir in boiling water slowly and cover for about 10 minutes. In small bowl, beat together egg, butter, ½ cup water and yogurt. Add egg mixture to cornmeal and stir until blended. Add flour and baking powder into mixture with a few strokes. Cook on a griddle at medium to low heat, about 5 minutes on each side. Make sure pancakes are thoroughly cooked. Due to the cornmeal, they need to cook at a lower temperature and a little longer than other pancakes. Be patient, they're worth it.

༆ *For Cinnamon-Banana Pancakes, add 1 mashed banana to egg mixture and add ½ teaspoon cinnamon with flour.*

Egg Souffle

6 slices 100% sprouted grain bread
8 large eggs
½ cup kefir cheese
¾ teaspoon salt
¼ teaspoon hot pepper sauce (optional)
½ teaspoon dry mustard
½ cup yogurt or Yogurt Cheese
1 ¼ cups water
½ cup chives, snipped

DEEP CLEANSER
4 servings
Overnight

Remove crust and cube bread. Place cubed bread in a greased 1½ quart souffle or casserole dish. In a bowl, beat eggs well and then beat in kefir, seasonings, yogurt, water, and chives. Pour over bread. Cover and refrigerate over night. Bake uncovered at 350 degrees until golden and set, about 1 hour. Serve immediately.

Granola

3 cups quinoa flakes
½ cup maple syrup
¼ cup melted butter
1 teaspoon vanilla or almond extract
⅛ teaspoon cinnamon

SUPER CLEANSER
8 servings
1 hour

Preheat oven to 250 degrees. In a medium bowl mix dry ingredients. In a separate small bowl, mix syrup, butter, extract, and cinnamon. Add to dry ingredients and mix well. Spread on a greased cookie sheet. Bake for 1 hour, stirring occasionally. Cool in pan. Makes about 4 cups.

ᶜ⁓ *Depending on your level, when the granola is cool, ⅓–½ cup of any ONE of the following may be added: shredded coconut (can also be stirred in with dry ingredients), chopped dates, chopped dried bananas, or chopped dried apricots.*

Grilled Polenta

6 cups water
2 cups cornmeal, corn grits or polenta
1 teaspoon salt
butter and maple syrup

BASIC BALANCER
6 servings
Overnight

In a large saucepan bring water to a boil. Slowly add cornmeal and salt to boiling water, stirring constantly. Cook until thickened, stirring frequently. Cover and continue cooking over low heat for 5 minutes. Stir and pour into loaf pan and refrigerate overnight. Heat griddle to medium heat and slice cornmeal mush into ½-inch pieces. Spray griddle with cooking oil and cook slices on each side about 5–10 minutes or until crisp. Serve warm with butter and maple syrup.

⤷ *An old fashioned name for this recipe is "mush."*

Overnight French Toast

1 large egg
1 large egg white
3 tablespoons Yogurt Cheese or yogurt
  plus water to make ¾ cup
2 tablespoons maple syrup
1 teaspoon vanilla extract
¼ teaspoon ground cinnamon
⅛ teaspoon baking powder
8 slices sprouted bread, cut in half diagonally
1 tablespoon butter
syrup to taste

DEEP CLEANSER
4 servings
Overnight

In a medium bowl, whisk together egg, egg whites, yogurt and water, syrup, vanilla, cinnamon and baking powder. Place bread slices in a large, shallow baking dish and pour egg mixture over the top. Turn to coat evenly. Press a piece of wax paper directly on the bread to cover it. Then cover dish with plastic wrap. Refrigerate overnight. To cook, heat ½ tablespoon butter in a 12-inch nonstick skillet over medium-high heat. Add four slices of the soaked bread to the pan and cook until golden, about 2–3 minutes per side. Cook the additional four slices using the remaining butter. Serve warm with maple syrup.

⤷ *Homemade sprouted bread may be substituted for store-bought sprouted bread. Cut bread ½-inch thick for a heartier meal.*

Mushroom Scrambled Eggs

½ pound sliced mushrooms
8 large eggs
2 tablespoons butter

DEEP CLEANSER
4 servings
15 minutes

Heat butter in a large sauté pan over medium heat. Sauté mushrooms until tender, about 5 minutes. Place eggs in mixing bowl and whisk with fork until blended. Move mushrooms to side of sauté pan and add eggs to open side of pan. Let eggs cook 1–2 minutes undisturbed and then begin to scramble. Cool eggs to desired doneness and mix in mushrooms from side of pan. Serve.

℮ *Other ingredients can be added to mushrooms such as 2 chopped green onions, chopped chives and/or 2 slices smoked salmon/lox. Dried mushrooms can be reconstituted with boiling water, drained and used in this recipe.*

Pancakes

2 cups quinoa flour
½ teaspoon salt
1 tablespoon baking powder
¼ cup maple syrup
2 egg whites
2 tablespoons melted butter
1½ cups water
¼ cup Yogurt Cheese

SUPER CLEANSER
4 servings
25 minutes

In a large bowl, combine flour, salt and baking powder. In a small bowl, combine syrup, egg whites, butter, water and Yogurt Cheese. Add liquid ingredients to bowl containing dry ingredients. Mix just until blended. Add more water or flour to adjust consistency. Drop batter in ¼ cupfuls onto heated nonstick pan or greased griddle. Cook until bottoms are golden and small bubbles start to form on top, 3–4 minutes. Flip and cook until the other side is browned, 1–2 minutes. Serve topped with butter and maple syrup.

℮ *Basic Balancers may substitute corn flour for quinoa flour.*

Pumpkin Pancakes

½ cup yogurt
¾ cup water
1 large egg, lightly beaten
¾ cup canned or fresh cooked pumpkin, puréed
1 tablespoon soft butter
¼ cup maple syrup
1 cup quinoa flour
2½ teaspoons baking powder
½ teaspoon allspice
1 teaspoon vanilla extract
½ teaspoon cinnamon
¾ teaspoon salt (optional)
½ teaspoon pumpkin pie spice
butter to coat skillet

SUPER CLEANSER
4 servings
20 minutes

In a large bowl, mix together yogurt, water, egg, pumpkin, butter, and maple syrup. Add the remaining ingredients and blend. Melt the butter in a skillet over medium-low heat. Drop batter onto skillet in ¼ cup portions. Cook 4–5 minutes until bubbles begin to form on top. Turn pancakes and cook an additional 2–3 minutes. These pancakes need to be cooked longer and at a lower temperature than regular pancakes. Top with butter and maple syrup.

Quinoa Cereal

1 cup water
dash salt (optional)
⅓ cup quinoa flakes

SUPER CLEANSER
1 serving
6 minutes

Add quinoa flakes and salt to rapidly boiling water. Return to boil and cook for 90 seconds, stirring frequently. Remove from heat and allow to cool until cereal is slightly thickened. Increase/decrease water for desired consistency.

Pumpkin Quinoa Waffles

1 cup quinoa flour
1 cup quinoa flakes
2 teaspoons baking powder
2 teaspoons baking soda
2 teaspoons cinnamon
½ teaspoon salt
½ teaspoon nutmeg or pumpkin pie spice
½ cup maple syrup
¾ cup canned pumpkin
2 large eggs
3 tablespoons melted butter
⅓ cup Yogurt Cheese
1¾ cups water

SUPER CLEANSER
6 servings
20 minutes

Preheat waffle iron. Mix flour and flakes with powder, soda, cinnamon, salt, and spices. In a separate bowl, mix together syrup, pumpkin, eggs, butter, Yogurt Cheese, and water. Add to dry ingredients. Coat waffle iron with cooking spray and cook according to waffle iron directions.

❧ *For muffins, omit 3 tablespoons Yogurt Cheese and ½ of the water. Pour batter into greased muffin tins and bake at 400 degrees for 12–15 minutes.*

Smoked Salmon on Kefir Cheese Toast

4 slices sprouted grain bread
4 tablespoons kefir cheese
6 thin slices of smoked salmon

DEEP CLEANSER
2 servings
10 minutes

Toast bread slices. Spread one side of toast with kefir cheese and top with salmon.

❧ *Basic Balancers may add a slice of tomato and chopped red onions.*

Sprouted French Toast

8 slices sprouted sourdough bread
4 large eggs (or 6 egg whites)
½ teaspoon salt
¼ cup Yogurt Cheese
1 teaspoon vanilla extract
1 cup water
¼ teaspoon cinnamon
maple syrup and butter to taste

SUPER CLEANSER
4 servings
15 minutes

In a small bowl, lightly beat eggs. Add salt, Yogurt Cheese, water, vanilla, and cinnamon. Stir until blended. Heat skillet to medium-high heat. Melt 1 tablespoon of butter in skillet. Dip bread slices in egg mixture and place on skillet. Brown for 2–3 minutes on each side. Serve with butter and maple syrup.

ᕒ *Other diets may use any 100% sprouted grain breads.*

Waffles

2 large eggs
¼ cup Yogurt Cheese
1¼ cup water
3 tablespoons melted butter
¼ cup maple syrup
1 tablespoon vanilla extract
1¾ cups quinoa flour
½ teaspoon salt (optional)
1 tablespoon baking powder

SUPER CLEANSER
4 servings
20 minutes

In a large mixing bowl, lightly beat eggs. Add Yogurt Cheese, water, melted butter, syrup, and vanilla. Mix until smooth. Add the remaining dry ingredients to the egg mixture and mix well. Follow waffle iron instructions for cooking. Adjust consistency of batter by adding more water or flour as needed. Serve with butter and maple syrup.

ᕒ *Basic Balancers and beyond may substitute corn or sprouted spelt flour for quinoa flour. You may also use combinations of the listed flours. Make a double batch and freeze half. Toast to reheat. For variation, add 1 mashed banana or 1 cup blueberries, when they come back into your diet. Prepared batter can be stored overnight in the refrigerator. Extra waffles can be frozen and then popped in the toaster for a quick breakfast.*

Salads

Once raw vegetables are introduced in the Basic Balancer Diet, a wider selection of salads can be enjoyed. These recipes offer a variety of vegetable salads and introduce the wonderful ingredient quinoa (a grain that digests like a fruit) to salads.

Cooked Carrot Salad

1 pound cooked carrots, sliced
¼ cup vinegar-free salsa
⅛ cup sliced black olives
salt and pepper to taste

DEEP CLEANSER
4 servings
5 minutes

Mix ingredients in a large bowl. Chill or serve at room temperature.

Egg Salad

6 large hard-boiled eggs, peeled and diced
1 stalk celery, chopped
1 chopped green onion
1 teaspoon dried dill weed, sweet basil,
   marjoram, chili powder, curry powder or
   oregano (or use a combination of the herbs)
salt and pepper to taste
½ cup Essential Mayonnaise or kefir cheese

BASIC BALANCER
4 servings
10 minutes

Mix all ingredients together in order listed. Spread on sprouted bread or salad greens.

Green Bean and Olive Salad

½ cup black olives
4 ounces green beans
¼ cup chopped parsley
2 tablespoons Roasted Garlic Dressing

DEEP CLEANSER
4 servings
20 minutes

Steam green beans about 4 minutes until crisp, tender. Cool and slice beans into 1-inch pieces. In a bowl, toss all the ingredients together. If possible, cover the salad and set aside for 5–10 minutes to allow the flavors to infuse. Serve at room temperature or chilled.

ᶜ⌐ *Tomatoes, cut into wedges, can be added for Basic Balancers.*

Cucumber Carrot Salad

¼ cup dried cranberries
1 cup yogurt
½ teaspoon salt
¼ teaspoon pepper
½ teaspoon ground cumin
3 carrots, grated
1 cup diced cucumber

BASIC BALANCER
4 servings
15 minutes

Place cranberries in a small bowl and cover with warm water. Let cranberries soak while you combine yogurt, salt, pepper, and cumin in a medium bowl. Stir yogurt mixture. Add carrots, cucumber and drained cranberries to mix. Chill.

℘ *For variation, substitute ½ cup yogurt with kefir cheese or use diluted Yogurt Cheese. Phase Two Diet may substitute raisins for cranberries.*

Crab Salad

½ pound imitation crabmeat (pollack), shredded
½ cup Yogurt Cheese
2 teaspoons water
½ teaspoon onion powder
⅛ teaspoon garlic powder (optional)
½ teaspoon maple syrup
½ teaspoon salt
1 teaspoon dried dill weed
½ teaspoon dry mustard

SUPER CLEANSER
4 servings
15 minutes

Mix ingredients in a medium bowl. Makes about 2 cups.

℘ *Deep Cleansers and beyond may add 1 tablespoon tamari sauce. Phase Four diets may substitute Vegenaise for Yogurt Cheese.*

Herbed Quinoa Salad

4 cups cooked quinoa
2 drops lemon extract
1 tablespoon water
1 teaspoon dry mustard
2 tablespoons 100% cranberry juice
1½ tablespoons minced shallots
2 teaspoons kefir cheese
¼ cup olive oil
1 cup chopped cucumber
1 cup thawed frozen peas
3 tablespoons chopped parsley
1½ tablespoons fresh dill

BASIC BALANCER
6 servings
20 minutes

In a small bowl, combine the lemon extract, water, mustard, juice, shallots and kefir cheese. Whisk in the oil in a thin, steady stream. Season with salt and pepper. The dressing can stand at room temperature up to 3 hours. Steam peas or cook according to package directions. In a bowl, toss the quinoa with the cucumber, peas, parsley and dill. Just before serving, stir in the dressing.

Wild Rice Salad

2 cups cooked wild rice
½ cup cooked corn kernels
½ cup chopped tomatoes
½ cup diced sweet pepper
¼ cup cooked green peas
¼ cup finely chopped red onion
¼ cup green beans, cooked and coarsely chopped
1 tablespoon fresh chopped tarragon
    (or 1 teaspoon dried)
1 tablespoon fresh chopped parsley
    (or 1 teaspoon dried)
½ Cranberry Vinaigrette Recipe

BASIC BALANCER
4 servings
15 minutes

In a large bowl, combine all the ingredients. Toss with Cranberry Vinaigrette until mixed. Serve chilled.

Marinated Mushroom Salad

8 ounces sliced mushrooms
4 green onions, finely sliced
1 tablespoon dried coriander or parsley
4 drops lemon extract
1 clove garlic, minced
1 teaspoon maple syrup
1 tablespoon olive oil
2 tablespoons tamari sauce
1 tablespoon water
¼ teaspoon fresh ground pepper

BASIC BALANCER
4 servings
20 minutes

Combine mushrooms, onions and coriander in a bowl and mix well. Place the lemon extract in a small bowl and using a fork or wire whisk, beat in the garlic, syrup, oil, tamari, and pepper. Drizzle the dressing over the salad, tossing the ingredients thoroughly. Cover and set aside to allow the flavors to infuse, about 5–10 minutes.

↝ *⅓ cup chopped fresh coriander or parsley may be substituted for dried. Coriander is often called cilantro or Chinese parsley.*

Marinated Tomato and Potato Salad

1 pound tomatoes, cut into wedges
½ cup black olives (optional)
½ pound green beans, steamed until tender
2 scallions, chopped
½ pound small red potatoes
⅔ cup Cranberry Vinaigrette
½ cup chopped parsley

BASIC BALANCER
6 servings
50 minutes

Place potatoes in a large saucepan and cover with water. Bring to boil and simmer for 20 minutes, until tender. Drain and let cool. While potatoes are cooking, steam green beans until tender, about 4 minutes. Remove beans from pan, let cool slightly and slice into 2-inch lengths. Cut the potatoes into wedges and place in a large bowl with the remaining ingredients. Cover and set aside for 10 minutes to allow flavors to infuse.

Potato, Beet and Cucumber Salad

3 medium beets
¾ pound small new potatoes
1 cup sliced cucumber (1 small)
1 tablespoon chopped chives
1 tablespoon chopped dill weed
   (or 1 teaspoon dried)
Cranberry Vinaigrette
4 lettuce leaves

BASIC BALANCER
4 servings
5 hours

Clean beets leaving skins on, steam 45 minutes–1 hour, or until tender when pierced with a fork. Make sure to keep enough water in the pan to prevent burning as beets steam. Cool and slice beets and place in a medium mixing bowl. In a large saucepan, cook potatoes in boiling water for 20 minutes or until tender; drain. Leaving skins on or peeling potatoes before cooking is a personal preference. Cool potatoes, quarter and place in a large mixing bowl. Stir in cucumbers, chives and dill. Make Cranberry Vinaigrette. Pour ¼ cup of the dressing over the beets and ¼ cup over the potatoes. Toss to lightly coat ingredients in each bowl. Cover and chill both mixtures 4–24 hours, stirring each occasionally. Line 4 salad plates with lettuce leaves. Using a slotted spoon, arrange beets and potato mixture evenly between plates. Stir marinade used for potato mixture and pour over each salad and serve.

An easy salad for extra cooked beets and potatoes.

Roasted Corn Salad

3 cups fresh corn kernels (about 6 ears)
1 teaspoon olive oil
1 cup chopped tomatoes
½ cup chopped red pepper
½ cup chopped green onions
¼ cup Cranberry Vinaigrette

BASIC BALANCER
4 servings
30 minutes

Preheat oven to 425 degrees. Combine corn and oil and place on greased jelly roll pan. Bake 20 minutes or until browned, stirring occasionally. Let roasted corn cool slightly; then place in medium bowl with tomatoes, pepper, green onions and dressing. Toss to mix. Serve warm or at room temperature.

Slivered Endive Salad

2 Belgian endive
2 tablespoons kefir cheese or sour cream
2 teaspoons 100% cranberry juice
½ teaspoon dried tarragon
¼ teaspoon dried oregano
2 teaspoons maple syrup
salt & pepper

BASIC BALANCER
2 servings
15 minutes

Trim outer leaves of endive. Slice endive crosswise into thin rounds and separate. Combine remaining ingredients in a medium bowl, add endive and toss.

Spinach and Quinoa Salad

2 cups cooked quinoa
8 cups spinach leaves, torn into bite-size pieces
½ large red onion
½ cup sliced black olives
1 cup yogurt
3 tablespoons olive oil
1 clove garlic, minced (optional)
½ teaspoon ground cumin
3 tablespoons 100% cranberry juice
1 tablespoon maple syrup
2 teaspoons barley miso
½ teaspoon dry mustard
salt and pepper to taste

BASIC BALANCER
6 servings
20 minutes

Place quinoa, spinach, onion and olives in a large bowl. For the dressing, place the remaining ingredients in a small bowl; whisk until smooth. Add dressing to spinach mixture and toss well.

℮ *4 ounces (about 2 cups) of sliced mushrooms may be added.*

Spinach Avocado Salad

2 cups packed baby spinach leaves,
  (or regular leaves, torn into pieces)
½ cup cherry tomatoes (about 4 ounces)
2 scallions, sliced
½ cucumber, peeled and cut into chunks
3 large radishes, sliced
1 large ripe Hass avocado, peeled, pitted,
  and sliced
4 tablespoons Yogurt Chive Dressing
  (or to taste)

BASIC BALANCER
2 servings
15 minutes

Wash and dry spinach and place in a mixing bowl. Cut tomatoes in half and add to the mixing bowl along with the scallions. Add the cucumber, radishes and avocado to the bowl. Make dressing; pour into bowl and toss.

Tuna and Potato Salad

12 small new potatoes, scrubbed, not peeled
2 cans tuna (6 ounce cans), packed in water
2 tablespoons 100% cranberry juice
1 teaspoon maple sugar
2 teaspoons olive oil
½ teaspoon salt
¼ teaspoon pepper
½ cup finely chopped celery ribs
2 thinly sliced scallions
¼ cup chopped parsley
6 romaine lettuce leaves

BASIC BALANCER
6 servings
30 minutes

In a medium saucepan, cover the potatoes with cold water, bring to a boil and cook until tender, about 20 minutes. Drain potatoes and let them cool slightly, then quarter them or cut into 1-inch chunks. Drain the water from the tuna into a bowl and whisk in the cranberry juice, sugar, oil, ½ teaspoon salt and ¼ teaspoon pepper. Add the warm potatoes, tuna, celery, scallions and parsley and toss well. Serve on the lettuce leaves.

Shredded Carrot Salad

3 cups shredded carrots
¼ cup chopped dates
½ cup yogurt
1 teaspoon vanilla
⅛ teaspoon cinnamon
salt to taste

DEEP CLEANSER
4 servings
15 minutes

Mix all ingredients in a medium bowl. Cover and chill.

Tuna Fish Salad

1 can tuna packed in water, drained (6 ounce can)
½ cup Yogurt Cheese
½ teaspoon maple syrup
¼ teaspoon dry mustard
¼ teaspoon garlic powder (or to taste)
1 teaspoon dill weed
1 teaspoon onion powder (or to taste)
dash of cayenne pepper
salt
1 tablespoon 100% cranberry juice or water

SUPER CLEANSER
2 servings
10 minutes

In a medium mixing bowl, place all ingredients and mix until blended. Use more or less cranberry juice or water for desired consistency. Serve on toasted sprouted sourdough bread.

 ↶ *Basic Balancers may substitute ¼ cup kefir cheese for ¼ cup of the Yogurt Cheese. Phase Four may substitute Vegenaise for yogurt and omit syrup. Other additions for Basic Balancers and beyond are chopped celery and green onion. For variation, wrap salad in lettuce leaves to serve.*

Sandwiches

Aside from being refreshing, these sandwich ideas do not violate Nutritional Rule #5 of not mixing starches with proteins. Most traditional sandwiches of meat and wheat bread combine a starch with a protein, making it impossible for the body to digest it properly. By making sandwiches with sprouted grain bread, bread that digests like a vegetable, starches are avoided.

Try my favorite sandwich, the ALT (avocado, lettuce and tomato.) On sprouted toast, of course!

ALT Sandwich

4 slices sprouted grain bread
1 ripe avocado
1 small tomato
2 large lettuce leaves
2 tablespoons kefir cheese

BASIC BALANCER
2 servings
10 minutes

ALT—Avocado, lettuce and tomato! Lightly toast bread slices. Peel and thinly slice avocado. Slice tomato and wash lettuce. Lay a slice of toasted bread on separate plates and spread 1 tablespoon kefir cheese on each. Divide avocado, tomato and lettuce and layer over kefir cheese. Top with remaining slice of bread.

Cranberry Yogurt Cheese Sandwich

2 tablespoons Cranberry Spread
1 tablespoon Yogurt Cheese
2 slices sprouted sourdough bread, toasted

SUPER CLEANSER
1 serving
5 minutes

Toast bread slices. Make sandwich by spreading Cranberry Spread on one slice and Yogurt Cheese on another. Place slices together as a sandwich.

ᕙ *This sandwich can be made in a few minutes if you have Cranberry Spread and Yogurt Cheese on hand. It travels well and can be eaten at all times of the day. Deep Cleansers may substitute kefir cheese for Yogurt Cheese.*

Hazelnut Butter Sandwich

4 slices 100% sprouted grain bread
2 tablespoons hazelnut butter, divided
4 leaves lettuce

PHASE TWO
2 servings
10 minutes

Toast bread slices. Divide hazelnut butter between two slices of bread and spread evenly. Top each sandwich with two leaves of lettuce and the remaining slice of bread.

ᕙ *Cranberry Spread can be substituted for lettuce. Hazelnut butter can be found in most health food stores.*

Sprouted Bean Bruschetta

1 cup boiling water
¼ cup dried tomatoes
2 cups cooked sprouted beans
1 clove garlic
½ cup water from tomatoes
4 slices sprouted sourdough bread

DEEP CLEANSER
4 servings
30 minutes

Pour 1 cup boiling water over dried tomatoes, letting soak until soft, about 20 minutes. Drain, reserving ¾ cup water. With food processor running, drop garlic through feed tube and process until chopped. Add beans and ½ cup reserved tomato water and process until smooth. Add tomatoes, salt and pepper and pulse just to mix. Add more tomato water if dip is too thick. Scrape into a bowl. Heat broiler and arrange bread slices in single layer on cookie sheet. Broil 1–3 minutes, until lightly toasted. Spread each slice with bean purée and serve.

Basic Balancers may top bruschetta with chopped green onions and shredded lettuce if desired.

Grilled Kefir Cheese and Tomato Sandwich

8 slices sprouted grain bread
2 medium tomatoes, cut into 8 thin slices
4 tablespoons kefir cheese
4 teaspoons butter, softened

BASIC BALANCER
4 servings
20 minutes

Spread about ½ teaspoon softened butter on each of the 8 slices of bread. Turn four of the slices over and spread 1 tablespoon of the kefir cheese on each slice. Heat a griddle over medium heat and place the four bread slices with the kefir cheese on them, buttered side down on the griddle. Place two slices of tomatoes each on the kefir cheese and top with the remaining slices of bread, buttered side up. Cook for about 5 minutes, until slices start to brown. Turn sandwiches with a spatula and cook the other side until browned, about 5 minutes. Serve.

Portobello Mushroom Sandwich

2 large Portobello mushrooms, stems removed
1 medium tomato, sliced
2 large lettuce leaves
2 slices sweet onion
4 ounces sprouts
4 slices sprouted grain bread

DEEP CLEANSER
2 servings
25 minutes

Grill the mushrooms or roast on a baking sheet, turning once in a 500 degree oven for 15 minutes, until browned and cooked through. Slice mushroom ¼-inch thick and divide between two bread slices. Top with tomato, onion slices, lettuce, sprouts and remaining slice of bread.

Smoked Salmon Sandwich

8 slices smoked salmon
8 slices 100% sprouted sourdough bread
4 tablespoons Herbed Yogurt Cheese

SUPER CLEANSER
4 servings
15 minutes

Toast bread. Spread Herbed Yogurt Cheese on 4 slices. Divide salmon into fourths and layer on top of cheese. Put remaining bread slice on the top of each sandwich and slice sandwich in half. Serve.

✑ *Basic Balancers may add sprouts or lettuce. Radish sprouts taste great on this sandwich. Deep Cleanser and beyond may substitute kefir cheese with 1 teaspoon chopped chives for the Herbed Yogurt Cheese and use other sprouted breads.*

Fried Egg Sandwich

2 teaspoons butter
2 large eggs
4 slices sprouted sourdough bread
salt and pepper

SUPER CLEANSER
2 servings
10 minutes

In a small skillet, melt butter and cook eggs sunny-side up. When eggs are almost cooked, turn them over and cook until yolks are completely cooked. Meanwhile, toast and butter the bread. Place one egg between two slices of bread, cut in half and serve.

✑ *For variation, add a few steamed spinach leaves that have been patted dry.*

Salmon Spread

3 cups yogurt
½ pound smoked salmon
2 tablespoons minced radishes, radish sprouts,
   or green onions
2 teaspoons dill weed
1 clove garlic, minced (optional)
¼ teaspoon salt and grind of black pepper

BASIC BALANCER
6 servings
Overnight

Blend briefly in food processor; strain in yogurt strainer, cheese cloth or mesh strainer in refrigerator overnight. Shape in a mold or bowl. Remove from mold or serve in bowl.

ᴇ *Spread on sprouted sourdough toast.*

Veggie Sandwich Spread

5 ounces chopped fresh or frozen spinach
1 cup Yogurt Cheese
2 teaspoons chopped roasted peppers
2 teaspoons grated or finely chopped onion
¾ cup grated carrots (about 3 medium)
1½ teaspoons maple syrup
½ teaspoon dried oregano or tarragon
salt and pepper to taste

BASIC BALANCER
6 servings
30 minutes

Mix all ingredients in a medium bowl. Spread on toasted sprouted bread. Makes 2 cups.

ᴇ *Vegetables may be grated and chopped with a food processor.*

Soups

Soup is one of the best ways to increase cooked vegetable intake and cut down on fat in the diet. Soup is versatile, nurturing and convenient. Soup can be served as a meal, a snack, or an appetizer. Try Quick Gazpacho in the summer and Wholesome Chicken Soup in the winter.

In most cases, substitutions can be made for the seasonal availability of vegetables.

Soups can be as easy as mashing cooked vegetables together, adding broth and herbs. Making soup is still a labor of love, but these recipes are about love, not labor!

Avocado Cucumber Soup

½ cup sour cream
1 cup water
1 large avocado
1 small cucumber, peel and seed, and finely chop
¼ cup cilantro
¼ teaspoon salt

BASIC BALANCER
4 servings
15 minutes

Place all ingredients in a blender and blend until smooth. Serve chilled or at room temperature.

Beet Soup

1 pound beets (about 4 medium)
1 tablespoon butter
1 large red or yellow onion, chopped
1 medium sweet red or yellow pepper, chopped
1 pound tomatoes, chopped
1 clove garlic, minced
3 tablespoons barley miso
2 cups water
1 tablespoon maple syrup
1 tablespoon tamari sauce
¼ teaspoon pepper
6 teaspoons Yogurt Cheese or sour cream (optional)

DEEP CLEANSER
6 servings
1 hour 20 minutes

Clean beets, leaving skins on and cut in half or into large chunks. Small beets may be left whole. Steam beets in a large covered stock pot or vegetable steamer for 45 minutes, or until tender when pierced with a fork. Add water as needed. Cool to the touch; remove skins and coarsely chop. While the beets are cooking, melt butter and sauté onions and peppers in a large saucepan, about 8 minutes, until tender. Add tomatoes and garlic, sauté another 8 minutes. Mix miso with water and add to vegetables. Add syrup, tamari, pepper, and reserved beets. Simmer soup uncovered for 10 minutes. Cool slightly and serve as a chunky soup. For a smoother texture, mash soup with a potato masher or purée in a food processor. Serve warm or chilled, topped with Yogurt Cheese if desired.

Butternut Squash Soup

1 butternut squash (2–3 pounds), peel and cut
   into 1-inch cubes
1 pound sweet potatoes or yams, peel and cut
   into 1-inch cubes
1 cup chopped carrots
1 large onion
1 teaspoon butter
2 tablespoons tamari sauce
5 cups water or vegetable broth

DEEP CLEANSER
4 servings
25 minutes

Put squash, potatoes, carrots, and water in a saucepan and boil for 10 minutes until vegetables are soft. In a skillet, sauté onion in butter until tender, about 8 minutes. Pour vegetables with their liquid into a blender with the tamari sauce and onions. Blend until smooth. Serve warm or chilled.

Wholesome Chicken Soup

1 whole chicken (2–3 pounds)
2 quarts chicken broth
¾ cup onion, cut into 2-inch pieces
½ cup carrots, cut into 2-inch pieces
½ cup celery, cut into 2-inch pieces
¾ cup fresh or frozen corn kernels
½ cup chopped celery
½ cup thinly sliced carrots
1 tablespoon chopped fresh parsley
1 teaspoon crushed saffron threads (optional)
1 cup cooked elbow or spiral corn pasta
salt and pepper to taste

BASIC BALANCER
8 servings
1 hour 20 minutes

In a large stock pot, combine chicken, broth, onions, carrots, celery and saffron (if using). Bring to a boil, reduce heat and simmer about 1 hour, skimming the surface if necessary. While chicken is cooking, fill small saucepan with water and bring to a boil. Add pasta and cook, stirring occasionally until cooked, about 4–6 minutes. Drain and set aside. When the chicken is cooked, remove from the broth. When cool enough to handle, pick the meat from the bones and cut into bite-size pieces. Strain the broth through a sieve into a large saucepan. Bring the strained broth to a slow simmer and add chopped celery, corn, carrots, and parsley. Simmer 10 minutes until vegetables are tender. Add reserved chicken and cooked pasta. Salt and pepper to taste. Serve.

Carrot Celery Root Soup

1 tablespoon butter
1 large onion, peeled and chopped
1 pound carrots, peeled and chopped
1 pound celery root, peeled, sliced,
   and chopped into cubes
1 teaspoon salt
6 cups vegetable broth
¼ cup fresh chopped parsley
¼ teaspoon pepper

DEEP CLEANSER
10 servings
1 hour 20 minutes

Melt butter in a large saucepan over medium heat. Add onion and cook, stirring occasionally until wilted, about 6 minutes. Add carrots, celery root, salt, and ½ cup vegetable broth. Cover and cook until vegetables are tender, about 15–20 minutes. Add remaining stock, cover and simmer, stirring occasionally for 45 minutes. Remove from heat and purée until smooth. Sprinkle with parsley and pepper to taste. Serve warm.

൞ *Basic Balancers may substitute chicken broth for vegetable broth.*

Chicken Avocado Soup

7 cups chicken broth
½ cup chopped onion
½ cup chopped celery
1 clove garlic, minced
1 teaspoon pepper
¾ cup macaroni shaped corn pasta
2 boned and skinned chicken breasts
2 drops lemon extract (or to taste)
1 tablespoon chopped parsley
¼ cup chopped cilantro
1 firm ripe avocado, peel and pit

BASIC BALANCER
4 servings
45 minutes

In a 4–5 quart pan, bring broth, onion, celery, garlic and pepper to a boil. Add chicken and return to a boil. Reduce heat to low, cover pan, and simmer until chicken is white in thickest part, about 15 minutes. With tongs, lift out breasts and let stand. Reduce heat to very low to keep soup warm. When chicken is just cool enough to handle, tear into coarse shreds. Increase heat to a simmer under soup, add pasta and chicken, cook about 5–8 minutes until pasta is tender. Stir in lemon extract, parsley and cilantro. Ladle into bowls. Add thinly sliced avocados and serve.

"Creamy" Green Bean Soup

2 medium potatoes (about ⅓ pound), peeled and
   cut into ½-inch pieces
1 tablespoon butter
1 cup chopped yellow onions
1 pound fresh green beans, trimmed and cut into
   1-inch pieces (or two 10 ounce frozen packages)
1 quart vegetable or chicken stock
1½ teaspoons dried oregano
1 teaspoon salt
¼ teaspoon pepper
1 cup yogurt (or 4 tablespoons kefir cheese)

DEEP CLEANSER
6 servings
45 minutes

In a large saucepan, melt butter and sauté onions until tender, about 5 minutes. Add the potatoes, beans, stock or broth, oregano, salt and pepper. Bring to a boil over medium heat, cover, reduce heat to low and simmer for 30 minutes, or until vegetables are very tender. Purée in a blender or food processor. Return to the saucepan, stir in yogurt or kefir and reheat gently on low. Serve immediately or refrigerate and serve chilled.

  ↝ *Basic Balancers may substitute chicken broth for vegetable broth.*

Creamy Mushroom Soup

2 tablespoons butter
1½ cups chopped onions or shallots
2 pounds baby portobello, cremini or white
   mushrooms
3 tablespoons sprouted spelt flour
4 cups vegetable or chicken stock
1 tablespoon tamari
salt and pepper to taste
6 teaspoons kefir cheese

DEEP CLEANSER
6 servings
30 minutes

In a large saucepan, melt butter over medium heat; add the onions (or shallots) and reduce heat to low. Cook, stirring a few times, until softened, about 5 minutes. Increase the heat to moderately high and add mushrooms. Season with salt and pepper and cook, stirring, until wilted, about 4–6 minutes. Stir in the flour and mix well. Add the stock and continue to heat for 5 minutes. Remove from heat and purée in batches. Serve immediately or let cool and refrigerate. Garnish with kefir cheese.

  ↝ *Basic Balancers may substitute chicken broth for vegetable broth.*

Fish Stew

2 tablespoons butter or ghee
1 red bell pepper, chopped
2 large carrots, peel and slice thinly
1 cup chopped onion
1 cup chopped celery
1 28 ounce canned tomatoes
3 cups vegetable or fish broth
1 tablespoon tomato paste
4 cups russet potatoes (about 1½ pounds),
   peeled and diced
3 cloves garlic, minced
1 teaspoon dried oregano
1 bay leaf
dash cayenne pepper (or to taste)
1½ pounds flounder, cut 1-inch thick
¼ cup chopped parsley

DEEP CLEANSER
6 servings
1 hour

Heat oil in a heavy large pot over medium-high heat. Add peppers, carrots, onion and celery and cook, stirring frequently, until vegetables are tender, about 15 minutes. Mix in tomatoes, broth and tomato paste. Add potatoes, garlic, oregano, bay leaf and cayenne and bring to boil. Reduce heat and simmer until potatoes are tender, about 20 minutes. Add fish. Cover and cook until fish is cooked through and flakes with a fork, about 10 minutes. Sprinkle with parsley.

Cod or other lean white fish fillets may be substituted for flounder.

Quick Chicken Noodle Soup

8 cups chicken broth
½ pound chicken, cooked and shredded
1½ cups thinly sliced carrots
4 ounces corn spaghetti pasta, broken into
   2-inch pieces
¾ cup frozen peas

BASIC BALANCER
8 servings
40 minutes

In a medium nonstick skillet, sauté chicken tenders until cooked through. Cool slightly and shred. Meanwhile, in a large stock pot, combine broth and carrots. Bring to a boil over medium heat and cook for 5 minutes. Add pasta, boil 4 minutes, add chicken and peas. Continue cooking until pasta is tender and peas are cooked through, about 2 minutes.

This is an easy soup to make when you have extra cooked chicken.

Green Pea and Quinoa Soup

7 cups vegetable broth
4 cups peas, fresh or frozen
¼ cup chopped fresh mint or 2 teaspoons dried
¼ cup butter
1 clove garlic, minced (or more to taste)
1½ cups uncooked quinoa grain
¼ cup chopped fresh parsley
salt and pepper to taste

SUPER CLEANSER
8 servings
45 minutes

In a medium saucepan, bring the broth to a simmer. Add 2 cups of peas and 3 tablespoons of the mint and blanch over low heat for 1 minute. Using a slotted spoon, transfer the peas to a food processor and add ½ cup of the stock. Pulse the peas to a course purée while keeping the remaining stock warm. In a large heavy saucepan, melt the butter. Add the garlic and cook about 1 minute. Add the quinoa and the warm stock and simmer covered for 10 minutes. Add the remaining 2 cups of uncooked peas and 1 tablespoon of mint to the quinoa. Stir in the coarsely puréed peas and parsley. Simmer uncovered an additional 15 minutes and serve.

  Basic Balancers may substitute chicken broth for vegetable broth.

Green Pea Soup

3 cans (14½ ounce) vegetable broth or 6 cups
2 cups chopped snap peas
2 cups green peas (can be frozen)
2 cups chopped romaine lettuce
2 cups chopped zucchini
1 cup chopped celery
¼ cup chopped parsley
1 clove garlic, minced (optional)
salt and pepper to taste

SUPER CLEANSER
8 servings
45 minutes

In a medium saucepan, combine all ingredients except salt and pepper. Bring to a boil, then reduce heat and simmer the vegetables, partially covered for 15 minutes or until tender. Purée in a blender about 3 cups at a time until smooth. Season with salt and pepper. Serve warm or chilled.

  3 tablespoons Yogurt Cheese can be added prior to serving if a creamy texture is desired. Basic Balancers may substitute chicken broth for vegetable broth, or kefir cheese for yogurt cheese.

Miso Soup

6 cups vegetable broth
1 medium leek, thinly sliced crosswise
2 cloves garlic, thinly sliced or minced
1 medium carrot, thinly sliced
¼ cup loosely packed arame, rinsed (optional)
4 ounces fresh oyster mushrooms
1 tablespoon mellow barley miso (or to taste)
4 cups coarsely chopped spinach, loosely packed

DEEP CLEANSER
4 servings
30 minutes

Trim the tough ends from the mushrooms and tear or slice mushrooms into pieces. Set aside. In a large saucepan, heat broth to a boil, add leek, garlic, carrot, and arame. Cover and simmer gently until vegetables are tender, about 10–15 minutes. Add mushrooms and simmer 3–5 more minutes. In a small bowl, whisk miso with several tablespoons of soup stock. Stir back into soup along with the spinach. Serve immediately.

❧ *Arame is a sweet and mild sun dried sea vegetable sold in health food stores and Oriental sections of grocery stores. Barley miso is sold in a paste form that needs to be kept refrigerated. Shiitake mushrooms may be substituted for oyster mushrooms.*

Polenta Stew

1 tablespoon butter
1 medium finely chopped onion
1 garlic clove, minced
½ teaspoon dried thyme
salt and pepper to taste
8 cups coarsely chopped spinach
8 cups chicken broth
1 cup polenta or corn grits
1 pound cooked, baked or grilled boneless
    chicken breasts, shredded into bite-size pieces

BASIC BALANCER
4 servings
50 minutes

Melt butter in a large stockpot. Add the onion, garlic, thyme, salt, and pepper. Cook over medium heat, stirring often, until the onion softens, about 5 minutes. Add the broth and bring to a boil over medium-high heat. Gradually add the polenta, stirring constantly to avoid lumps. Lower heat and simmer, stirring occasionally, until the polenta thickens, 15–20 minutes. Stir in the chicken and spinach, simmer until heated, 3–5 minutes. Serve.

❧ *Phase Two may substitute kale for spinach, saute with onions.*

Potato and Greens Soup

1 pound red potatoes, cut into 1-inch cubes
1 large onion, chopped
1 clove garlic, minced
1 small jalapeno pepper, seeded and finely minced
3 cups coarsely chopped chard, beet greens, turnip greens or mustard greens
4 medium tomatoes, chopped
2 cups canned diced plum tomatoes
1 quart vegetable broth
1 teaspoon oregano
1 teaspoon salt
½ teaspoon pepper

DEEP CLEANSER
6 servings
50 minutes

Place all the ingredients in a large stock pot, cover and bring to a boil over high heat. Reduce heat and simmer for 40 minutes, or until the potatoes are soft. Cool slightly and purée in a blender or food processor, or serve chunky without puréeing.

Potato Leek Soup

¼ cup butter (less for lower fat)
2 pounds leeks, white portions only
6 cups vegetable stock
2 pound russet potatoes, cubed (peeling is optional)
¼ cup fresh chives, finely chopped
½ teaspoon onion powder
salt and white pepper

DEEP CLEANSER
8 servings
45 minutes

Cut leeks in half lengthwise and carefully wash; slice ½-inch crosswise. In large saucepan, melt butter over medium heat. Add the leeks and sauté just until they begin to soften, 3–5 minutes. Meanwhile cut potatoes into bite-size pieces. Add stock and potatoes, bring to boil, reduce heat to low and simmer until the potatoes are very tender, about 20 minutes. Season to taste with onion powder, salt and pepper. Ladle into bowls and garnish with chives.

Basic Balancers may substitute chicken broth for vegetable stock.

Pumpkin Soup

1 cup finely chopped chives (or onion)
2 stalks celery, finely chopped
1 medium carrot, finely chopped
2 teaspoons butter
2½ cups vegetable (or chicken) broth
2 tablespoons quinoa flour (or any sprouted flour)
1½ cups canned pumpkin
2 teaspoons maple syrup
⅛ teaspoon ground ginger
⅛ teaspoon ground nutmeg
⅛ teaspoon ground cloves
⅛ teaspoon ground pepper
salt to taste
3 tablespoons Yogurt Cheese
water to dilute yogurt

SUPER CLEANSER
4 servings
40 minutes

Clean onion, celery and carrot. Chop finely by hand or cut into chunks and put into food processor and pulse until finely chopped. In a large saucepan, melt butter over medium heat. Add onion (if using chives, add with yogurt), celery, carrot and 3 tablespoons of broth. Cook, stirring frequently, 5 minutes or until vegetables are soft. Add a tablespoon of broth if liquid evaporates too quickly. Remove pan from heat and add flour, stirring to combine well. Return pan to heat. Slowly add remaining stock, stirring so that no lumps form. Stir in pumpkin, syrup, spices and salt. Bring to a boil. Lower heat and simmer, covered, about 20 minutes or until vegetables are tender. In a glass measuring cup, place Yogurt Cheese and enough water to make 1 cup, mix and add to soup. Do not return soup to boil after adding yogurt. Serve warm or refrigerate for up to two days. Remember, do not boil soup when reheating.

༄ *½ teaspoon pumpkin pie spice can be substituted for ginger, nutmeg and cloves. Deep Cleansers and Basic Balancers may substitute ingredients in parenthesis.*

Quick Gazpacho

5 large ripe tomatoes, cut into wedges
1 large cucumber, seeded and peeled
1 sweet pepper, seeded and peeled
½ cup chopped red onion
1 clove garlic, diced
3 tablespoons olive oil
2 drops lemon extract
½ teaspoon salt
1½ cups ice water
2 teaspoons chopped fresh cilantro
3 teaspoons chopped fresh parsley

BASIC BALANCER
6 servings
25 minutes

Prepare cucumber and sweet pepper. In large bowl, mix together the tomatoes, cucumber, sweet pepper, onion and garlic. Purée this mixture in blender, about 2 cups at a time, blending until smooth. Pour puréed vegetables into a large bowl; add oil, lemon extract and salt. Beat with wire whisk until well mixed and smooth. Whisk in ice water to desired consistency and chill until serving time. Just before serving, stir in cilantro and parsley.

Three tablespoons of cooked quinoa grain may be used to garnish each bowl of soup.

Spinach and Corn Soup

3 cups fresh spinach, cut or torn into 1-inch pieces
2 ears of corn, kernels cut off
4 cups water or vegetable broth
2 teaspoons tamari sauce
½ teaspoon ground coriander
½ cup cooked wild rice

BASIC BALANCER
4 servings
20 minutes

In a stock pot, bring water to a boil and add spinach and corn. Cover, turn off heat and let sit for 5 minutes. Add tamari sauce, coriander and rice. Serve warm.

Quinoa Vegetable Soup

¼ cup quinoa, rinsed and drained
½ cup diced carrots
¼ cup diced celery
¼ cup diced green or red pepper
2 cloves garlic, chopped (optional)
1 tablespoon butter
4 cups water or vegetable broth
¼ cup chopped chives
1 teaspoon salt (optional)
chopped parsley (optional)

SUPER CLEANSER
6 servings
45 minutes

In a saucepan, sauté quinoa, carrots, celery, pepper and garlic in butter until golden brown. Add water and bring to a boil. Simmer 20–30 minutes or until vegetables are tender and quinoa is cooked. Season to taste, sprinkle with chives and parsley if desired.

✎ *Deep Cleansers and beyond may sauté ½ cup chopped onions with peppers and add ½ cup chopped tomatoes with water.*

Tomato Pomodoro Soup

2 tablespoons butter
2 medium onions (about 2 cups), chopped
1 clove garlic
1 pound tomatoes, chopped
2 cans diced tomatoes (28 ounce cans)
3 tablespoons maple sugar or syrup
½ cup finely chopped basil leaves
3 cups sprouted bread, crusts removed
    and cubed (3–4 slices)
1 teaspoon salt
½ teaspoon pepper

DEEP CLEANSER
8 servings
1 hour

In a large stock pot, heat butter over medium heat. Add onions and garlic and sauté until slightly browned, about 10 minutes. Add basil, fresh and canned tomatoes and sugar; simmer 30 minutes. Remove pan from heat. Cool slightly. Purée in blender in batches until smooth. Return purée to pan and add bread cubes, salt and pepper. Simmer 15 minutes until bread soaks up purée and thickens soup. Stir to break up bread cubes. Serve.

✎ *This thick tomato bread soup is great for a main course. Try with homemade Sprouted Spelt Bread.*

Sweet Potato Soup

2 large cooked sweet potatoes or yams, peeled
   (about 1½ pounds)
4 cups vegetable or chicken broth
½ cup yogurt or Yogurt Cheese
½ teaspoon salt
¼ teaspoon pepper
1 cup corn kernels

BASIC BALANCER
4 servings
20 minutes

Combine sweet potatoes, stock and yogurt in a large sauce pan. Season with salt and pepper. Mash ingredients with a potato masher creating a chunky texture. Add corn and cook over medium-low heat, stirring occasionally, until warm. Do not boil.

If sweet potatoes or yams are not cooked, peel and chop them into chunks and cook in simmering broth until potatoes are tender. Reduce heat and cool until no longer simmering; add yogurt, salt, pepper, and corn. Serve warm. For a smooth textured soup, purée all ingredients except corn in a food processor before putting in the saucepan. But this takes longer and makes more dishes to wash!

Sweet Root Vegetable Soup

4¼ cups vegetable broth
1½ cups chopped onions
1 stalk chopped celery
½ cup parsnips, peel and cube
½ cup winter squash, peel and cube (optional)
1 cup cubed red potatoes
1 medium carrot, cut into 1-inch chunks
2 tablespoons maple syrup
1 cup tomato sauce, canned or fresh
½ cup yogurt
salt
fresh ground pepper

DEEP CLEANSER
6 servings
1 hour 15 minutes

In large sauce pan, bring ¼ cup broth to a boil; add onions. Cook 3 minutes over medium-high heat, stirring frequently. Add 1 cup of broth, parsnips, celery, squash, potatoes and carrot. Simmer, stirring occasionally, 10 minutes, then add remaining broth. Bring soup to boil, lower heat and simmer, covered, until vegetables are soft, about 40 minutes. Stir in salt, pepper, maple syrup and tomato sauce; simmer 10 more minutes. Add seasonings; serve hot with a dollop of yogurt.

Roasted Squash and Tomato Chowder

2 butternut squash (1 pound), peel and seed
2 medium tomatoes
2 tablespoons olive oil
2 cups chopped onions
2 cups corn kernels
2 teaspoons minced garlic (optional)
1 teaspoon ground coriander
1 teaspoon ground cardamom
½ teaspoon ground cumin
½ teaspoon ground cloves
salt and pepper
6 cups vegetable broth or chicken broth
1 large baked potato, peeled

BASIC BALANCER
8 servings
1 hour 15 minutes

Heat oven to 400 degrees. Lightly grease 3 cookie sheets with 1 tablespoon olive oil or cooking spray. Cut the squash in half and remove the seeds. Then cut the squash in 1-inch strips and peel off the skin with a knife. Finally, cut squash into 1-inch cubes and place on prepared cookie sheets. Place whole tomatoes on one of the sheets with the squash. Season with salt and pepper. Roast until squash is nearly soft, 20–25 minutes, tossing with spatula to prevent burning. Meanwhile, chop onions. In large stock pot heat 1 tablespoon oil and sauté onions and garlic over medium heat about 8 minutes. While onions are sautéing, add coriander, cardamom, cumin and cloves to stock pot. Add vegetable broth, corn, squash and tomato mixture to stock pot. Bring to boil and simmer 30 minutes, breaking up tomato and squash pieces with back of fork or spatula. Dice potato and add to soup. Heat to warm potato for 5 minutes and serve.

℮ *Fresh, canned or frozen corn may be used. Acorn squash may be substituted for butternut squash. If potato is not already baked, cut in 1-inch cubes and roast with squash.*

Tomato Florentine Soup

1 large onion, chopped
1 teaspoon olive oil
2 stalks celery, chopped
1 can tomatoes (28 ounce can)
1 can tomato paste (6 ounce can)
3½ cups vegetable or chicken broth
1 teaspoon dried oregano
½ teaspoon dried basil
2 bay leaves
3 tablespoons maple syrup
salt and pepper
1 package chopped frozen spinach (10 ounces),
   thawed and drained
1 cup sprouted bread croutons, divided among
   servings (optional)
8 teaspoons kefir cheese garnish, 1 teaspoon
   per serving (optional)

BASIC BALANCER
8 servings
30 minutes

Sauté onion and celery in olive oil and 3 tablespoons broth, about 3–5 minutes. Add tomatoes, tomato paste, broth, herbs, syrup, salt and pepper. Simmer 20 minutes. Purée soup, thin with additional broth if needed. Return soup to pan and add spinach. Heat through and serve with croutons and kefir cheese garnish.

Vegetable Soup

1 tablespoon butter or broth
1 ½ cup chopped carrots
1 cup chopped celery
1 large onion, chopped
5 medium potatoes, cubed
3 ears corn, cut off cob
⅓ cup chopped parsley
5 cups vegetable or chicken broth
8 tablespoons tamari sauce
2 teaspoons paprika
¼ teaspoon thyme
salt and pepper to taste
10 ounces spinach (about 1 bunch), chopped
4 teaspoons Yogurt Cheese (sour cream or kefir)

BASIC BALANCER
4 servings
30 minutes

In a large skillet, melt butter or add broth and sauté carrots, celery and onions until tender, about 8 minutes. Add potatoes, corn and parsley; cook until tender, about 10 minutes. Add 5 cups broth, tamari, paprika, thyme, salt and pepper; simmer for 10 minutes longer. Stir in spinach and simmer until wilted, about 1 minute. Remove from heat. Garnish each serving with a teaspoon of yogurt (sour cream or kefir).

If you plan to reheat soup, do not add yogurt (sour cream or kefir) until it is reheated.

Vegetable Lentil Soup

2 tablespoons butter or ghee
1 cup diced onion
1 clove garlic, minced
2 stalks celery, diced
2 large carrots, diced
1 ½ cups sprouted, cooked lentils
5 cups water or broth
1 teaspoon dried thyme
½ teaspoon dried oregano
1 teaspoon dried basil
4 cups diced tomatoes or 28 ounce can
   diced tomatoes
3 tablespoons tomato paste
salt and pepper to taste
8 tablespoons kefir cheese (optional)

DEEP CLEANSER
6 servings
1 hour

In a large stock pot, melt the butter and sauté the onion, garlic, celery, carrots and tomatoes for 10 minutes, stirring frequently. Add the remaining ingredients, except the kefir cheese and bring to a boil. Reduce heat, cover and simmer for 20 minutes until all vegetables are tender. Let cool slightly and put half of the mixture in a blender or food processor and blend until smooth. Return the lentil purée to the stock pot. If a chunkier soup is desired, omit puréeing. Serve and garnish each bowl with 1 tablespoon kefir cheese if desired.

℘ *Using already cooked, sprouted lentils makes this an easy and quick soup to prepare. Refer to Sprouting Beans, Legumes and Seeds in the recipe section.*

Tortilla Soup

⅓ cup chopped onions
2 cloves garlic, chopped (optional)
1 teaspoon dried oregano
¾ teaspoon ground cumin
⅛ teaspoon chili powder (or to taste)
¼ teaspoon pepper
8 cups vegetable or chicken broth
1 can diced tomatoes (14 ounce can)
1 can diced green chilies (4 ounce can),
   hot or mild
10 corn tortillas
1 ripe avocado
2 tablespoons chopped fresh cilantro or parsley
1 cup corn kernels
kefir cheese or Yogurt Cheese

BASIC BALANCER
6 servings
30 minutes

Heat a nonstick 6 quart pan over medium heat. Add onion, garlic, oregano, cumin, chili powder, and pepper. Sauté 1 minute. Add broth, tomatoes (including juice), and chilies. Cover and bring to a boil over medium-high heat. Stack tortillas and cut into ⅛-inch strips. Add tortillas to boiling broth. Reduce heat, cover and simmer for 15 minutes, stirring occasionally. Peel, pit, and coarsely chop the avocado. Add avocado to soup with corn, cilantro or parsley. Serve garnished with a teaspoon of kefir cheese or Yogurt Cheese.

ᵔ *When tomatoes are in season, substitute 2 cups of chopped fresh tomatoes and their juices for canned tomatoes.*

Vegetable Wild Rice Soup

2 quarts vegetable stock (8 cups)
1 clove garlic, minced
¼ cup dried tomatoes, snipped into small pieces
2 large carrots, halved and thinly sliced
½ cup thinly sliced celery
½ cup trimmed green beans, cut into ½-inch pieces
1 large leek, thinly sliced, white part only
1 cup shredded spinach, kale or chard
1 cup wild rice
2 new potatoes, quartered
½ cup fresh or frozen green peas
salt and pepper to taste

DEEP CLEANSER
8 servings
1 hour 15 minutes

In a large pot, bring broth to a boil. Reduce heat to simmer and add garlic and tomatoes. Stir; bring soup back to steady simmer. Add ingredients in the following order, bringing back to a simmer between each addition: carrots, celery, green beans, leeks, and spinach; simmer 8 minutes. Add rice and potatoes, simmer 35–40 minutes. If liquid seems to be evaporating too fast, cover soup, but maintain simmer. Add salt and pepper to taste. Add peas and cook until soup returns to simmer. Remove from heat and serve.

Spicy Pumpkin Soup

1 cup chopped onions
1 clove garlic, minced
½ teaspoon curry powder
½ teaspoon salt
⅛ teaspoon crushed red pepper
⅛ teaspoon ground coriander
1 can pumpkin (16 ounce can)
3 cups vegetable broth
1 cup yogurt

DEEP CLEANSER
6 servings
30 minutes

Melt butter in a large saucepan and sauté onion and garlic until soft. Add curry powder, salt, pepper and coriander. Cook for one minute. Add broth and boil gently, uncovered, for 15 minutes. Stir in pumpkin and cook 5 more minutes. Reduce heat and stir in yogurt. Be careful not to boil yogurt. Serve warm.

෴ *For a creamier soup, purée in a blender after adding the yogurt. Do not boil when reheating. Basic Balancers may use chicken broth and garnish soup with a dollop of sour cream or kefir cheese.*

Carrot Soup

1 clove garlic, minced (optional)
2 tablespoons butter or ghee
½ teaspoon sage
½ teaspoon oregano
¼ teaspoon crushed red bell pepper (optional)
3 cups chopped carrots
2 cups vegetable broth
1 teaspoon onion powder
¼ teaspoon curry powder (or to taste)
fresh ground pepper
4 teaspoons Yogurt Cheese

SUPER CLEANSER
4 servings
40 minutes

In a large saucepan over medium heat, sauté garlic in butter, about 2 minutes. Add sage, oregano, red pepper and carrots; briefly sauté again, about 5 minutes. Add a small amount of the vegetable broth if the vegetables begin to stick to the pan. Add broth and curry powder and bring to a boil. Reduce heat and simmer until the carrots are tender, about 20 minutes. Cool slightly and pour into a blender and purée. Add Yogurt Cheese and blend further. Return soup to the pan and reheat. Do not boil or Yogurt Cheese will separate. Add salt and pepper to taste.

ᶜ⁓ *Basic Balancers may substitute kefir cheese for Yogurt Cheese and chicken broth for vegetable broth. Basic Balancers may sauté 1 large, chopped onion with garlic for 7–8 minutes. Soup can be prepared ahead and refrigerated; but do not add the kefir cheese until soup is reheated. Cream cheese can be substituted for kefir cheese when it is back in the diet.*

Sprouted Beans, Legumes and Seeds

Sprouting dried beans and growing sprouts offers year round accessibility to fresh, organic food that is rich in vitamins and enzymes. Sprouting changes beans from a starch product which is indigestible to a vegetable that is pure digestive delight. The best part is that you don't need a green thumb to sprout them!

Use any amount of dried beans, legumes, peas, or lentils when sprouting. Use whole peas as they are easier to sprout than split peas. Large beans such as lima, navy, kidney and black beans have low yields and spoil quickly. The husks of oats, barley, and millet are commonly removed and will not sprout. Make sure packaged dried beans are fresh. Some packaged beans are sterilized and will not sprout.

To sprout beans, place in a large bowl, rinse, removing any foreign matter and drain in a colander. Put the beans back in the bowl and cover with several inches of water. Let them soak overnight or 8–12 hours. Drain beans in a colander and cover with a damp towel so they don't dry out. Rinse every morning and evening with room temperature water to remove any bacteria, mold or fungus build-up. While sprouting beans, place them in indirect light and at a room temperature no lower than 70 degrees. Sprouted tails need to be ¾–1-inch long. For most beans this will take 3–4 days in the colander. Sprout only one variety of beans per colander as certain beans sprout at different times.

Once the beans have sprouted, cook them according to the Cooking Beans Recipe. Sprouted beans and legumes may be used in any of the recipes that call for regular beans and legumes.

In addition to sprouted beans, sprouted seeds, such as alfalfa, radish, basil, and leek seeds can be added to a variety of recipes to enhance their nutritional value. Stackable seed tray sprouters, flax sprouting bags, and ball jars can be used to sprout seeds.

The stackable seed trays are designed so that water flows from one tray to the next leaving enough dampness to encourage seed to germinate. Sprout bags offer an easy way to rinse and drain seeds twice daily. When sprouted, seeds will expand to four times their initial volume.

Chlorophyll-developing plants, such as alfalfa, radish, clover, fenugreek, and other vegetable seeds, have better results in a vertical growing method than a seed sprouter tray or ball jar affords.

When using a seed sprouter or bag sprouter follow the instructions included with the equipment. If a ball jar is being used, examine seeds and remove any foreign matter. Soak seeds in a clean jar covered with pure water. Soak overnight or 8–12 hours. Rinse seeds for approximately 10 seconds under room temperature water. With a rubber band, secure a piece of cheesecloth over the top of the jar. Drain off water and return seeds to an even level on the bottom of the jar. While sprouting, keep at room temperature, no lower than 70 degrees, in a neutral spot. Indirect light is the best. Rinse under running, room temperature water twice a day, no more than 12 hours apart, for a minimum of 30 seconds. Drain. Depending on the type of seeds, shoots take about 2–5 days. Fresh sprouts may be kept in the refrigerator for a few days.

Sprouting requires quality beans and seeds and conscientious rinsing. Roasted, salted, and processed seeds will not sprout. Seed sprouters and seeds for sprouting are available at most health food stores. (See Sources)

A word of caution. Many of the sprouted bean recipes use hot peppers and/or chilies. The acids from some chili peppers can literally burn the skin when handling. Use gloves or wash hands with a pumice soap every few minutes. Also, be careful not to touch eyes or any sensitive skin areas when working with hot peppers or chilies.

Bean Balls

4 cups cooked, sprouted adzuki beans
½ red pepper, coarsely chopped
6 scallions, coarsely chopped
1 tablespoon tamari sauce
2 cloves garlic, minced (optional)
1 teaspoon grated ginger root (or ¼ teaspoon dried)
2 tablespoons tomato paste
1 cup quinoa flakes
pepper
1 tablespoon melted butter

DEEP CLEANSER
6 servings
30 minutes

Using a food processor, pulse the beans, pepper and scallions into a coarse meal texture. Transfer mixture to a bowl and add the remaining ingredients. Form the mixture into balls about the size of a walnut and place on a prepared baking sheet. Place the tray in the freezer for 10–15 minutes to allow the balls to harden. Heat the oven to 400 degrees. Brush the balls with a little melted butter and bake them for 15–20 minutes, rolling once or twice to prevent burning. Makes about 40 balls.

ॐ *These balls can be served with a red sauce as an appetizer. Basic Balancers may serve over corn or quinoa pasta.*

Cooking Sprouted Beans

4 cups sprouted beans

DEEP CLEANSER
4 servings
50 minutes

Place beans in a saucepan and add water to cover by 1-inch. Bring to a boil. Continue boiling, uncovered, for about 10 minutes. Add more water as needed. Reduce the heat and simmer the beans for 30–50 minutes, or until tender. Drain excess liquid into a container and retain for soup stock.

ॐ *The cooking time of sprouted beans is usually half that of unsprouted beans. Cooked beans may be frozen for future use.*

Kidney Bean Salad

¼ cup Essential Mayonnaise
2 tablespoons minced onion
1 tablespoon minced parsley
2 cups sprouted kidney beans, cooked and chilled
½ cup chopped celery
2 large hard-boiled eggs, chopped
¼ teaspoon pepper
½ teaspoon oregano
¼ teaspoon marjoram and basil
dash cayenne

BASIC BALANCER
4 servings
15 minutes

In a large bowl mix together Essential Mayonnaise, onion and parsley; mix in beans, celery and eggs. Add seasonings and chill well.

‿ *Variations: Use pintos, anasazi, or a combination of all as a substitute. ½ cup finely chopped carrots, green peppers and/or cucumbers may be added.*

Refried Beans

5 cups sprouted kidney beans
1½ cups water
1 large onion, chopped
¼ cup chopped chili peppers
1 clove garlic, chopped
¼ teaspoon cayenne pepper
¼ teaspoon cumin seeds
1 cup yogurt or kefir

DEEP CLEANSER
4 servings
1 hour

In a large saucepan, simmer beans, water, onion, chili peppers, garlic, cayenne and cumin seeds for 30 minutes. Let cool slightly. Using a blender, purée the bean mixture with yogurt. To blend the beans they need to be somewhat liquid, but the extra liquid will cook off. Pour the blended mixture into a skillet and cook at low heat for 5 minutes or more, scraping the bottom of the pan constantly until they hold together in the pan. Remove from heat and let stand for 30 minutes.

‿ *Basic Balancers may spread on warmed corn tortillas and top with chopped tomatoes, scallions, and sour cream.*

Shelley's Chili

3 cups sprouted pintos beans
3 cups sprouted kidney beans
1 cup chopped celery
1 cup chopped green peppers
2 cans tomato sauce (15 ounce cans)
4 cups chopped tomatoes
2 cups tomato juice
2 large onions, chopped
2 cloves garlic, minced
1 teaspoon chili powder or more to taste
½ teaspoon ground cumin
¼ teaspoon cayenne

DEEP CLEANSER
12 servings
3 hours

In a large stock pot, add all ingredients; bring to a boil, reduce heat and simmer for 3 hours.

Sprouted Baked Beans

2 tablespoons butter
1 large chopped onion
2 cloves garlic, minced
½ pound sprouted Pinto or Northern beans,
    cooked (about 4 cups)
1 cup crushed tomatoes
2 tablespoons tomato paste
¼ cup maple syrup
1 teaspoon salt
½ teaspoon dry mustard
¼ teaspoon pepper
dash chili pepper (optional)

DEEP CLEANSER
4 servings
40 minutes

In a medium skillet, melt butter and sauté onion and garlic until soft. In a medium bowl combine remaining ingredients. Add onions and garlic and place in a casserole dish. Baked covered at 350 degrees for 25–30 minutes, or until hot.

Sprouted Bean Burgers

4 cups sprouted pinto beans, cooked
4 teaspoons butter or ghee
⅔ cup minced onion
2 tablespoons ground coriander
4 teaspoons sprouted spelt flour
4 teaspoons ground cumin
¼ teaspoon salt
½ teaspoon pepper

DEEP CLEANSER
6 servings
30 minutes

Place beans in a mixing bowl and mash with a fork. In a medium nonstick skillet, melt butter or ghee over medium heat. Add onion; sauté 3 minutes or until tender. Add coriander, flour, cumin, salt and pepper. Cook, stirring constantly for 1 minute. Preheat broiler. Add onion mixture to beans and stir well. Cut 6 (4-inch) squares of wax paper. Divide bean mixture into 6 equal portions, shape into 3½-inch patties and place each on a wax paper square. Invert patties onto a baking sheet coated with cooking spray; remove wax paper. Broil 4 minutes; turn carefully and broil an additional 2–3 minutes.

Remember, butter will burn at a lower temperature than ghee. Basic Balancers may substitute olive oil for butter or ghee.

Sprouted Bean and Tomato Bisque

3 medium-size firm ripe tomatoes
  (about 1¼ pound) or one 16 ounce can
  chopped tomatoes
1 large chopped onion
1 clove garlic, minced
2 large chopped carrots (about ½ pound)
4 cups cooked sprouted pinto beans
2 cans vegetable broth (14½ ounce cans),
  or 4 cups homemade
⅓ cup fresh basil leaves (or coriander)
salt and pepper
pinch of maple sugar

DEEP CLEANSER
4 servings
40 minutes

In a 4–5 quart pan, add 1 tablespoon butter, onion and garlic. Stir often over high heat until onion is faintly browned, about 6–8 minutes. Add chopped tomatoes, carrots, pinto beans and broth. Bring to a boil; then reduce heat and simmer, covered, until carrots are very soft, about 10 minutes. In a blender or food processor, smoothly purée soup a portion at a time. Return to pan, add salt and pepper to taste. Add a pinch of maple sugar or a teaspoon of maple syrup if bisque is too acidic. Warm soup and serve or refrigerate up to two days.

Sprouted Bean Dip

2 cups cooked sprouted beans
1 clove garlic
¼ cup dried tomatoes, reconstituted
½ cup water from tomatoes (or more
   to thin as needed)

DEEP CLEANSERS
8 servings
30 minutes

Pour 1 cup boiling water over dried tomatoes and let soak until soft, about 20 minutes. Drain, reserving ¾ cup water. With food processor running, drop garlic through feed tube and process until chopped. Add beans and ½ cup reserved tomato water and process until smooth. Add tomatoes, salt and pepper and pulse just to mix. Add more tomato water if dip is too thick. Scrape into a bowl.

ℰ *Basic Balancers may layer top with sour cream, chopped green onions and/or shredded lettuce. Spread on sprouted toast or use as dip for vegetables and corn tortillas.*

Sprouted Pea Soup

4 cups water
3 cups sprouted peas
1 large onion, chopped
1 stalk celery, chopped
1 bay leaf
½ teaspoon marjoram
½ teaspoon oregano
¼ teaspoon sweet basil
pinch of dried sage
1 cup water
2 cups sliced mushrooms
1 tablespoons butter
1 tablespoon maple syrup
¼ teaspoon garlic powder
½ teaspoon tamari sauce
pepper to taste

DEEP CLEANSER
6 servings
2 hours

In a large stock pot, add water, peas, onion, celery, bay leaf, marjoram, oregano, basil, and sage; bring to boil, cover and simmer for 1–1½ hours, until peas are soft. Add more water if needed. In a blender or food processor, purée soup in batches. Return soup to stock pot and add water to make desired consistency. In a small skillet sauté mushrooms in butter; add to soup with syrup and seasonings. Heat and serve.

Sprouted Pea Stew

6 cups water
4 vegetable broth cubes
2 cups sprouted peas
½ hot chili pepper, minced (optional)
3 large onions
1 small rutabaga
2 stalks celery
3 large carrot
3 small sweet potatoes or yams
1 tablespoon butter
½ cup parsley
1½ teaspoons maple syrup
1 tablespoon tamari sauce (or to taste)
dash of cayenne
Yogurt Cheese (optional)

DEEP CLEANSER
10 servings
3 hours 30 minutes

In a large saucepan, add water, vegetable cubes, peas and chili pepper; simmer 3 hours adding more water if needed. As peas cook, uniformly chop onions, rutabaga, celery, carrots and sweet potatoes. In a large skillet, melt butter and sauté these vegetables until soft. In a blender, purée cooked peas in batches. Return to saucepan and add sautéed vegetables, parsley, syrup, tamari and cayenne. Serve over slices of toasted sprouted bread. Put a dollop of Yogurt Cheese on top if desired.

ᶜ⌐ *Basic Balancers may substitute sour cream for yogurt cheese.*

Sprouted Soyburgers

5 cups sprouted soybeans, cooked
¾ cup sprouted spelt flour
1 large onion, chopped
2 tablespoons tamari sauce
2 teaspoons oregano
1 teaspoon basil
2 teaspoons garlic powder
⅛ teaspoon cayenne (or to taste)

DEEP CLEANSER
6 servings
25 minutes

Using a juicer or vegetable grinder, mash soybeans. Add remaining ingredients and mix well. Form into thin patties and fry in pan or grill. These patties freeze well.

ᶜ⌐ *Basic Balancers may substitute corn flour for sprouted spelt flour.*
Edamame may be substituted for sprouted soybeans. Edamame are soybeans that have not been dried therefore digest as a vegetable.

Sauces, Spreads and Marinades

Quite possibly, one of the best ingredients is Yogurt Cheese. Yogurt Cheese is one of the easiest foods to digest and it can be substituted in many recipes for milk, cream, sour cream, cheese, and kefir. It can be added to cooked soups, used in dressings, cheesecake, icings, dips, and more.

Once the whey is drained from the yogurt, leaving Yogurt Cheese, the overpowering yogurt taste that is hard to disguise in recipes disappears. Yogurt Cheese is the base for Essential Mayonnaise and the Baked Potato Topper recipes.

One hundred percent cranberry juice is another wonderful ingredient. Cranberries fall into the vegetable category, due to the enzymes used to digest them. The tartness of pure cranberry juice is used in Cranberry Vinaigrette as a substitute for vinegar.

I must make special mention of the Cranberry Spread Recipe. It consists of cranberries and maple syrup, making it mostly a vegetable. My mother created this recipe years ago for the first Thanksgiving after I "converted" to essential eating. This spread can be served warm as a side dish, on toast as a jam, in sandwiches with kefir cheese, or in frozen desserts and parfaits. Cranberry Spread is worth making and having on hand. Keep a six month supply in the freezer at all times!

Asparagus Guacamole

7 ounces fresh asparagus, steamed
5 ounces fresh peas, steamed
2 teaspoons tamari sauce
2 tablespoons kefir cheese
2 tablespoons chopped cilantro
1 clove garlic, minced
¼ teaspoon ground cumin
1 medium tomato, chopped
2 tablespoons chopped red onion

BASIC BALANCER
10 servings
20 minutes

Steam asparagus and peas for 5 minutes, until tender. Purée asparagus, peas, tamari, kefir cheese, cilantro, garlic and cumin in a blender or food processor until smooth. Empty into a small bowl and add tomato and onion. Serve the same day with baked corn chips.

Can also be used as a sandwich filling. Half of a 10 ounce package frozen peas can be substituted for fresh peas.

Avocado Dressing

1 cup yogurt
1 large avocado
¼ cup chives
dash of garlic powder
dash of chili powder (optional)

SUPER CLEANSER
6 servings
10 minutes

Purée all ingredients in a blender or food processor. Thin with water if needed. Chill.

Deep Cleansers may add 1 teaspoon tamari and may substitute kefir cheese for yogurt. Diluted Yogurt Cheese may be substituted for yogurt. Basic Balancers may substitute 1 green onion for chives or sour cream for yogurt.

Baked Potato Topper

1 cup Yogurt Cheese or plain yogurt
½ teaspoon dried dill weed
1 tablespoon fresh chives (or 2 teaspoons dried)
¼ teaspoon salt
⅛ teaspoon pepper

DEEP CLEANSER
8 servings
5 minutes

In a small bowl, combine all ingredients and mix well. Chill.

❧ *For variation, try ½ cup Yogurt Cheese and ½ cup kefir cheese.*

Cucumber Dill Dressing

1 cup cucumber, peeled, seeded, and finely diced
½ cup yogurt, Yogurt Cheese, or sour cream
½ teaspoon dill weed
⅛ teaspoon garlic powder
⅛ teaspoon salt
¼ teaspoon dry mustard
⅛ teaspoon pepper

BASIC BALANCER
4 servings
10 minutes

Place diced cucumber on paper towels; pat to dry. Allow to dry on towels while combining other ingredients. In a medium bowl, whisk together all remaining ingredients until blended. Add cucumbers and mix well. Chill.

Essential Mayonnaise

1 cup Yogurt Cheese
¼ teaspoon dry mustard
¼ teaspoon onion powder (or to taste)
¼ teaspoon pepper
2 drops vanilla extract
2 drops lemon extract
dash of garlic powder and cayenne pepper

SUPER CLEANSER
4 servings
2 minutes

Mix all ingredients. Use in egg or tuna salad.

❧ *Basic Balancers may substitute yogurt with sour cream or kefir cheese thinned to consistency of sour cream. For a thicker mayonnaise that you would use on sandwiches, substitute Yogurt Cheese for yogurt.*

Basil Dressing

½ cup sour cream
¼ cup water
8 large leaves of fresh basil
1 green onion
1 tablespoon olive oil
½ teaspoon thyme
½ teaspoon dried dill
1 drop lemon extract
dash of cayenne pepper (optional)
salt and pepper to taste

BASIC BALANCER
6 servings
10 minutes

Purée all ingredients in a food processor or blender. Chill.

↬ *Fresh parsley may be substituted for basil.*

Basil Tomato Sauce

2 teaspoons butter
1 medium onion, chopped
3 cloves garlic, minced
½ cup vegetable broth
1 can crushed tomatoes (28 ounce can)
¼ teaspoon maple sugar
1 tablespoon dried oregano
½ teaspoon dried rosemary
½ cup loosely packed fresh basil leaves,
    torn into small pieces
salt and pepper

DEEP CLEANSER
4 servings
50 minutes

In a large saucepan, melt butter over medium heat. Add onion and garlic and cook, stirring often, until onion is soft, about 5 minutes. Add broth, tomatoes, sugar, oregano and rosemary. Simmer over low heat, uncovered, stirring occasionally, until mixture thickens slightly, about 30 minutes. Add basil and cook 3 minutes. Salt and pepper to taste. Yields 4 cups.

Crabmeat Dip

¾ cup Yogurt Cheese
¼ cup kefir cheese
1 tablespoon tamari sauce
1 teaspoon onion powder
½ teaspoon paprika
1 teaspoon dried dill
¼ teaspoon maple syrup
½ pound imitation crabmeat (pollack),
    finely chopped
salt and pepper to taste

DEEP CLEANSER
8 servings
10 minutes

Blend all ingredients together. For a smoother dip, pulse in a food processor.

↪ *Serve with cold, cooked or raw vegetables.*

Cranberry Spread

8 cups fresh, whole cranberries
2½ cups maple syrup
3 tablespoons arrowroot (optional)
3 tablespoons cold water (optional)

SUPER CLEANSER
20 servings
1 hour 30 minutes

In a large saucepan, place cranberries and syrup. Bring to a boil and simmer 1 hour stirring occasionally. Pan may be partially covered to prevent splattering. A splatter screen works well. If spread needs to be thickened, mix arrowroot in cold water and add to cranberries. Let simmer 15 more minutes to thicken and remove from heat. Let cool and put in containers. Can be frozen or will keep in the refrigerator for a month.

↪ *Fresh cranberries are best but their buying season is limited to November through January in most stores. The next best thing to fresh is frozen sliced cranberries which can be ordered from a large grocery store's bakery department. Sometimes grocers carry whole cranberries in the frozen foods section after January.*

Cranberry Vinaigrette

6 tablespoons 100% pure cranberry juice
2 tablespoons maple syrup
½ teaspoon salt
1 teaspoon dry mustard
6 tablespoons olive oil
2 teaspoons barley miso

BASIC BALANCER

12 servings

10 minutes

In a cruet or jar, mix all ingredients and shake well. Pour over greens and serve. Yields ⅔ cups.

℮ *For a creamy dressing add 1 cup yogurt and ½ teaspoon cumin.*

Creamy French Dressing

½ cup tomato or vegetable juice
¾ cup Yogurt Cheese or kefir cheese
2 tablespoons 100% cranberry juice
2 teaspoons maple syrup
¼ teaspoon salt
¼ teaspoon pepper
1 teaspoon dry mustard
½ teaspoon dried oregano
¼ teaspoon dried basil

DEEP CLEANSER

6 servings

10 minutes

Place all ingredients in a small jar or cruet and shake well. Refrigerate.

℮ *A combination of yogurt and kefir cheeses may be used. Basic Balancers may substitute ¼ cup olive oil for cheese.*

Fruit Dressing

1 cup Yogurt Cheese
¼ cup 100% cranberry juice
¼ cup maple syrup

SUPER CLEANSER

8 servings

5 minutes

Mix all ingredients and serve over fresh apricots or bananas cut into bite-size pieces when they come back into the diet.

Fruit Preserves

1 pound dried apricots, unsulphured, organic maple syrup to taste

SUPER CLEANSER

10 servings

40 minutes

In a medium saucepan, place apricots and enough water to cover them. Cook, simmering until soft, about 10 minutes. Drain off excess liquid. Purée in blender adding maple syrup if a sweeter taste is desired. Keep refrigerated.

℮ *For variation use other dried fruits. Spices like nutmeg and cinnamon or extracts like lemon or orange may be added.*

Miso Dressing

1 cup vegetable broth
1 tablespoon arrowroot
2 tablespoons miso paste
2 teaspoons tamari sauce
2 teaspoons minced green onion
1 drop lemon extract

BASIC BALANCER

6 servings

15 minutes

Put vegetable broth in a small saucepan and whisk in arrowroot. Heat over medium heat, whisking constantly until mixture thickens. Remove from heat and cool. Whisk in remaining ingredients and chill. Adjust consistency with water if needed.

℮ *Serve over greens or as a fish sauce.*

Roasted Garlic Dressing

½ cup yogurt or Yogurt Cheese
1 clove Roasted Garlic (or to taste)
½ teaspoon dried dill
1 drop lemon extract

SUPER CLEANSER

4 servings

5 minutes

Place all ingredients in a blender or food processor and purée until smooth. Chill.

℮ *Basic Balancers may blend with ½ cup chopped cucumber.*

Gazpacho Dressing

1 medium tomato
¼ green pepper
1 green onion
2 thick (1-inch) slices of cucumber
¼ cup water
2 tablespoons tomato paste
1 tablespoon parsley
¼ teaspoon dill weed
¼ teaspoon basil
⅛ teaspoon tamari sauce
⅛ teaspoon garlic powder

BASIC BALANCER
4 servings
15 minutes

Purée all ingredients in a food processor or blender. Chill.

Mushroom Gravy

2 tablespoons butter
1 medium onion, chopped
1 clove garlic, minced
1½ cups chopped cremini mushrooms
2¼ cups water
3 tablespoons tamari sauce
2 teaspoons arrowroot, dissolved in ¼ cup water
salt and pepper

DEEP CLEANSER
8 servings
25 minutes

In a medium saucepan, melt butter over medium heat. Add onion and garlic and cook, stirring often, until onion is soft, about 5 minutes. Add mushrooms and cook, stirring often, until they begin to release their juices. Add water, tamari sauce and dissolved arrowroot; stir well. Simmer until slightly thickened, about 10 minutes. Salt and pepper to taste. Yields about 3 cups.

Guacamole

2 cloves garlic, minced
2 roasted red peppers, finely chopped
½ teaspoon dried coriander
½ cup snipped chives
2 drops lemon extract
salt and pepper to taste
3 large avocados, ripened
   (about 1½ pounds)

SUPER CLEANSER
8 servings
10 minutes

In a small bowl, mix garlic, peppers, coriander, chives, extract and salt. Just before serving, cut avocados in half lengthwise; remove pit and scoop meat from the skin with a spoon. In a large bowl, mash avocados with a fork (or potato masher); stir in the garlic mixture. Serve on sprouted sourdough toast points or with Veggie Sticks. To make toast points, cut a piece of toast with an x to make four triangles.

  Roasted peppers in a jar may be substituted. Deep Cleansers and beyond may add ¾ cup no-vinegar salsa. Basic Balancers may serve with baked corn chips.

Quick Tomato Sauce

2 cans diced or whole tomatoes (28 ounce cans)
2 cloves garlic, minced (or to taste)
3 tablespoons butter
4 tablespoons chopped fresh basil (about 8 leaves)
½ teaspoon maple sugar
1½ teaspoons salt

DEEP CLEANSER
6 servings
20 minutes

If using whole tomatoes, drain and reserve liquid. Coarsely chop tomatoes and add back enough liquid if necessary to make 4 cups. Use diced tomatoes directly from can. Mince garlic and mix in a small bowl with 2 teaspoons water. In a 10-inch skillet, melt butter and add garlic, sautéing over medium-low heat until fragrant but not brown, about 2 minutes. Stir in tomatoes and simmer until thickened slightly, about 10 minutes. Stir in remaining ingredients and cook, stirring occasionally for 1 minute. Serve over quinoa pasta.

Roasted Tomato Basil Pesto

2 medium ripe tomatoes (about ¾ pound)
1 cup loosely packed basil leaves
⅓ cup flat leaf parsley
1 clove garlic, minced
2 tablespoons 100% cranberry juice
½ teaspoon maple sugar
¼ teaspoon salt
¼ teaspoon pepper

BASIC BALANCER
4 servings
30 minutes

Heat the oven to 425 degrees. Cut the stem core out of the tomatoes and cut the tomatoes in half. Place them in a greased square baking pan, cut side up. Roast tomatoes for 15–20 minutes until tomatoes start to lose their shape. Remove from oven and cool. Place basil, parsley and garlic in a food processor and pulse to finely chop vegetables. Add tomato, juice, sugar, salt, and pepper. Pulse until well mixed. Makes about 1 cup.

ↄ *Pesto may be used over quinoa or corn pasta, with vegetables, on pizza or as a dip.*

Vinaigrette

½ cup balsamic vinegar
3 tablespoons water
3 tablespoons fresh lemon juice
1 tablespoon Dijon mustard
1 tablespoon maple syrup
1 teaspoon dried oregano
½ teaspoon salt
¼ teaspoon pepper
½ cup olive oil

PHASE THREE
10 servings
15 minutes

In a jar or cruet, mix all ingredients and shake well until blended. For variation you can add 2 tablespoons grated Vadalia onion.

Vinegar-Free Catsup

1 can tomato paste (6 ounce can)
1 tablespoon maple syrup
3 tablespoons water

DEEP CLEANSER
10 servings
5 minutes

Mix all ingredients together in a small bowl.

White Gravy

4 tablespoons butter
4 tablespoons quinoa flour
½ cup Yogurt Cheese
¾ cup water
1 teaspoon tarragon, thyme, dill, onion powder,
   or garlic powder

SUPER CLEANSER
6 servings
10 minutes

In a small skillet over medium heat, melt butter. Add flour, whisking constantly until it starts to bubble. In a small bowl, blend cheese and water until smooth. Gradually add liquid to skillet, whisking constantly until mixture is thick. Add herb of choice. Makes about 1½ cups.

ᕙ *Deep Cleansers may add 1 teaspoon tamari sauce and ½ cup finely chopped mushrooms.*

Yogurt Chive Dressing

1 cup Yogurt Cheese
¼ cup snipped fresh chives, or 2 tablespoons
   freeze-dried
2 tablespoons chopped fresh tarragon or
   2 teaspoons dried
¼ teaspoon salt
¼ teaspoon pepper
1 drop lemon extract

SUPER CLEANSER
8 servings
5 minutes

Combine all ingredients in a bowl and whisk until blended. Thin with water if needed.

Grains and Pasta

Oh, the wonders of pasta—another "comfort" food! These recipes use quinoa and corn pastas to create exciting alternatives for hard-to-digest wheat pastas.

Quinoa, a grain that digests like a fruit, is easy to prepare and a nutritious addition to Quinoa Pilaf and Quinoa Stuffing.

Buttered Noodles

2 cloves garlic, minced
¼ cup butter
1 pound quinoa pasta
2 tablespoons chopped fresh parsley
salt and pepper to taste

BASIC BALANCER
4 servings
20 minutes

Bring a large stock pot of water to a boil for pasta. In a medium saucepan, heat butter and add garlic. Cook gently, stirring all the time, until golden. Do not let the garlic burn or become too brown. Meanwhile, cook pasta in the boiling water according to the package directions. Drain and rinse with hot water. Toss pasta with garlic and butter mixture. Add salt, pepper and parsley. Serve.

‿ *Deep Cleansers and beyond may substitute corn pasta for quinoa.*

Cranberry Stuffing

½ cup vegetable broth
¼ cup chopped onions
¼ cup chopped celery
½ teaspoon dried sage
½ teaspoon ground cinnamon
¼ teaspoon salt
3 cups 100% sprouted bread, cubed
3 ounces dried cranberries
½ cup vegetable broth

DEEP CLEANSER
4 servings
1 hour

In a medium skillet, bring ½ cup broth to boil. Add onions and celery. Simmer over medium heat for 4 minutes, or until vegetables are tender. Remove from heat. Put onion mixture into large bowl; stir in sage, cinnamon and salt. Add bread cubes and cranberries and toss well. Moisten mixture with remaining ½ cup broth according to the amount of moisture desired. Spoon into a lightly greased 1½–2 quart baking dish. Cover and bake at 350 degrees for 40 minutes. Yields about 6 cups stuffing.

‿ *Basic Balancers and beyond may use chicken broth.*

Green Quinoa

3 cups cooked quinoa
2 bunches spinach or arugula (about 1 pound)
1 clove garlic, minced
3 tablespoons melted butter
½ teaspoon salt
¼ teaspoon pepper

SUPER CLEANSER
4 servings
40 minutes

Bring a large saucepan of water to a boil. Blanch spinach until bright green, about 5 seconds. Immediately transfer to a bowl filled with ice water to stop the cooking process. Drain, squeeze out excess water, and finely chop. (Spinach may be steamed instead.) In a medium pan, melt butter and sauté garlic for 1 minute over medium-low heat. Add spinach and quinoa, stirring until heated through, about 3 minutes. Serve.

Sprouted Grain Stuffing

12 slices stale, 100% sprouted grain bread
   (about 10 cups), torn into small pieces
2½ cups water or vegetable broth
2 tablespoons maple sugar
1 teaspoon salt
2 teaspoons poultry seasoning
1 tablespoon butter
2 cups chopped celery
1 cup chopped onion
¼ cup chopped parsley
pepper to taste
¼ cup melted butter

DEEP CLEANSER
8 servings
1 hour 25 minutes

To make bread stale, let sit out uncovered overnight or toast lightly in oven. Tear or cut into thumbnail size pieces. Place bread pieces in large bowl and add water or broth. Remove bread from bowl and squeeze slightly, draining off excess liquid. Put moistened bread in separate bowl and add sugar, salt and seasoning. In a medium skillet, melt 1 tablespoon butter and add onion, celery and parsley. Sauté until vegetables are tender, about 8 minutes. Add additional ¼ cup butter and pepper. Add vegetable mixture to bread and stir to blend. Recipe makes about 8 cups of stuffing. Stuffing can be used in baking whole chicken or Cornish hens. Stuffing can also be heated in covered casserole dish at 350 degrees for 45 minutes.

Recipe can be prepared up to two days ahead, wrapped airtight and refrigerated.
Basic Balancers may substitute chicken broth for vegetable broth

Cooked Quinoa

1 cup quinoa, rinsed
2 cups water or vegetable broth

SUPER CLEANSER
5 servings
25 minutes

Rinse quinoa thoroughly in a small strainer or by running water over the quinoa in a pot. Drain. Place quinoa and water in 1½ quart saucepan and bring to boil. Reduce to simmer, cover, and cook until all water is absorbed, about 10–15 minutes. When done, the grain appears translucent and a tiny white ring will be visible.

Depending on the brand of quinoa, the water may have to be adjusted. Compare this recipe to the directions on the package. Yields about 2½ cups cooked quinoa. For variation, try substituting carrot juice for half of the water or broth.
Basic Balancers may substitute chicken broth for vegetable broth.

Curried Quinoa with Zucchini and Peas

2 tablespoons butter
1 cup quinoa
1 teaspoon curry powder
4 cups diced zucchini
1 cup carrot juice
salt to taste
2 cups boiling water
1 cup fresh or frozen peas
¼ cup snipped chives
2 tablespoons chopped parsley or cilantro

SUPER CLEANSER
4 servings
30 minutes

Using a sieve, rinse quinoa in a bowl, changing water until it is clear. In a small sauce pan over medium heat, melt 1 tablespoon of the butter; add the quinoa, ½ teaspoon curry powder, and salt to taste. Add 2 cups boiling water. Cover, lower the heat, and simmer for 15 minutes until water is absorbed.

Meanwhile, over medium heat, melt remaining butter in a 10-inch skillet. Add the zucchini and remaining ½ teaspoon curry powder. Cook stirring frequently for 5 minutes. Add the carrot juice, and salt to taste. Cook on simmer for 5 minutes, then add the peas and cook for 3–5 minutes longer, until peas are cooked. Stir in the chives and the parsley. Mix vegetables with quinoa and serve.

Pasta with Olive Mushroom Sauce

1 tablespoon butter (or olive oil)
1 clove garlic, minced
8 ounces mushrooms, coarsely chopped
¾ cup black olives, pitted
2 tablespoons chopped fresh parsley
1 red chili, seeded and chopped
1 pound quinoa or corn pasta
8 ounces cherry tomatoes (about 2 cups)

BASIC BALANCER
4 servings
20 minutes

Bring a stock pot filled with water and ½ teaspoon salt to a boil. In a large pan melt butter over medium heat. Add garlic and cook for one minute. Add the mushrooms, cover, and cook until soft, 6–8 minutes. Place the mushrooms, olives, parsley and red chili in a blender or food processor and blend until smooth. Cook the pasta according to package directions. Drain, rinse with hot water and return to the stock pot. Add the olive mixture and toss until the pasta is coated. Cover and keep warm. In an ungreased frying pan, heat tomatoes and shake pan until they start to split, about 2–3 minutes. Serve the pasta topped with the tomatoes.

Pasta with Quick Red Sauce

1 tablespoon butter
2 green onions, chopped
1 clove garlic
2 teaspoons dried oregano
1 teaspoon dried basil
½ teaspoon maple sugar
1 can cut or diced tomatoes in juice (28 ounce can)
½ cup chopped parsley
salt and pepper
1 pound quinoa or corn pasta

BASIC BALANCER
4 servings
30 minutes

In a large saucepan, melt butter over medium heat. Add green onions and garlic and cook, stirring often, until onions are soft, about 3 minutes. Stir in oregano, basil and sugar. Add tomatoes with juice and simmer just until slightly thickened, about 10 minutes. In a large stock pot, bring water to a boil and add pasta. Cook according to package directions. Drain and rinse under hot water. Serve topped with sauce and parsley. Yields 4 cups.

Quinoa Stuffing

1 large chopped onion
1 cup chopped carrots
1 teaspoon butter
1 teaspoon ground coriander
½ teaspoon ground cumin
½ teaspoon ground ginger
¼ teaspoon ground cinnamon
3¾ cups vegetable broth
2 cups quinoa
½ cup chopped dried apricots
⅓ cup chopped fresh cilantro (optional)
salt and pepper to taste

DEEP CLEANSER
8 servings
30 minutes

In a 5–6 quart saucepan, melt butter. Sauté onion and carrot over medium heat until vegetables are soft, about 8 minutes. Add coriander, cumin, ginger, cinnamon, broth, quinoa, and apricots and bring to a boil. Reduce heat to simmer, cover and cook until all the liquid is absorbed, about 15–20 minutes. When done, the quinoa grain will look translucent. Salt and pepper to taste. Fluff with a fork; mix in cilantro if desired.

ᕦ *Basic Balancers and beyond may use chicken broth.*

Quinoa with Asparagus and Basil

2 cups water
1½ cups quinoa, rinsed and drained
2 tablespoons melted butter
1 pound asparagus, steamed
½ cup chopped fresh basil
¼ cup snipped chives
½ cup diced roasted red peppers

SUPER CLEANSER
6 servings
40 minutes

Bring water to a boil in a 2 quart saucepan. Add quinoa and return to a boil. Reduce heat, cover and simmer until the quinoa is tender but still crunchy, about 15 minutes. Meanwhile, steam the asparagus in a separate pan for about 4 minutes. Chop the basil and chives and melt butter. Transfer the quinoa to a large bowl and toss with the melted butter. When the quinoa has cooled slightly, add the remaining ingredients. Toss and serve.

Pasta Primavera

1 cup chopped onion
2 cloves minced garlic
4 tablespoons vegetable broth, divided
2 cans tomato sauce (15 ounce cans)
4 tablespoons maple syrup
2 teaspoons dried oregano
2 teaspoons dried basil
¼ teaspoon pepper
1 tablespoon butter
1 sweet red pepper, cut into 1-inch strips
1½ cups sliced mushrooms
1½ cups yellow summer squash or zucchini,
   cut into 1½-inch thin strips
1½ cups carrots, peeled and sliced
¾ cup peas
10 ounces quinoa or corn pasta, cooked
¼ cup chopped green onions
2 tablespoons chopped fresh parsley

BASIC BALANCER
6 servings
45 minutes

In a medium saucepan, over medium heat, cook onion and garlic in 2 tablespoons broth about 5–7 minutes, until softened. Add tomato sauce, syrup, oregano, basil and pepper. Bring to a boil, reduce heat and simmer for 20 minutes. Put pasta water on to boil. Clean and chop vegetables. In a skillet or wok, over medium-high heat melt butter and add 2 tablespoons broth, red pepper, mushrooms, squash and carrots. Stir fry until crisp yet tender, about 10 minutes. Add peas and stir fry an additional 2 minutes. Set aside. Add pasta to boiling water and cook according to package directions, about 4–6 minutes. Drain and rinse under hot water. Put in serving bowl. Pour sauce over pasta and toss thoroughly. Add cooked vegetables and toss again. Sprinkle with green onions and parsley and serve.

Tomato and Fennel Quinoa

½ cup quinoa, cooked
2 tablespoons butter
½ cup finely chopped fennel
¼ cup chopped onion
3 plum tomatoes, finely chopped
¾ teaspoon finely chopped tarragon
⅛ teaspoon crumbled dried tarragon
salt and pepper to taste

DEEP CLEANSER
2 servings
15 minutes

In a heavy skillet heat butter over moderate heat until hot. Cook fennel, onion, tomatoes and tarragon until fennel is tender, about 5 minutes. In a bowl, combine quinoa with fennel mixture, season with salt and pepper and serve.

Vegetable Quinoa Pilaf

4 cups cooked quinoa
1 tablespoon butter
1 cup grated carrots
1 bunch spinach, chopped (about 10 ounces)
¼ cup vegetable broth
1 cup chopped chives
½ cup Yogurt Cheese

SUPER CLEANSER
6 servings
35 minutes

Cook quinoa according to package directions or Cooked Quinoa recipe. In a large sauté pan, melt butter over medium heat. Add carrots and sauté until crisp-tender, about 6–8 minutes. Add spinach; cover and steam 5–7 minutes, until tender. If vegetables begin to stick to the pan, add broth a tablespoon at a time. Add cooled quinoa, chives, and cheese to vegetable mixture; mix well. Remove from heat. Serve warm, chilled, or at room temperature.

Basic Balancers may sauté onions with carrots, and omit chives. Kefir cheese may be substituted for Yogurt Cheese, and chicken for vegetable broth. Deep Cleansers and beyond may add ½ pound coarsely chopped mushrooms with spinach.

Vegetable Entrees

Vegetables, once the accompaniments of the meal are now the "main event." These recipes, built around fresh, seasonal vegetables, are quick to prepare and to some, an introduction to lesser known vegetables.

Recipes like Spaghetti Squash With Red Sauce, Mushroom Crusted Quiche, and Portobello Pizzas invite new taste excitement.

Caponata

2 tablespoons butter
1 medium eggplant, peeled and cubed
½ large green pepper, chopped
1 medium onion
1 cup chopped mushrooms
2 cloves garlic, minced
1 can tomato paste (6 ounce can)
¼ cup water
½ cup sliced black olives
½ teaspoon oregano
½ teaspoon salt
¼ teaspoon pepper
3 dashes cayenne pepper (or to taste)

DEEP CLEANSER
4 servings
1 hour

Melt butter in a large skillet. Sauté eggplant, pepper, onion, mushroom, and garlic for 10–15 minutes, covered on medium-low heat. Mix in remaining ingredients and simmer 30 minutes.

✐ *A medium cooked and diced potato may be added with the vegetables.*

Confetti Rice with Corn Tortillas

2 cups wild rice
4 cups chicken broth
1 tablespoon onion powder
1½ cups frozen corn kernels, thawed and drained
1 cup vinegar-free salsa
12 corn tortillas

BASIC BALANCER
6 servings
1 hour

Heat a large skillet coated with cooking spray and add rice. Heat for 2–3 minutes, stirring occasionally. Pour in broth, sprinkle with onion powder and mix well. Stir in salsa. Reduce heat to low, cover and simmer 20 minutes. Add corn to rice mixture and mix lightly. Continue cooking until all liquid is absorbed, about 25–35 minutes. Warm tortillas and serve with rice as filling. Garnish with a dollop of kefir cheese.

Hash Brown Omelet

1 pound russet potatoes, peeled, dried,
   and coarsely grated
¼ teaspoon salt and pepper
1 tablespoon butter
1 medium tomato, diced
1 tablespoon chopped fresh basil
¼ cup kefir cheese

DEEP CLEANSER
4 servings
30 minutes

Wrap the grated potatoes in a clean dish towel, using two hands to twist tightly in opposite directions to release the water. In a medium bowl, toss the grated potatoes with salt, and pepper. Melt half of the butter in a 12-inch skillet over medium heat. Scatter potatoes evenly over entire pan bottom. Using a spatula, firmly press potatoes to flatten. Reduce heat to medium and continue to cook until golden brown and crisp, 7–8 minutes.

Invert hash browns, browned side up, onto a large plate. Add remaining butter to pan. Once butter has melted, slide hash browns back into pan. In a small bowl, mix tomatoes with basil and kefir cheese. Put tomatoes on top of hash browns as soon as they are inverted back into the pan. Continue to cook until remaining side is golden brown, about 5–6 minutes. Fold the potato round in half. Cook about 1 minute. Slide hash browns onto cutting board, cut into wedges and serve.

Italian Omelet

½ cup finely chopped green or yellow sweet pepper
½ teaspoon dried oregano
½ teaspoon dried basil
1 cup red tomato sauce
1 cup sliced mushrooms
4 large eggs

DEEP CLEANSER
2 servings
20 minutes

Coat a 7–8 inch omelet pan with cooking spray. Add pepper, onion and seasonings. Cook, covered, over medium heat until peppers are soft, about 2–3 minutes. Meanwhile in a small saucepan, stir together sauce and mushrooms. Cook over low heat until mushrooms wilt and sauce is heated. Keep warm while preparing omelet. Pour eggs over pepper mixture. With an inverted pancake turner, carefully lift cooked portions at edges toward center so uncooked portions can reach hot pan surface, tilting pan and moving cooked portions as necessary. When top of omelet is thickened and no visible liquid egg remains, spoon ½ of the sauce onto omelet. With pancake turner, fold omelet in half or roll. Slide from pan onto plate. Spoon on remaining sauce. Serve hot.

Mushroom Curry

1 tablespoon butter
1 large onion, chopped
1 clove garlic (optional)
1 carrot, diced
½ pound mushrooms, sliced
2 medium tomatoes, chopped
2 teaspoons fresh grated ginger root
    (or ½ teaspoon dried)
½ teaspoon cumin or curry powder to taste
¼ teaspoon cardamom powder
¼ teaspoon paprika
dash cayenne pepper
2 teaspoons tamari sauce
½ cup Yogurt Cheese

DEEP CLEANSER
2 servings
20 minutes

In a medium skillet, melt butter and sauté onion, garlic and carrot, about 7 minutes. (Broth may be substituted for butter.) Add mushrooms, tomatoes, ginger, cumin, cardamom, paprika, cayenne, and tamari; cover and simmer for 10 minutes. Remove from heat. Stir in Yogurt Cheese. Serve over quinoa or corn pasta, cooked quinoa or sprouted bread toast.

Portobello Pizzas

½ 10 ounce package frozen spinach
½ cup kefir cheese
¼ cup chopped black olives
1 teaspoon dried basil
¼ teaspoon pepper
12 portobello mushrooms (3–4-inch diameter),
    cleaned and stems removed
2 tablespoons melted butter

DEEP CLEANSER
6 servings
30 minutes

Preheat oven to 350 degrees. Thaw spinach and mix with cheese, olives, basil and pepper. Place mushrooms bottom side up on a greased baking sheet. Divide spinach mixture evenly between mushrooms. Drizzle with butter and bake for 15–20 minutes, until heated through.

‿ *Smaller mushrooms may be used for appetizer size portions. Super Cleansers may substitute Yogurt Cheese for kefir cheese.*

Mushroom-Crusted Quiche

¾ pound mushrooms, finely chopped
2 tablespoons butter, divided
½ cup sprouted bread crumbs
1 medium onion, chopped (about 1 cup)
½ cup kefir cheese (4 ounces)
½ cup Yogurt Cheese
3 large eggs
1 cup yogurt
dash cayenne pepper (optional)

DEEP CLEANSER
6 servings
50 minutes

Preheat oven to 325 degrees. For crust: In a medium skillet, sauté mushrooms in 1 tablespoon butter; remove from heat and add bread crumbs. Press mixture evenly on sides and bottom of 9-inch pie pan. For filling: In the same skillet used for the mushrooms, sauté onion in 1 tablespoon butter until soft, about 8 minutes. Sprinkle onions over crust. Layer spoonfuls of kefir cheese and Yogurt Cheese over onions. Blend eggs with yogurt and cayenne and pour over onion-cheese layer. Bake 35–45 minutes, until knife in center comes out clean.

⌐ *An additional ½ cup of kefir cheese may be used in place of Yogurt Cheese.*

Poached Eggs on Wild Rice

1 tablespoon butter
¼ cup vegetable broth
4 cups cooked wild rice
1 cup frozen peas
1 cup shredded carrots
1 cup chopped zucchini
4 large eggs
salt and pepper

SUPER CLEANSER
4 servings
20 minutes

In a 10–12-inch skillet, melt butter and add ¼ cup vegetable broth. Add peas, carrots and zucchini and cook for 5 minutes over medium-low heat, until vegetables are crisp-tender. Add rice, stirring until warmed. With the back of a large spoon, spread the rice mixture evenly over the skillet and make 4 slight indentations in the top. Crack one egg at a time into each indentation. Cover skillet and let eggs steam 3–5 minutes, until desired doneness. Salt and pepper to taste.

⌐ *You can use your choice of vegetables, or whatever you have on hand to make three cups. Great for left-over steamed vegetables.*

Potato, Onion and Kefir Cheese Frittata

3 medium potatoes, cooked and cooled
1 teaspoon butter or ghee
1 small onion, peeled and sliced ¼-inch thick
1 minced garlic clove (optional)
8 chopped basil leaves
6 large eggs, slightly beaten
salt and pepper to taste
4 ounce kefir cheese

DEEP CLEANSER
4 servings
30 minutes

Preheat oven to 350 degrees. Melt butter in a 10-inch ovenproof frying pan over medium-high heat. Add onion and sauté, stirring occasionally until tender, about 6 minutes. Add potatoes, garlic and basil; sauté 1–2 minutes longer. Add eggs, salt and pepper to taste. Add kefir cheese in ½ teaspoonfuls to mixture. Stir just to mix, leaving cheese in chunks. Place pan in oven and bake 18–20 minutes until frittata is set.

This is an easy recipe for when you have extra cooked potatoes. If you don't have an ovenproof frying pan, transfer mixture to a greased baking pan prior to putting frittata in the oven.

Roasted Sweet Potato Tortillas

2 sweet potatoes or yams (about 1½ pounds) scrubbed clean
½ pound shallots or small onions, (about 1 cup) cut into quarters or 1-inch chunks
8 corn tortillas
8 teaspoons sour cream or Yogurt Cheese
8 teaspoons vinegar-free salsa
½ cup sliced black olives

BASIC BALANCER
4 servings
1 hour 20 minutes

Preheat oven to 425. Place whole potatoes in a small baking pan. Lightly grease another small baking pan and add shallots. Put pans with potatoes and shallots in heated oven. Bake 15 minutes, stirring shallots once. Remove shallots from oven. Increase oven heat to 450 and continue baking potatoes 45 minutes or until tender when pierced with a fork. Remove potatoes from oven and let cool slightly. Remove skins from potatoes. With a potato masher or fork, mash potatoes into the roasted shallots. Add salt and pepper to taste. Heat tortillas in a skillet over medium-high heat, a few seconds per side until heated through. Place a ⅓ cup of potato/shallot mixture on each tortilla, top with sour cream, salsa, and black olives.

Potatoes and shallots may be roasted days ahead. Refrigerate and then reheat when ready to use.

Potato Vegetable Patties

1 cup peeled and grated potato
1 cup peeled and grated sweet potato
1 cup grated carrots
½ cup finely chopped onion
1 cup finely chopped fresh kale, arugula,
   spinach or chard
1 teaspoon dried sage
1 teaspoon dried thyme
1 clove garlic, minced, (optional)
1 small green or red chili pepper, seeded
   and minced
2 large eggs, lightly beaten
1 teaspoon salt
¼ teaspoon pepper
1 tablespoon tamari sauce
1 cup quinoa flakes

DEEP CLEANSER
4 servings
30 minutes

Mix together all ingredients in a large bowl. To save time, a food processor may be used to grate potatoes and carrots, and chop onions and greens. In a large, greased, nonstick skillet, heated to medium low, place ¼ cup of the mixture for each patty onto the skillet and press into 4-inch diameter; cook patties about 8–10 minutes per side, or until golden. Press patties down with a spatula as they cook. Yields about 12 patties. Cook patties in batches or use two skillets.

༺ *Super Cleansers may omit onions and tamari sauce. Basic Balancers may substitute crushed corn flakes for quinoa flakes. For the continuous kitchen, double the recipe and freeze half.*

Quesadilla

2 teaspoons butter
4 fresh corn tortillas
4 rounded tablespoons vinegar-free salsa
2 tablespoons kefir cheese

BASIC BALANCER
2 servings
15 minutes

In a skillet over medium-high heat, melt 1 teaspoon butter. Divide and spread salsa and cheese on two tortillas. Top with remaining two tortillas. Warm quesadillas one at a time, cooking about 2 minutes per side. Turn gently. Add the additional 1 teaspoon butter to skillet prior to warming second quesadilla. Remove from skillet and cut into fourths. Serve.

༺ *For variation, try mashed avocado, chilies, green onions, and/or chopped olives. The tortillas will be easier to handle if the ingredients are spread in a thin layer.*

Quinoa Stuffed Peppers

4 cups cooked quinoa
4 large red or green peppers, cut ½-inch
   from top, remove seeds and membranes
1 medium onion, chopped
1 clove garlic, minced
½ pound mushrooms, sliced
1 tablespoon butter
1 can diced tomatoes (28 ounce can)
1 teaspoon dried oregano

DEEP CLEANSER
4 servings
1 hour

Heat oven to 325 degrees. In a large stock pot with a steamer tray, partially steam peppers, about 4–5 minutes. In a large skillet, melt butter and sauté onion, garlic and mushrooms until tender. Add oregano and tomatoes, simmer about 8 minutes. Fold in cooked quinoa. Fill peppers with quinoa mixture and stand up with their sides touching in a greased baking dish. Cover loosely with foil and bake until peppers are tender, about 25–30 minutes.

Peppers may also be cut in half instead of stuffing whole. Stuffed peppers may be frozen. To create a Super Cleanser version, omit onions and mushrooms. Substitute 1 cup of vegetable broth for tomatoes and stir in ½ cup chopped chives with cooked quinoa.

Spinach Frittata

4 tablespoons butter
1 clove garlic, minced (optional)
1 bunch finely chopped spinach (10–12 ounces)
8 large eggs
¼ cup water
½ cup snipped chives
salt and pepper

SUPER CLEANSER
6 servings
25 minutes

In a 10–12-inch nonstick skillet, melt butter and sauté garlic for two minutes. Add spinach and sauté just until wilted, turning while cooking. In a medium bowl, lightly beat eggs. Add water, chives, salt, and pepper to taste. Add egg mixture to skillet when spinach is wilted and stir to mix. Cook over low heat until set and golden on the bottom, about 10–15 minutes. Invert the omelet onto a plate, slide it back into the pan and cook until set, a few minutes.

Instead of turning the frittata to cook the other side, it can be baked in a 350 degree oven for 15–20 minutes. Make sure your pan is ovenproof!

Spaghetti Squash with Asparagus

1 spaghetti squash (about 2½ pounds), rinsed
1 pound asparagus
2 tablespoons butter
1 cup thinly sliced red pepper
1 clove garlic, minced (optional)
½ teaspoon ground ginger
½ cup snipped chives
salt and pepper to taste

SUPER CLEANSER
4 servings
1 hour 30 minutes

Preheat oven to 350 degrees. Cut squash lengthwise and remove seeds. Fill a baking dish with ¼-inch of water. Place squash in dish cut side down. Bake until flesh is soft, about an hour. While the squash is cooking, rinse asparagus and cut into 2-inch pieces. Combine asparagus with ½ cup water in a pan and stir often over high heat just until crisp-tender, about 3–4 minutes. Drain asparagus in a colander. To the same pan, add butter, peppers, and garlic; sauté over medium heat about 5–8 minutes until peppers are crisp-tender. Mix in reserved asparagus, ginger and chives. When squash is cooked, remove from oven and drag a fork through the flesh, pulling the strands apart. Toss squash with the asparagus mixture, season to taste and serve.

Spaghetti Squash with Red Sauce

1 spaghetti squash (about 2½ pounds), rinsed
1 can tomato sauce (8 ounce can)
½ teaspoon dried oregano
½ teaspoon dried basil
⅛ teaspoon garlic powder
1 tablespoon kefir cheese (optional)

DEEP CLEANSER
4 servings
1 hour

Preheat oven to 375 degrees. Pierce squash in several places with a knife and place in a baking dish. Bake 45 minutes–1 hour until flesh is soft. Cut squash in half lengthwise and remove seeds. Using a fork, remove squash in strands into a baking dish. While squash is baking, combine remaining ingredients. Pour over squash strands. Bake 10 minutes until hot.

Stir-Fried Carrots, Jicama and Watercress

2 tablespoons ghee
2 cloves garlic, minced
2 tablespoons chopped ginger
3 carrots, peeled and julienned
1 pound jicama, peeled and julienned ¼-inch thick
3 tablespoons vegetable broth
½ teaspoon maple syrup
1 bunch watercress, chopped (remove large stems)
salt and pepper to taste
2 cups cooked quinoa

SUPER CLEANSER

2 servings

20 minutes

Melt ghee in sauté pan or wok over medium-high heat. Add garlic and ginger. Stir fry for 1 minute. Add the carrots and continue to stir fry for 2 minutes. Add the jicama, broth, and syrup; continue to stir fry until carrots are firm-tender. Add the watercress and stir fry for 30 seconds. Season to taste and serve over cooked quinoa.

Spinach may be substituted for watercress.

Soft Polenta with Mushrooms

4 cups water or broth
1 ⅓ cups polenta or finely ground cornmeal
½ teaspoon salt
1 tablespoon finely chopped fresh parsley
    (or 1 teaspoon dried)
½ teaspoon dried oregano leaves
¼ teaspoon dried thyme
¼ teaspoon pepper
1 pound sliced wild or domestic mushrooms
1 tablespoon butter or water
¼ cup Yogurt Cheese, kefir cheese, or sour cream

BASIC BALANCER

4 servings

35 minutes

In a large saucepan, bring water and salt to a boil. Slowly stir in polenta with a whisk or fork, taking care to avoid lumps. Return to a boil and then lower heat. Add herbs and simmer about 20 minutes, stirring occasionally. While polenta is cooking, cook mushrooms in a small sauté pan in 1 tablespoon butter or water, about 6 minutes, until tender. When polenta is cooked, stir in Yogurt Cheese; transfer to serving bowls; top with mushrooms.

Any vegetable you choose may be sautéed and used in this recipe instead of the mushrooms.

Vegetable Enchiladas

1 tablespoon butter
¼ cup water or broth
8 cups mixed chopped vegetables such as:
    bell pepper, carrots, celery, peas, onions,
    parsnips, radishes, squash and/or mushrooms
3 tablespoon tamari sauce
¼ teaspoon cayenne (or to taste)
12 corn tortillas
1⅓ cups Yogurt Cheese or sour cream

BASIC BALANCER
6 servings
20 minutes

Chop vegetables into bite-size pieces. Melt butter in a medium skillet. Add vegetables and sauté adding water or broth to loosen vegetables if they begin to stick. Add tamari and cayenne. Steam or lightly fry tortillas. Hold tortillas cupped in your hand and fill with ½ cup sautéed vegetables and Yogurt Cheese or sour cream.

Winter Squash Burgers

1 cup cooked acorn or butternut squash
1 cup cooked quinoa
1 tablespoon butter
1 cup chopped onion
½ cup green pepper, cored, seeded and chopped,
    or grated carrots
½ teaspoon curry powder
2 tablespoons dried unsweetened coconut
1½ cups Sprouted Bread Crumbs
salt and pepper

DEEP CLEANSER
4 servings
35 minutes

This recipe is quick if you have extra cooked squash and quinoa on hand. It will take longer if you have to bake the squash and cook the quinoa before you begin. In a medium skillet, melt butter over medium heat. Add onion and cook until wilted, about 8 minutes. Add the bell pepper and curry powder and stir to mix. Reduce heat and cook, covered, 5 minutes or until the pepper is tender. Add squash. Cook uncovered, 3 to 5 minutes, stirring constantly. Add the coconut and mix well. Remove from heat. Cool slightly. Place squash mixture and quinoa in food processor and pulse until blended. Transfer to a large bowl and mix in breadcrumbs. Season to taste with salt and pepper. Form into patties 3-inches in diameter and ½-inch thick. Place patties on a greased broiler pan or large cookie sheet. Broil 3–5-inches from heat, 5–7 minutes per side or until lightly browned. Check often to prevent burning. Makes 8 patties. Serve on sprouted bread as a sandwich or as an entree.

Vegetable Pizza

CRUST:

2 teaspoons maple syrup
1 cup warm water (110–115 degrees)
2 teaspoons active dry yeast
2 teaspoons melted butter
1 teaspoon salt
3 cups quinoa flour, sprouted wheat flour,
   or sprouted spelt flour,
   or any combination of these flours

TOPPING:

1½ cups tomato sauce
½ teaspoon each of dried basil and marjoram
6 teaspoons Yogurt Cheese or Kefir Cheese

OPTIONAL TOPPINGS:

1 medium onion, chopped
1 cup mushrooms, sliced
1 cup black olives, sliced
2 medium tomatoes, sliced
1 bell pepper, sliced
½ cup chopped spinach, cooked and drained

DEEP CLEANSER
4 servings
55 minutes

FOR THE CRUST: In a food processor with a metal blade or in a large bowl, combine maple syrup and water. Water should be warm to the touch but not hot. Add the yeast and let stand 5 minutes. Add the melted butter and salt. Add 2½ cups flour and process or stir until mixture forms a ball, adding additional ½ cup of flour as needed. This takes about 30 seconds by machine or 5 minutes by hand. Turn onto a lightly floured work surface and knead until the dough is smooth and elastic, about 5 minutes. Add more flour if dough is still too sticky. Coat large bowl with cooking spray, add the dough and turn to coat all sides. Cover with plastic wrap or a cloth and let rise in a warm place 15–20 minutes. Punch down dough and spread by hand or roll out with a rolling pin. Place on a ungreased cookie sheet sprinkled with 2 teaspoons of cornmeal. Pinch up the sides ½-inch to hold in the toppings. Dough may also be divided into four balls and rolled into individual pizzas. Preheat oven to 425 degrees.

FOR THE TOPPING: Add herbs to tomato sauce and spread over crust. Optional vegetable toppings are listed above. Vegetables may be used raw or sautéed first. Bake pizza 10–15 minutes, or until done. For the cheese: Cook the pizza for 8 minutes, remove from oven and drop small pieces of yogurt/kefir cheese onto pizza. Return pizza to oven for 5 minutes, until cheese melts and pizza is hot.

Basic Balancers may use 1 pound cooked, ground chicken with a teaspoon each of dried sage and thyme. After rising, dough may be wrapped in plastic wrap and then aluminum foil and frozen for up to two months. Thaw at room temperature, knead, and let set 10 minutes.

Vegetable Omelet

1 tablespoon butter
½ cup finely chopped vegetables,
   such as, sweet peppers, asparagus tips
   or artichoke hearts
½ teaspoon dried oregano
½ teaspoon dried basil
6 large eggs
salt and pepper to taste

SUPER CLEANSER
2 servings
20 minutes

Melt butter over medium heat. Add vegetables and seasonings. Cook, covered, until vegetables are soft, about 2–3 minutes. Pour eggs over vegetable mixture. With an inverted pancake turner, carefully lift cooked portions at edges toward center so uncooked portions can reach hot pan surface, tilting pan and moving cooked portions as necessary. When top of omelet is thickened and no visible liquid egg remains, fold omelet in half or roll with a spatula. Slide from pan onto plate. Serve hot.

ᴄ⁓ *9 egg whites may be substituted for whole eggs.*

Veggie Patties

1 cup chopped carrots
1 stalk chopped celery
½ cup chopped red pepper
1 cup onion
1 bunch spinach (about 10 ounces)
1 cup chopped zucchini
4 large eggs
2 tablespoons tamari sauce
2½ cups crushed quinoa flakes
2 cups cooked quinoa
salt and pepper

DEEP CLEANSER
6 servings
30 minutes

In food processor, chop carrots; add celery, pepper, onion, spinach and zucchini. Pulse the food processor to chop the vegetables into small pieces. Mix in salt, pepper, eggs, tamari, quinoa flakes and quinoa. Shape into 3–3½-inch burgers about ¾-inch thick. Cook on griddle, in nonstick pan or under broiler for 5–8 minutes, turning once until golden brown. Makes 12 burgers. Mixture can also be placed in a loaf pan and baked at 350 for 45 minutes. Let loaf cool before slicing.

ᴄ⁓ *Super Cleansers may substitute 2 teaspoons onion powder for fresh onion and quinoa flakes for corn flakes. Omit tamari sauce.*

Vegetables

These recipes will introduce a wider variety of vegetables into your repertoire. Celery Root Mashed Potatoes, Fried Wild Rice, and Fresh Beets are a few of my favorites.

Vegetables are very versatile and can almost always be substituted with a seasonal variety. Almost any vegetable tastes wonderful simply steamed with a touch of salt and pepper.

Vegetable cookery is limitless. Just use fresh produce, cook simply, and enjoy.

Apricot Cheese Stuffed Celery

4 stalks celery, cut into 2-inch pieces
¼ cup finely chopped dried apricots
½ cup kefir cheese
1½ teaspoons maple sugar
⅛ teaspoon salt

DEEP CLEANSER

8 servings

10 minutes

Cut a thin slice from the bottom of celery pieces to prevent tipping; set aside. In a food processor or blender, process apricots until finely chopped. Add cheese, sugar, and salt and process until smooth. Fill celery pieces with cheese mixture. Cover and refrigerate up to 3 hours before serving. Makes about 20 pieces.

↩ *Additional chopped apricots may be sprinkled on top if desired.*

Artichokes with Potatoes, Carrots and Leeks

3 tablespoons butter
1 box frozen artichokes (10 ounce), cut in half,
    if not already
¾ pound new potatoes (about 8) scrubbed
    and cut in half
½ pound carrots, split lengthwise and cut
    in 2-inch pieces
½ pound leeks, white and light green parts
    only, split lengthwise, thoroughly cleaned,
    sliced into 2-inch pieces
salt and pepper to taste
⅓ cup finely chopped fresh parsley
¼ cup finely chopped fresh dill
1 tablespoon finely chopped fresh mint
1½ cups vegetable broth or water
3 drops lemon extract

DEEP CLEANSER

6 servings

35 minutes

In a large sauté pan, melt butter over medium-high heat. Add the artichokes, potatoes, carrots, leeks, salt and pepper. Cook, stirring until the leeks are limp, about 5 minutes. Add broth or water, reduce heat to medium low and simmer, partially covered, until the vegetables are tender, about 20 minutes. Add parsley, dill and lemon extract. Season with salt and pepper. Can be served at room temperature.

Baked Potato Fries

1 teaspoon chili powder (or to taste)
½ teaspoon onion powder
⅛ teaspoon salt
⅛ teaspoon pepper
2 large potatoes, cut into ½-inch sticks
¼ cup vegetable broth

DEEP CLEANSER
4 servings
40 minutes

Preheat oven to 425. Mix chili powder, onion powder, salt and pepper. Set aside. In a large bowl, toss potatoes with broth. Drain. Place potatoes on baking sheet. Sprinkle with seasoning mixture. Toss to coat evenly. Arrange potatoes in a single layer. Bake 30 minutes, or until browned.

℮ *Basic Balancers may use chicken broth. For herbed fries, add ¼ teaspoon dried thyme, marjoram, tarragon and rosemary in place of chili and onion powder.*

Butternut Squash, Potato and Tomato Gratin

1 medium butternut squash (about 1½ pounds),
   peel, halve, seed, slice crosswise ⅛-inch thick
4 medium potatoes (about ¾ pounds)
   slice ⅛-inch thick
3 medium tomatoes, thinly slice crosswise
1 cup vegetable or chicken broth
2 cloves garlic, minced (optional)
½ teaspoon dried thyme
¼ teaspoon dried nutmeg (optional)
salt and pepper to taste

DEEP CLEANSER
8 servings
1 hour 30 minutes

Heat oven to 350 degrees. Grease a 4 quart baking dish with cooking spray. Layer half of the squash slices in the baking dish, overlapping them slightly. Cover with half of the potato slices, overlapping them slightly. It works best when squash and potato slices are uniform. Top with half of the tomato slices, overlapping slightly and season with salt and pepper to taste. Repeat the three layers with the remaining vegetables. In a medium saucepan, bring the broth, garlic and herbs to a boil over moderate heat. Pour the broth over the vegetables. Cover and bake about 45 minutes–1 hour, or until the vegetables are tender when pierced with a knife. Let rest for 10 minutes prior to serving.

℮ *The gratin can be refrigerated overnight. Reheat, covered, in a 300 degree oven for 35–40 minutes until warmed.*

Carrot Loaf

1 pound carrots, shredded (about 4 cups)
1 small onion, grated
2 slices sprouted grain bread, crumbled
4 large eggs
1 tablespoon tamari sauce
½ teaspoon onion powder
½ teaspoon dried dill
¾ teaspoon salt
2 tablespoons sprouted spelt flour

DEEP CLEANSER
4 servings
1 hour 15 minutes

Preheat oven to 350 degrees. Shred carrots and grate onion; place in a large bowl. In a blender, combine remaining ingredients and blend until smooth. Pour over carrots and mix well. Put carrot mixture in a 4 × 8-inch greased loaf pan. Bake 50 minutes, until loaf is set and lightly browned. Let cool 5 minutes before cutting and serving.

Chard with New Potatoes

1 bunch chard (1½ pounds)
24 small new potatoes (2 pounds)
2 cloves garlic, minced (optional)
1 small onion, finely chopped
1 tablespoon ghee or butter
¼ cup water
salt and pepper to taste

DEEP CLEANSER
6 servings
55 minutes

In a large pot, steam potatoes with skins on until tender, about 20 minutes. When cool enough to handle, cut in half. Meanwhile, remove stems and thick ribs from chard. Discard stems; ribs may be finely diced and used if desired. Rinse chard several times to clean. In a large pot or stir-fry pan, melt ghee or butter over medium heat. Add garlic and onion and cook, stirring frequently, for 2–3 minutes. Add chard, cover and steam until tender, adding water as needed. Steam time varies greatly, so check frequently, but estimate 10–15 minutes. Drain and transfer to colander. Remove and discard garlic cloves. When cool enough to handle, squeeze out liquid, then transfer to a cutting board and chop leaves. In a serving bowl, combine chopped chard, potatoes and toss to mix. Season with salt and pepper and serve.

    Regular size potatoes can be used if new potatoes are not available. Just cut potatoes in halves or quarters prior to steaming, depending on their size.

Cottage Potatoes

2 large baked potatoes, skins on or off
1 tablespoon butter
¼ cup water
salt and pepper to taste

DEEP CLEANSER
4 servings
20 minutes

Cut cooked potatoes into 1-inch chunks. Melt butter in a large sauté pan. Add water and potatoes. Bring to a simmer and cover for 10–15 minutes, until potatoes are heated. Water will evaporate. Salt and pepper to taste.

✍ *Try with scrambled eggs.*

Curried Sweet Potatoes

2¼ pounds sweet potatoes (4–5 medium),
   peeled and cut into 1-inch pieces
½ teaspoon salt
½ cup dried apricots cut into ¼-inch slivers
1 tablespoon butter or ghee
1 medium onion, finely chopped
1 teaspoon curry powder
ground pepper to taste

DEEP CLEANSER
6 servings
45 minutes

Place sweet potatoes in a large pan and add cold water to cover by 1-inch. Add salt and bring to boil over high heat. Reduce heat to medium and cook, uncovered, until tender but not mushy, 8–12 minutes. Drain well. While potatoes are cooking, combine apricots and 1 cup boiling water in a small bowl. Let sit 10 minutes. In a large, wide skillet, heat butter or oil over medium-high heat. Add onion and cook, stirring often, until softened, about 6 minutes. Stir in curry powder and cook 2 minutes. Add the cooked sweet potatoes, apricots and their liquid. Season with salt and pepper. Stir gently over medium-low heat until warmed through.

✍ *Recipe can be prepared ahead and stored, covered, in the refrigerator for up to two days. Reheat on the stovetop over medium-low heat until warmed through.*

Celery Root Mashed Potatoes

2 pounds potatoes, peeled and cut
   into 2-inch cubes
½ pound celery root, peeled and cut
   into 2-inch cubes
2 tablespoons butter
1 cup cooking liquid
salt and pepper

DEEP CLEANSER
8 servings
30 minutes

Place potatoes and celery root in a large saucepan; add cold water to cover by 1-inch and bring to a boil. Boil, partially covered, until tender, about 20–25 minutes. Drain, reserving 1 cup of the liquid. Add butter to vegetables and mash with a potato masher. While mashing, add enough reserved cooking liquid to make a smooth consistency. Salt and pepper to taste.

  Potatoes do not have to be peeled. Basic Balancers may mix in 2 tablespoons of sour cream.

Eggplant, Tomato and Onion Gratin

1 large sweet onion, finely diced
1 clove garlic, minced (optional)
1 teaspoon dried thyme
1 bay leaf
2 tablespoons melted butter, divided
salt and pepper to taste
1 medium eggplant sliced crosswise ¼-inch thick
2 large tomatoes, sliced ¼-inch thick

DEEP CLEANSER
4 servings
1 hour

Preheat oven to 400 degrees. In large skillet over medium heat, sauté onions, garlic, thyme, bay leaf, salt and pepper in half of the butter until soft, about 5 minutes. Remove bay leaf from mixture. Grease shallow 9-inch baking dish with cooking spray. Spread onion mixture over bottom of dish. Cover with overlapping rows of alternating eggplant and tomato slices. Each slice should cover ⅔ of the preceding one. Season with salt and pepper and drizzle with remaining melted butter. Cover and bake until eggplant is soft enough to cut with a spoon, about 30 minutes. Uncover and bake an additional 15 minutes. The gratin should be moist but not watery.

Fried Wild Rice

1 cup wild rice, uncooked
4 cups water
2 tablespoons butter
1 large egg
½ cup chopped green onions (about 4)
½ cup frozen green peas
2 tablespoons tamari sauce

DEEP CLEANSER
4 servings
55 minutes

In a small saucepan, combine rice and 4 cups water. Bring to a boil, reduce heat and simmer 30–45 minutes until rice is tender. Drain and set aside to cool. In a medium skillet, melt butter and scramble the egg. Add the onions and peas; sauté until vegetables are tender. Add the rice and drizzle with tamari. Serve.

Fresh Beets

4 large beets
2 teaspoons butter (optional)
salt and pepper to taste

SUPER CLEANSER
4 servings
1 hour

Scrub beets, leaving skins on. Steam beets in a large stockpot or vegetable steamer 30–45 minutes, covered, until tender when pierced with a fork. Steaming time will vary depending on the size of beets. Add water as needed. When beets are cool to the touch, slip the skins off. Salt and pepper to taste and melt butter over if desired.

↶ *Water used for steaming beets (or other vegetables) may be used for vegetable stock. Beets are like asparagus—they remind you later that you have eaten them!*

Herbed Mixed Peas

2 cups fresh or frozen green peas
1 cup sugar snap peas, trimmed and halved
   crosswise
½ cup diced carrot
1 cup snow peas, halved crosswise
1 teaspoon dried mint
½ teaspoon dried oregano
1 tablespoon butter
½ teaspoon salt
¼ teaspoon pepper

SUPER CLEANSER
4 servings
20 minutes

In a large stockpot with a strainer insert, or in a vegetable steamer, steam green peas, sugar snap peas and carrots, covered, about 4 minutes. Add snow peas. Cover and steam an additional 2 minutes or until crisp-tender. Place vegetables in a serving bowl and add herbs, butter, salt, and pepper; toss until butter is melted.

Italian Green Beans

1 pound green beans, trimmed and cut
   into 2-inch pieces
½ cup vegetable broth
1 medium onion, chopped
1 clove garlic
1 ½ teaspoons dried oregano
¾ cup diced tomatoes
1 tablespoon tomato purée (optional)
¼ teaspoon salt
¼ teaspoon pepper

DEEP CLEANSER
4 servings
20 minutes

Fill the bottom of a large stockpot (with a vegetable steamer tray) with ½-inch of water; bring to a boil. Place beans in tray and steam until tender, about 4 minutes. Remove the beans from the heat and refresh under cold water. Drain and set aside. In a large sauté pan, bring vegetable stock to a boil; add onion and simmer, covered, about 10 minutes until translucent. Add garlic, oregano, tomato and optional tomato purée; simmer about 5 minutes. Add the beans and simmer about 2 minutes, until some of the sauce is absorbed and beans are heated. Season with salt and pepper.

Maple Acorn Squash

1 acorn squash
4 tablespoons maple syrup, or to taste
2 teaspoons butter

SUPER CLEANSER
2 servings
40 minutes

Preheat oven to 425 degrees. Wash and cut squash in half crosswise and remove seeds. If needed, slice a tiny piece off the bottom of each half to prevent squash from rolling when placed on a flat surface. Fill a small baking pan with ¼-inch of water, place halves in pan, cut side down. Bake 25–35 minutes, or until tender when pierced with the tip of a sharp knife. Remove pan from oven, turn squash over and place 2 tablespoons syrup and 1 teaspoon butter in each squash half. Allow butter to melt. Serve.

℮ *Maple sugar may be substituted for syrup.*

Mashed Potatoes

1 ½ pounds potatoes (about 3 medium)
   with skin on or off, cut into 2-inch cubes
½ cup vegetable broth
1 tablespoon butter
salt and pepper to taste

DEEP CLEANSER
4 servings
40 minutes

In a medium saucepan, cover potatoes with water. Bring to a boil over high heat. Reduce heat and simmer for approximately 20–25 minutes, or until potatoes are tender. Drain water off potatoes. Leaving potatoes in saucepan, add butter and let melt over potatoes. Add ¼ cup broth and mash with potato masher or electric hand mixer. If needed, add the remaining ¼ cup broth slowly until potatoes are desired consistency.

℮ *Basic Balancers may substitute chicken broth. For variety, a 7 ounce jar of drained roasted red peppers can be mashed into potatoes. For a creamier texture, add 2 tablespoons of kefir cheese or sour cream with the broth.*

Mashed Yams

2½ pounds yams
¾ cup sour cream
¼ teaspoon nutmeg
salt and pepper to taste

Basic Balancer
8 servings
55 minutes

Peel yams and cut into ½-inch pieces; steam until tender when pierced with a fork, about 30 minutes. Place yams in a large bowl. Add sour cream, nutmeg, salt and pepper to the bowl and beat with an electric mixer on medium speed until smooth, about 3 minutes. A hand-held potato masher can be used instead of the mixer. Spoon into a buttered 1½–2 quart casserole. Place covered casserole in a 350 degree oven until yams are hot, about 15 minutes.

Recipe can be assembled, covered and kept refrigerated up to one day ahead. It will take about 30–45 minutes to heat when dish is chilled. Super Cleansers and Deep Cleansers may substitute vegetable broth and 2 tablespoons melted butter for sour cream.

Mediterranean Mushrooms

2 cloves garlic, crushed
½ small yellow onion, chopped
4 tablespoons butter or ghee
1 pound white mushrooms, sliced
¼ cup sprouted breadcrumbs
¼ cup finely chopped parsley
salt and pepper to taste

Deep Cleanser
6 servings
15 minutes

In a medium sauté pan, melt butter and sauté garlic and onion until tender, about 8 minutes. Add mushrooms and sauté until tender, about 4 minutes. Stir in breadcrumbs and parsley; heat through. Serve.

Polenta Bites

2 cans chicken broth, 14½ ounce each
1 cup cornmeal
⅓ cup dried tomatoes, finely chopped
½ cup kefir cheese
2 tablespoons olive oil

BASIC BALANCER
20 servings
1 hour 25 minutes

Coat a 9 × 13-inch pan with cooking spray. Line pan with plastic wrap, allowing longer side to extend over edges. In medium saucepan, bring broth to boil. Whisk in cornmeal and tomato bits. Reduce heat and simmer, whisking constantly about 5 minutes until mixture is very thick. Remove from heat; whisk in kefir cheese and blend thoroughly. Spread polenta evenly in pan; cover loosely with plastic wrap and refrigerate at least one hour and up to 24 hours. Lifting edges of plastic wrap, remove polenta from pan to cutting surface. Cut into squares, other shapes or use cookie cutters. Heat broiler. Place polenta on baking sheet, brush lightly with oil. Broil about 1 minute just until lightly browned, watching closely. Serve hot. Makes about 36 pieces.

Potato Pancakes

3 russet potatoes, peel and shred
1 small yellow onion, grated
1 tablespoon sprouted spelt flour
2 tablespoons chopped parsley
1 large egg
1 egg white
¼ teaspoon salt
¼ teaspoon pepper
1 tablespoon butter, divided

DEEP CLEANSER
2 servings
25 minutes

In a colander, rinse shredded potatoes; dry on paper towels. In a large bowl, combine onion, flour, and parsley. Stir in egg, egg white, salt, and pepper. Add potatoes; mix. Heat skillet over medium-high heat and melt 1 teaspoon of butter. Place about 3 tablespoons of potato mixture per pancake in skillet; flatten with spatula. Cook until golden brown on both sides. Repeat with the remaining butter and potato mixture.

Oven Fried Potatoes

2 pounds potatoes, cut into 1-inch pieces
2 tablespoons melted ghee or butter
2 tablespoons minced oregano
2 tablespoons minced basil
salt and pepper to taste

DEEP CLEANSER
4 servings
1 hour

Preheat oven to 425 degrees. In a 10 × 15-inch baking pan, mix potatoes with melted butter. Bake until the potatoes are a rich brown, 35–45 minutes; do not disturb until potatoes begin to brown; then use a wide spatula to turn pieces over several times. Put potatoes into a bowl and sprinkle with oregano and basil. Season to taste with salt and pepper.

Roasted Celery Root, Onions and Mushrooms

1½ pounds red onions (about 3 medium),
   cut into 1-inch pieces
3 pounds celery root, cut into 1-inch cubes
3 tablespoons melted ghee or butter
1 teaspoon salt
1½ pounds button mushrooms
2 tablespoons chopped fresh sage leaves

DEEP CLEANSER
8 servings
1 hour 20 minutes

Preheat oven to 400 degrees. In two large roasting pans place like amount of celery root and toss with 1 tablespoon butter and ½ teaspoon salt per pan. Place pans in oven, stirring occasionally and switch positions of pans halfway through roasting if they are on two separate shelves. Roast a total of 25 minutes. In a large bowl, toss mushrooms, onions and sage with 1 tablespoon butter, salt and pepper to taste. Divide mushroom mixture between the two roasting pans, tossing with celery root. Continue to roast, stirring occasionally and switch pans half way through roasting, about 30 minutes, or until vegetables are tender and slightly browned.

   To prepare celery root, sometimes called celeriac, cut off ends with a sharp knife and place one of the cut sides down on a cutting board. Cutting top to bottom, remove skin. Cut celery root as desired. ½ pound fresh exotic mushrooms, such as portobello or morels, can be substituted for ½ pound of button mushrooms. Basic Balancers may substitute olive oil for butter.

Roasted Garlic

1 whole head of garlic
1 teaspoon butter
¼ teaspoon dried thyme
¼ teaspoon pepper
¼ teaspoon salt
½ cup water or vegetable broth

SUPER CLEANSER
8 servings
1 hour 20 minutes

Slice off the top ½-inch of the garlic head. Leave the root bottom. Remove some of the outer paper skin from the garlic head. Do not separate the cloves—leave intact. Arrange the head in a small covered baking dish or garlic roaster. Pour the stock over the garlic. Dot the heads with butter, thyme, pepper and salt. Turn on oven to 350 degrees; do not preheat. Cover garlic and bake, basting every 15 minutes for 1 hour. Uncover and bake 15 minutes longer.

❧ *Roasted garlic can be used in dressings, on bread or substituted in recipes where fresh garlic is used. Basic Balancers may substitute chicken broth for vegetable broth.*

Roasted Root Vegetables

4 large carrots, cut into 2-inch chunks
3 russet potatoes (8 ounces each), peel and quarter
2 parsnips (6 ounces each), peel and cut into
   2-inch chunks
2 onions, peel and quarter lengthwise
1½ pounds rutabaga, peel and cut into
   1-inch chunks
1 sweet potato or yam (8 ounces), peel and cut
   into 8 pieces
2 garlic cloves, minced
¼ cup melted ghee or butter
salt and pepper
1 teaspoon dried oregano

DEEP CLEANSER
8 servings
55 minutes

Preheat oven to 410 degrees. Position racks in upper and lower thirds of the oven. In a large bowl, toss vegetables with the butter, salt, pepper and oregano. Transfer to 2 large baking sheets. Roast vegetables, stirring twice, for about 45 minutes, or until all are tender and browned. Switch baking sheets half way through. Using slotted spoon, transfer vegetables to a platter and serve.

❧ *The choice of vegetables can vary, just keep the volume at about 7 pounds. Basic Balancers may substitute olive oil for butter. Fresh or frozen pearl onions may be substituted for onions.*

Wild Rice with Apricots

1 cup uncooked wild rice
3 cups water
¼ teaspoon salt
2 tablespoons butter
2 medium green onions, minced
1 cup canned apricot halves, drained
   and chopped
¼ cup chopped parsley
¼ teaspoon pepper

DEEP CLEANSER
8 servings
1 hour 30 minutes

Place rice, water, and salt in a medium saucepan. Cover and bring to a boil. Reduce heat and simmer about 60 minutes until grains split open. Drain any excess water and allow rice to cool. Preheat oven to 350 degrees. In a small skillet, melt butter and sauté onions about 1 minute. Transfer onions to a medium baking dish and add rice, apricots, parsley, and pepper; mix well. Cover and bake 15 minutes. Serve hot or at room temperature.

✐ *To create a Super Cleanser version, omit onions and add ¼ cup chopped chives with parsley.*

Sautéed Greens

2 tablespoons butter
½ pound beet greens, trimmed and
   cut into 2-inch strips
1 medium head of red leaf lettuce,
   cut into 2-inch strips
½ pound spinach, tough stems discarded
2 drops lemon extract, diluted
   in 2 tablespoons water
salt and pepper

SUPER CLEANSER
6 servings
15 minutes

Heat the butter in a large saucepan. Add the greens, in batches if necessary, and sauté over moderate heat until wilted, about 3 minutes. Stir in the lemon extract and season with salt and pepper.

Spanish Wild Rice

1 teaspoon butter
½ cup chopped onions
¾ cup uncooked wild rice
2 medium tomatoes, diced
½ teaspoon chili powder
2 cups vegetable broth or water
1 cup blanched fresh or frozen peas

DEEP CLEANSER
4 servings
45 minutes

Melt the butter in a medium saucepan and sauté the onions about 2 minutes. Stir in the rice and sauté 2–3 minutes. Add the tomatoes, chili powder and broth; bring to a boil over medium-high heat. Reduce heat and simmer, covered, about 35 minutes, until all the liquid is absorbed and rice has split open. Meanwhile, blanch peas in a small saucepan and add to rice when cooked.

 Basic Balancers may substitute corn for peas.

Sautéed Spinach

1 bunch spinach (about 10 ounces), washed
2 tablespoons butter
1 clove garlic, peel and mince
salt and pepper to taste

SUPER CLEANSER
2 servings
10 minutes

In large sauté pan melt butter over medium heat. Add the garlic and sauté until it starts to turn color, about 30 seconds. Add the spinach; cook until the leaves turn bright green and slightly wilt, about 2 minutes. Turn spinach as it cooks. Season with salt and pepper; serve immediately.

 Mustard greens may be substituted for spinach. Mustard greens have a slight radish taste.

Simply Steamed Beans

1 pound green beans, ends trimmed
1 teaspoon butter

DEEP CLEANSER
4 servings
15 minutes

In a large pot with fitted steamer pan or steamer insert, fill bottom with ½-inch of water and bring to boil. Add beans and steam for 5–6 minutes until tender. Immerse or run cold water over beans for a few seconds. Place steamed beans in serving dish and toss with 1 teaspoon butter. Serve warm.

∾ *Super Cleansers can use sugar snap peas.*

Sweet Potato Casserole

3 cups sweet potatoes (4 large)
2 tablespoons melted butter
2 large eggs, beaten
1 cup yogurt
2 teaspoons vanilla
1 cup maple sugar
½ teaspoon cinnamon
½ teaspoon salt
4 tablespoons melted butter
⅓ cup sprouted spelt flour

DEEP CLEANSER
6 servings
1 hour 45 minutes

Bake 4 large sweet potatoes in a 400 degree oven until tender when pierced with a fork, about 1 hour. When potatoes are removed from the oven, turn down temperature to 325 degrees. When the potatoes are cool enough to touch, remove skins. Put potatoes, 2 tablespoons melted butter, eggs, yogurt, vanilla, salt and cinnamon in a bowl and mash with a potato masher. Grease a 1½ quart casserole baking pan with cooking spray and put potato mixture in the bottom. In a separate bowl, mix sugar, 4 tablespoons melted butter and flour until crumbly. Sprinkle over potatoes and bake uncovered at 325 degrees for 30 minutes.

∾ *Yams may be substituted for sweet potatoes.*

Sweet Potato Fries

3 drops orange extract
3 tablespoons water
2 teaspoons olive oil
½ teaspoon ground ginger
¼ teaspoon salt
⅛ teaspoon ground pepper
2 large sweet potatoes (about 1½ pounds),
   peeled and cut into ⅛-inch strips

BASIC BALANCER
4 servings
45 minutes

Preheat oven to 400 degrees. In a small saucepan, combine extract, water, oil, ginger, salt and pepper. Bring to a boil, reduce heat to simmer and cook for 2 minutes. Remove from heat and let cool. Combine potatoes and oil mixture in a large bowl and toss well. Remove potatoes from bowl and arrange in a single layer on a baking sheet coated with cooking spray. Discard remaining oil mixture. Bake 30 minutes or until edges are crisp.

Vegetable Herb Rice

1 cup uncooked wild rice
2¼ cups vegetable broth or water
1 bay leaf
2 cups chopped fresh spinach
½ cup finely chopped chives
1 cup chopped flat-leaf parsley
¼ cup chopped basil
1 tablespoon chopped fresh tarragon
salt and pepper to taste

SUPER CLEANSER
4 servings
45 minutes

In a medium saucepan, combine the rice, broth and bay leaf; bring to a boil. Reduce the heat and simmer, covered, about 35 minutes, until all the liquid is absorbed and the rice has split open. Remove from heat. As the rice cooks, clean and chop the vegetables and herbs. In a small saucepan, bring 3 tablespoons of water to a boil, add spinach, chives or onions and, herbs. Cover and steam just until spinach begins to wilt. Drain any excess water and add to cooked rice. Mix well, season, and serve.

Deep Cleansers may substitute green onions for chives.

Vegetable Mashed Potatoes

1 tablespoon butter
2 leeks, white and light green part only,
    cut into 1-inch slices
2 large russet potatoes (1 pound), peel and cube
1 parsnip, peeled and cut into 1-inch pieces
1 carrot, peeled and cut into 1-inch pieces
1 cup spinach, chopped or torn into small pieces
1 teaspoon oregano
1 teaspoon salt
¼ teaspoon pepper

DEEP CLEANSER
4 servings
50 minutes

In a medium saucepan, melt the butter and add the leeks, potatoes, parsnips, carrots, oregano, salt and pepper. Add enough water to barely cover vegetables. Bring to a boil, partially covered, over high heat. Reduce the heat and simmer covered, for 10 minutes. Uncover and simmer for 10–15 minutes longer, until the vegetables are fork tender. During the last 5 minutes of cooking the vegetables, add the spinach to the top of the pan, cover and cook until wilted. Drain water off of the vegetables saving 1 cup of the liquid. Using a potato masher, mash the vegetables until only the small pieces remain, using reserved liquid to thin as needed. Serve hot.

↝ *Other vegetables can be substituted, such as chard for spinach, sweet potatoes for white potatoes and onions for leeks. Vegetable broth can be used when mashing vegetables instead of reserved water.*

Vegetable Stuffed Squash

3 acorn squash, halved and seeds removed
1 tablespoon butter
2 cups chopped onions
2 cups chopped mushrooms

DEEP CLEANSER
6 servings
1 hour

Heat oven to 350 degrees. Halve and seed squash. Place in large baking dish that has been greased with cooking spray. Bake squash 35 minutes. Melt the butter in a skillet and sauté onions 3–5 minutes, add mushrooms and cook until soft, about 5 minutes. Remove the squash from the oven and stuff with the mushroom mixture. Return squash to the oven and bake for an additional 20 minutes.

Veggie Sticks

2 large carrots
1 large red, yellow or green pepper
½ pound zucchini, with skin left on

SUPER CLEANSER
4 servings
15 minutes

Clean and cut carrots and zucchini into 3-inch length julienne strips about the size and width of a green bean. Clean and cut pepper into strips. The key is to cut the vegetables as uniform in size as possible so they cook evenly. Put a large steamer pot on the stove. Bring to a simmer, steam carrots about 2 minutes, then add peppers and zucchini, steam an additional 4 minutes until vegetables are crisp tender. Plunge into cold water to stop cooking. Drain and chill. Serve with yogurt cheese as a dip if desired.

℮ *Deep Cleansers may add ½ pound cleaned green beans with peppers and zucchini, or serve with kefir cheese.*

Zucchini Pancakes

3 cups grated zucchini, with skin left on
½ cup quinoa flour
1 teaspoon baking powder
salt and pepper to taste
1 large egg, beaten

SUPER CLEANSER
6 servings
15 minutes

Combine zucchini, flour, baking powder, salt and pepper. Mix in egg. Drop mixture by large rounded tablespoonfuls onto a medium heated skillet. Cook until browned, about 3 minutes on each side. Makes 12 pancakes.

℮ *Deep Cleansers may substitute sprouted flour for quinoa flour. Basic Balancers may substitute corn flour for quinoa flour.*

Fish and Chicken

These fish and chicken recipes are easy to prepare in a variety of basic and delicious ways. Remember to be selective when purchasing quality fish and chicken.

For a hearty meal try Herb Roasted Chicken And Vegetables. If something lighter is desired, serve Baked Trout.

Use these recipes as inspiration to create your favorite fish and chicken entrees.

Baked Trout

4 whole trout, heads removed
1 tablespoon butter
2 teaspoons dried dill weed
1 drop lemon extract, diluted in ¼ cup water

SUPER CLEANSER

4 servings

25 minutes

Preheat oven to 450 degrees. Spray baking sheet with cooking oil. Lay open trout, skin side down, on prepared pan. If trout does not lay open easily, use a knife to cut through the bones on the inside of the spine. Pour water mixed with lemon extract over fish. Cut butter into small bits and drop on top. Sprinkle with dried dill. Bake for 15 minutes.

✑ *¼ cup lemon juice may be substituted for lemon extract and water, if it is a "YES" food for you.*

Crab Cakes

2 large egg whites
2 tablespoons Yogurt Cheese
2 tablespoons melted butter
1½ teaspoons vinegar-free horseradish
dash of Tabasco (optional)
¼ cup quinoa flakes
1 teaspoon dried mustard
1 teaspoon dried parsley
1 teaspoon Old Bay seasoning
½ teaspoon pepper
salt to taste
1 pound package imitation crab meat (pollack)

SUPER CLEANSER

4 servings

20 minutes

In a large mixing bowl, beat together egg whites, cheese, butter, horseradish and Tabasco. Add quinoa flakes, mustard, parsley, and remaining seasonings. Add crab and toss to mix. Form into patties; cook over medium heat, in a nonstick skillet until golden, about 3 minutes on each side. Makes 8 patties.

✑ *Deep Cleansers and beyond may add 2 teaspoons Worcestershire sauce to butter mixture.*
   Basic Balancers may substitute ground corn flakes for quinoa flakes.

Crab Quiche

FOR CRUST:
- 1 cup sprouted seed flour
- ⅓ cup cornmeal
- ¼ teaspoon salt
- ⅓ cup butter
- ½ cup cold water

FOR FILLING:
- 2 teaspoons butter
- 2 leeks, cleaned and chopped, about 2 cups
- ½ pound imitation crabmeat
- 1 ¼ cups yogurt
- ¼ cup kefir cheese
- 4 large eggs, lightly beaten
- ½ teaspoon onion powder
- ½ teaspoon dry mustard
- ¼ teaspoon salt
- ¼ teaspoon pepper
- ½ teaspoon paprika

BASIC BALANCER
6 servings
1 hour 30 minutes

Preheat oven to 325 degrees. For the crust: combine flour, cornmeal and salt. Cut ⅓ cup butter into flour mixture and mix with a pastry cutter or fork until it resembles coarse crumbs. Add water, one tablespoon at a time, stirring gently with a fork until mixture forms a ball. On a lightly floured surface, roll out pastry to form a 12-inch circle. Fit loosely into a 9-inch pie plate; fold under and flute edges.

For the filling: cut off and discard coarse green stems of leeks, split lengthwise, wash thoroughly, and chop remaining tender stalks. Melt butter in a sauté pan over medium-high heat; add leeks and cook until soft. Shred crabmeat and gently mix with leeks and spoon into pastry shell. In a large mixing bowl, combine yogurt, cheese, eggs, onion powder, mustard, salt and pepper. Pour over crabmeat. Sprinkle top with paprika.

Bake for 55–60 minutes or until egg mixture is set in the center and appears firm when the pan is shaken. Remove from oven and let cool at least 10 minutes. Serve warm or at room temperature.

Fish Burgers

2 slices sprouted grain bread
½ pound cod
½ pound red snapper
¼ cup tamari sauce
¼ cup finely chopped green onions
2 teaspoons wasabi powder (optional)

DEEP CLEANSER

4 servings

25 minutes

Place the bread in a food processor and pulse into crumbs; about 1 cup. Put crumbs in a large mixing bowl. Add fish to the food processor and pulse until ground. Add the fish, tamari, green onion and wasabi to the bowl with the crumbs. Mix and form into 4 patties. Place patties on greased broiler tray and broil about 5 minutes per side, or until browned and cooked inside.

Salmon, tuna or flounder may be substituted for fish.

Fish Florentine

1 package chopped spinach (10 ounces),
   thawed and drained
½ pound thin slices or fillets of salmon,
   haddock, snapper or flounder
1 large egg, lightly beaten
½ teaspoon onion powder
1 teaspoon dried tarragon, dill or thyme
salt and pepper to taste
2 teaspoons butter
paprika

SUPER CLEANSER

2 servings

25 minutes

Preheat oven to 350 degrees. Spread spinach evenly over bottom of greased pie plate. Lay fish over the spinach. Mix seasonings together with egg; brush over fish. Dot with butter and sprinkle with paprika. Cover and bake for 10 minutes. Remove cover and bake for 5 minutes or until fish is done and spinach is heated.

Herbed Baked Fish

1 ½ pounds flounder (4–6 fillets)
¼ cup melted butter
2 drops lemon extract, diluted in ¼ cup water
½ cup vegetable broth or water
1 teaspoon dill weed
½ teaspoon onion powder
1 teaspoon dried oregano
½ teaspoon paprika plus a dash for top
salt and pepper

SUPER CLEANSER
4 servings
25 minutes

Preheat oven to 450 degrees. Place fish in a greased, shallow baking dish. Melt butter in a small saucepan over low heat. Stir in remaining ingredients and spread the mixture evenly over the fish. Sprinkle extra paprika over tops of fish. Bake uncovered for 10–15 minutes, until fish is done.

Mediterranean Fish

2 tablespoons butter
1 ½ pounds fish fillets (salmon, flounder, halibut)
1 medium green pepper, sliced ¼-inch thick
1 medium onion, sliced ¼-inch thick
4 medium mushrooms, sliced ¼-inch thick
1 can diced tomatoes (28 ounce can)
salt and pepper

DEEP CLEANSER
4 servings
20 minutes

Melt butter in large skillet over medium-high heat. Salt and pepper fish and place in skillet. Add green pepper, onion and mushrooms around pan with fish. Sauté vegetables, stirring frequently along sides of fish until tender, about 10 minutes. Turn fish and add tomatoes. Simmer, covered, 3–6 minutes, until fish is just opaque. Do not overcook fish.

Salmon with Vegetables

4 salmon steaks or fillets (6 ounces each)
½ cup water
4 ounces kefir cheese
1 cup chopped tomatoes
1 cup chopped mushrooms
½ cup chopped green onions or chives
2 tablespoons chopped parsley
salt and pepper to taste

DEEP CLEANSER
4 servings
25 minutes

Preheat oven to 400 degrees. Pour ½ cup water into a greased baking dish large enough to hold salmon. Place salmon in prepared dish. In a small bowl, combine chopped vegetables, parsley, kefir cheese, salt and pepper. Top salmon with vegetable mixture. Bake, uncovered, until fish flakes easily, about 12–16 minutes depending on thickness of fish.

Salmon Loaf

1 can salmon (14 ounce can), drained and flaked
2 large eggs, beaten
2 slices sprouted sourdough bread, crumbled
⅓ cup yogurt
½ cup water
½ cup chopped chives
2 drops lemon extract
1 tablespoon melted butter
½ teaspoon celery salt
½ teaspoon dried parsley
½ teaspoon dried basil
½ teaspoon dry mustard
¼ teaspoon pepper
paprika

SUPER CLEANSER
4 servings
1 hour 15 minutes

Preheat oven to 350 degrees. In a large bowl combine all ingredients. Mix well. Spread mixture into a 4 × 8-inch greased loaf pan. Top with paprika. Bake 1 hour or until top of loaf is light brown.

ℰ *Deep Cleansers may substitute green onions for chives.*

Poached Salmon with Dill

4 salmon fillets or steaks (4 ounces each)
6 cups water
1 teaspoon peppercorns
1 bunch fresh dill, chopped (about ¾ cup)
1 cup yogurt

SUPER CLEANSER
4 servings
25 minutes

In a pan large enough to hold the fillets, add 6 cups of water and peppercorns; bring to a boil. Add fish to boiling water (make sure water is covering fish) and poach at a rolling boil until desired doneness, about 6–12 minutes depending on thickness of fish. Meanwhile, place yogurt and dill in blender and blend until mixed. Remove fish to serving plates and garnish with dill sauce.

℘ *Fish stock may be substituted for water.*

Salmon Burgers

1 large egg, lightly beaten
2 tablespoons yogurt
4 teaspoons chopped fresh basil
   (or ¾ teaspoon dried)
⅛ teaspoon pepper
⅓ cup sprouted bread crumbs
1 can pink salmon (6 ounces), skinless
   and boneless, drained and flaked
2 teaspoons tamari sauce
1 green onion, chopped
2 tablespoons quinoa flakes
1 tablespoon butter

DEEP CLEANSER
2 servings
20 minutes

In a large mixing bowl, combine all ingredients except quinoa flakes and butter; mix well. Melt butter in a skillet over medium heat. Spread quinoa flakes on a plate. Form mixture into two patties and lay briefly on the plate with the quinoa flakes, turning once to coat. Melt butter in skillet over medium heat. Place patties in skillet and cook about 5 minutes on each side, until browned and heated through.

℘ *Basic Balancers may substitute cornmeal for quinoa flakes and serve with tomato wedges and red onion slices.*

Salmon Appetizer Rolls

3 ounces Yogurt Cheese (⅓ cup)
2 tablespoons kefir cheese
3 teaspoons minced onion, or 1 green onion
1 teaspoon minced parsley
8 slices smoked salmon (about ½ pound)

BASIC BALANCER
8 servings
30 minutes

Beat the yogurt and kefir cheeses with the onion and parsley until smooth. Spread some of the mixture on each slice of smoked salmon and roll up. Secure with a toothpick if necessary. Refrigerate 10–15 minutes to firm up rolls. Serve whole or slice into bite-size pieces.

‎ *Phase Two Diet may substitute cream cheese for Yogurt Cheese.*

Salmon Potato Cakes

1 large onion
2 teaspoons butter
1 large potato, peeled or not peeled
¼ cup Yogurt Cheese
1 can salmon (6 ounce can)
2 tablespoons chopped parsley
salt and pepper to taste

DEEP CLEANSER
2 servings
20 minutes

Cut potato into cubes and steam until soft, about 10 minutes. (Or use a previously baked potato cut into cubes.) In a medium skillet, melt butter and sauté onions. Place sautéed onions in a medium bowl; add drained salmon, yogurt, parsley, salt and pepper. Add more yogurt if too dry. Form mixture into patties and fry in the same pan used to sauté onions until they are golden.

Oriental Salmon Fillets

4 salmon fillets (about 1 ½ pounds)
¼ cup water
3 tablespoons tamari sauce
2 green onions, chopped
1 clove garlic, finely chopped
2 teaspoons fresh ginger, peeled and finely
    chopped (or ½ teaspoon dried ground ginger)

DEEP CLEANSER
4 servings
1 hour 15 minutes

Mix water, tamari, garlic, green onions, and ginger to make a marinade; pour over fish steaks and marinate for 1 hour in the refrigerator. Bake filets at 425 degrees for about 10–15 minutes, basting marinade while cooking.

Striped Bass with Tomato Sauce

4 striped bass fillets (about 4 ounces each)
2 large ripe tomatoes
1 cup yogurt
½ teaspoon vanilla extract
¼ teaspoon maple syrup
¼ cup finely chopped fresh dill
salt to taste

DEEP CLEANSER
4 servings
20 minutes

Preheat oven to 450. Place cleaned fillets on a baking pan greased with cooking spray. Bake fish for 10–15 minutes, until it flakes easily. In a blender, purée tomatoes, yogurt, vanilla, maple syrup, dill and salt. Pour over fish and serve.

Sauce may be served over hot or cold cooked fish. Salmon may be substituted for striped bass.

Stuffed Fish Rolls

6 fillets of sole or flounder
1½ cups grated carrots (about 3)
1 cup chopped onion
10 ounces frozen spinach, thawed
1 tablespoon butter
¾ cup Yogurt Cheese, kefir cheese,
   or sour cream
1 teaspoon dill
½ teaspoon paprika
3 tablespoons butter melted

DEEP CLEANSER
4 servings
45 minutes

In a large sauté pan, melt butter over medium heat. Add carrots, onions and spinach. Sauté until onions are tender, about 6–8 minutes. Mix the cheese into the vegetables and turn off stove. Wash and pat dry each fillet and spoon ½ cup of the vegetable mixture onto the center of each fillet. Roll ends over the filling and secure with a toothpick. Place in a baking dish toothpick side down. In a small saucepan melt butter, add dill and paprika and spread over fish rolls. Bake at 450 degrees for 10–15 minutes.

༄ *Any combination of the three cheeses may be used to equal the ¾ cup depending on the diet you are on.*

Sushi Rolls

3 cups cooked quinoa
6 sheets toasted nori
1½ cups julienne cucumbers
2 ripe avocados, thinly sliced
¾ pound imitation crabmeat (pollack), shredded

BASIC BALANCER
6 servings
20 minutes

To make a roll, dampen a sheet of nori and place on waxed paper. Spread a small mound of quinoa, about ½ cup lengthwise down the center. Lay strips of crabmeat and vegetables down the center on top of the quinoa. Start to roll the nori sheet using wax paper to control. Wet the outside seam of the roll to seal. Slice roll into 1-inch pieces using very sharp, smooth knife. Moistening the knife with water is helpful.

༄ *Toasted nori is a sea vegetable or seaweed. Try other roll combinations using smoked salmon, cream cheese, cucumbers and green onions—or use your imagination! Deep Cleansers and beyond may serve with tamari sauce, wasabi paste and pickled ginger. Wasabi is a powdered horseradish that is sold in health food stores and some grocery stores. Just mix it with water to form a paste.*

Lemon Oregano Sea Bass

2 teaspoons melted butter
4 drops lemon extract
2 tablespoons finely chopped fresh oregano
  (or 1 teaspoon dried)
4 sea bass fillets (5 ounces each)
salt and pepper

SUPER CLEANSER
4 servings
25 minutes

Preheat oven to 450 degrees. In glass baking dish, combine butter with the lemon extract and oregano. Add the sea bass, turn to coat and let marinate for 5 minutes. Coat broiling pan with cooking spray. Place bass on the pan and broil 5 minutes on each side or until browned and just cooked through.

Tuna Pasta Nicoise

2 cups macaroni shaped corn pasta
2 cups small red potatoes (about 10 ounces),
  quartered
2 cups green beans (about ½ pound),
  cut into 1-inch pieces
⅓ cup chopped green onions
1 cup black olives, sliced
1 can tuna (6 ounce can), packed in water,
  drained and flaked
2 tablespoons 100% cranberry juice
1 tablespoon 100% maple syrup
¼ teaspoon salt
¼ teaspoon dry mustard
¼ cup olive oil

BASIC BALANCER
4 servings
35 minutes

Put a large pot of water on to boil for the pasta. When water boils, cook pasta according to directions on package. Drain and rinse with warm water. Put potatoes in a medium saucepan, cover with water. Bring to a boil, reduce heat and simmer 10–15 minutes, until almost tender. Add beans; cook an additional 3–5 minutes or until beans are crisp-tender. Drain and rinse with cold water. In a large bowl, place pasta, potatoes, beans, green onions, black olives, and tuna; set aside. In a small bowl, make cranberry vinaigrette by whisking remaining ingredients, cranberry juice, maple syrup, salt, dry mustard and ¼ cup olive oil; gently toss with pasta mixture.

✐ *Serve at room temperature or chilled. Try over a bed of lettuce.*

Tuna Burger

2 cans tuna (6 ounce cans) packed
   in water, drained
3 tablespoons fresh minced chives
1 tablespoon melted butter
2 large egg whites, lightly beaten
1 tablespoon tamari sauce
pepper
4 slices 100% sprouted bread, toasted
garnish with sprouts, lettuce and tomatoes

DEEP CLEANSER
4 servings
20 minutes

In a large bowl, lightly mix tuna with the chives, butter and egg whites. Season with tamari, and a pinch of pepper. Shape the mixture into 4 patties 3½–4-inch in diameter. Preheat a nonstick skillet at medium heat and cook patties 8 minutes on each side, turning carefully. Put on toasted bread and serve as an open-faced sandwich topped with sprouts.

   Super Cleansers can make Tuna Burgers by omitting tamari sauce and garnishes.

Tuna Casserole

2 cups uncooked elbow quinoa pasta
2 cans tuna (6 ounce cans) packed
   in water, drained
8 ounces fresh mushrooms, sliced
2 green onions, minced or
   ½ teaspoon onion powder
2 tablespoons tamari sauce
½ cup kefir cheese
1 cup Yogurt Cheese
salt and pepper to taste

DEEP CLEANSER
4 servings
50 minutes

Preheat oven to 325 degrees. In a large sauce pan bring 2 quarts of water to a boil; add pasta and cook 4–6 minutes as directed on package. Drain and rinse with cool water. In a 2 quart greased baking dish, place tuna, mushrooms, onions, and cooked pasta. In a separate bowl, mix tamari, kefir, and Yogurt Cheese. Mix until blended and stir into tuna mixture. Bake covered for 20–30 minutes, until heated through. Let sit for 10 minutes before serving.

   Basic Balancers may use corn pasta. For variation, add ½ cup sliced black olives with mushrooms.

Tuna Quiche

1 cup sprouted spelt flour
⅓ cup cornmeal
¾ teaspoon salt, divided
¼ cup butter (4 tablespoons)
¼ cup cold water
1 package frozen chopped spinach
  (10 ounces), thawed
1½ cups yogurt
1 can tuna (6 ounce can), drained and flaked
3 large eggs, beaten
¼ cup kefir cheese
1½ teaspoons onion powder
½ teaspoon dill weed
¼ teaspoon pepper

BASIC BALANCER
6 servings
1 hour 15 minutes

Heat oven to 350 degrees. Combine flour, cornmeal and ¼ teaspoon salt. Cut small chunks of butter into flour mixture and mix with a pastry cutter or fork until it resembles coarse crumbs. Add water, 1 tablespoon at a time, stirring lightly with fork until mixture forms a ball. On lightly floured surface, roll out pastry to form a 12-inch circle. Fit loosely into 9-inch glass pie plate; turn under edges and flute. Drain and squeeze excess water out of spinach; combine with ½ teaspoon salt and remaining ingredients. Pour mixture into pastry shell. Bake 50–55 minutes or until knife inserted in center comes out clean. Let stand 10 minutes before serving.

Yogurt Baked Halibut

1 cup yogurt
⅓ cup chives, chopped
2 teaspoons grated fresh ginger
2 halibut steaks (4 ounces each)
salt and pepper

SUPER CLEANSER
2 servings
30 minutes

Preheat oven to 325 degrees. Mix yogurt, chives, ginger, salt and pepper. Spread ½ of the yogurt mix in the bottom of a small baking dish. Place halibut on top and spread remaining yogurt mixture on top. Bake 20 minutes or until fish is done in the center.

℃ *Deep Cleansers may substitute scallions for chives.*

Veggie Fish Packets

¾ pound thin white fish fillets, cut bite-size
   (sole, snapper or flounder)
8 spinach leaves
4 plum tomatoes, quartered
1 green onion, sliced
3 tablespoons tamari sauce
2 tablespoons water
½ teaspoon ground ginger
¼ teaspoon pepper

DEEP CLEANSER
2 servings
30 minutes

Preheat oven to 350 degrees. On two 12-inch square pieces of foil, divide and layer spinach, then fish, tomatoes and onion. In a small bowl, mix tamari, water, ginger, and pepper. Pour half of the tamari mixture over each fish packet. Seal packets by pulling up sides of the foil and folding together in ½-inch folds. Repeat with the ends of the foil. Make sure to leave an inch or two air space in the top of the packet for the steam. Bake 20 minutes. Serve in the packets.

Chicken Burgers

1¼ pounds ground chicken, uncooked
1 tablespoon minced onion flakes
1 teaspoon dried oregano
1 teaspoon dried basil
1 teaspoon onion powder
½ teaspoon salt
½ teaspoon paprika
½ teaspoon garlic powder
¼ teaspoon pepper

BASIC BALANCER
4 servings
25 minutes

Preheat oven to 350 degrees. In a large bowl, combine all ingredients. Mix well and shape into 8 patties. Place patties in shallow baking pan greased with cooking spray. Bake 10–12 minutes, until burgers are cooked through, turning once while baking.

ᕙ *Burgers may also be fried in a skillet over medium-high heat. Cook 5 minutes on each side and then cover for 2–3 minutes longer, or until no longer pink in the center. Serve with a red sauce or as an open-faced sandwich on sprouted toast with lettuce, tomato and Essential Mayonnaise. For variation, mash in half of an avocado or add some Tabasco sauce.*

Chicken Cacciatore

6 skinless chicken breasts (or other pieces)
2 tablespoons olive oil
1 cup sliced onion
1 cup diced celery
1 tablespoon parsley
1 cup chicken stock
3 cups chopped tomatoes or 28 ounce
  can tomatoes, with juice
½ cup sliced green onions
½ tablespoon oregano
½ teaspoon fennel seed (optional)

BASIC BALANCER
6 servings
1 hour 30 minutes

Put oil in a large frying pan and sauté chicken until lightly browned. You can sauté in batches depending on size of pan. If chicken pieces stick and pan gets dry, add a little chicken stock and loosen. Remove chicken from frying pan and place in baking dish. Add onions, celery, and parsley to frying pan and sauté with pan drippings until slightly tender.

Add remaining chicken stock and pour over chicken in baking dish. Add tomatoes or tomato sauce; mix together. Bake in 350 degree oven 45 minutes–1 hour or until chicken is tender.

Chicken Hash

1 pound ground chicken, white meat
½ cup chicken broth
2 chopped green onions or 2 teaspoons
  onion powder
2 stalks celery, finely chopped
2 large baked potatoes, diced
1 tablespoon dried parsley
1 teaspoon dried thyme
1 teaspoon dried sage
½ teaspoon salt
¼ teaspoon pepper

BASIC BALANCER
6 servings
20 minutes

Sauté chicken, onion and celery in a large skillet adding chicken broth as needed to keep from sticking. When chicken is almost cooked, add potatoes, herbs and seasoning. Add rest of broth, cover and steam until warm.

Chicken Paella

1 tablespoon ghee or butter
4 boneless chicken breasts (about 1 pound)
1 cup wild rice
1 small chopped onion
1¼ cups chicken broth
½ cup tomato sauce
1 large diced roasted red pepper
2 cups green beans, cut into 2-inch pieces
2 small tomatoes, cored and quartered
1 cup black olives

BASIC BALANCER
4 servings
1 hour

In a 10 × 12-inch frying pan or paella pan, melt butter over medium heat. Add chicken, brown each side about two minutes. Remove chicken and set aside. To the pan, add rice and onion; stirring often for 2 minutes. Stir in broth, tomato sauce, and roasted peppers, then lay chicken over rice. Bring broth to a boil, reduce heat and simmer 30–35 minutes, covered, or until grain of rice cracks open. Lay green beans, tomatoes, and olives on top of rice and chicken. Cover and cook 10 minutes more. Uncover and cook until most of the liquid is absorbed, about 4 minutes.

ᕊ *Ghee can be heated to a higher temperature than butter without burning. One teaspoon of saffron threads may be added with broth.*

Chicken with Herb Sauce

2 tablespoons butter
4 tablespoons finely chopped onion
4 tablespoons chopped parsley
1 teaspoon dried oregano
1 teaspoon poultry seasoning
½ teaspoon dried tarragon
½ teaspoon dried marjoram
1 cup vegetable or chicken broth
4 split chicken breasts
1 teaspoon paprika

BASIC BALANCER
4 servings
55 minutes

Preheat oven to 350 degrees. In a small sauce pan, melt butter; add onion and cook over medium heat until tender, about 5 minutes. Stir in herbs, seasonings (except paprika) and broth. Bring to a boil and simmer for 5 minutes until liquid is reduced by a third. Arrange chicken in a nonstick or greased square baking pan. Brush sauce over top and sprinkle with paprika. Bake 35–45 minutes, until chicken is done.

Chicken Spinach Loaf

1 ½ pounds ground chicken, white meat
½ cup sprouted bread crumbs
½ cup tomato juice
3 tablespoons minced onions
½ teaspoon garlic salt
½ teaspoon pepper
1 large egg
1 package frozen chopped spinach (10 ounces),
  thawed and drained
1 cup kefir cheese or cream cheese
1 can tomato paste (6 ounce can)
1 tablespoon maple syrup
4 tablespoons water
1 teaspoon dry mustard

BASIC BALANCER
8 servings
1 hour 20 minutes

Heat oven to 350 degrees. In a large bowl, combine chicken, bread crumbs, tomato juice, onion, salt, pepper, and egg. Place meat mixture on a piece of waxed paper and shape into a 9 × 12-inch rectangle. In a medium bowl, combine spinach and cheese; mix. Spread spinach mixture evenly over meat. Roll up from 9-inch side, press ends and seams to seal. Place seam side down in shallow baking pan coated with cooking spray. Bake 1 hour. Meanwhile, in a small bowl combine tomato paste, maple syrup, water and dry mustard. Spread over top of loaf at the end of one hour and return pan to oven; cook an additional 4 minutes until topping is heated. Let cool ten minutes before slicing.

Marinated Chicken

1 cup yogurt
3 tablespoons chopped fresh mint
2 cloves garlic, minced
1 teaspoon dried cumin
1 teaspoon dried coriander
1 teaspoon paprika
2¾ pounds whole chicken legs (4)

BASIC BALANCER
4 servings
4–24 hours

In a small bowl, combine yogurt, mint, garlic, and herbs. Make 2–3 diagonal cuts down to the bone in each chicken leg. Place in plastic bag or glass dish. Pour marinade over and turn legs to coat. Marinate in refrigerator 4–24 hours. Grill or broil in oven, turning and basting four times during cooking.

Chicken Vegetable Loaf

LOAF:

3 slices sprouted bread
1 large carrot, cut into ½-inch pieces
1 stalk celery, cut into ½-inch pieces
1 medium onion, roughly chopped
1 clove garlic, minced (optional)
½ cup flat-leaf parsley, loosely packed
1 can tomato paste (6 ounce can)
¼ cup water
4½ teaspoons dry mustard
1½ pounds ground chicken (white meat)
1 teaspoon salt
1 teaspoon pepper
2 large eggs (or three egg whites)
1 teaspoon Tabasco sauce (optional)

TOPPING:

3 tablespoons tomato paste
2 tablespoons water
4 tablespoons maple syrup

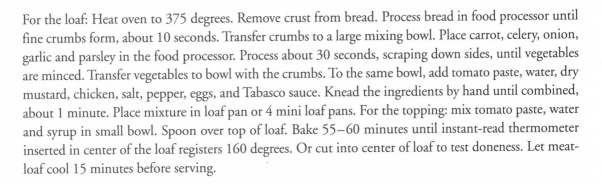

BASIC BALANCER
6 servings
1 hour 20 minutes

For the loaf: Heat oven to 375 degrees. Remove crust from bread. Process bread in food processor until fine crumbs form, about 10 seconds. Transfer crumbs to a large mixing bowl. Place carrot, celery, onion, garlic and parsley in the food processor. Process about 30 seconds, scraping down sides, until vegetables are minced. Transfer vegetables to bowl with the crumbs. To the same bowl, add tomato paste, water, dry mustard, chicken, salt, pepper, eggs, and Tabasco sauce. Knead the ingredients by hand until combined, about 1 minute. Place mixture in loaf pan or 4 mini loaf pans. For the topping: mix tomato paste, water and syrup in small bowl. Spoon over top of loaf. Bake 55–60 minutes until instant-read thermometer inserted in center of the loaf registers 160 degrees. Or cut into center of loaf to test doneness. Let meatloaf cool 15 minutes before serving.

Herb Roasted Chicken and Vegetables

1 whole chicken, about 4½ pounds
1 teaspoon salt
1 medium onion, cut in half
1 stalk celery
3 cloves garlic, slightly crushed
2 tablespoons melted butter or olive oil
1 teaspoon dried oregano
1 teaspoon dried parsley
1 teaspoon dried rosemary
½ teaspoon pepper
1 tablespoon paprika
8 ounces carrots, cleaned and cut
   into 1-inch pieces
1 pound small potatoes, cut in halves

BASIC BALANCER
4 servings
1 hour 40 minutes

Preheat oven to 350 degrees. Rinse chicken, remove excess fat and pat dry. Set the chicken in a large roasting pan. Salt the cavity and insert onion, celery and garlic cloves. In a small dish, combine oregano, parsley, rosemary, pepper, and paprika; drizzle melted butter over and mix. Brush herb butter mixture over outside of chicken. Bake chicken for 40 minutes, basting once, then place carrots and potatoes around the chicken. Baste vegetables with chicken juice. Continue baking for 45 minutes, basting occasionally, until juice runs clear when chicken is pierced with a fork and leg moves easily when twisted.

One Pan Chicken and Vegetables

4 skinless chicken breast halves
1 cup vegetable or chicken broth
1 tablespoon chopped fresh parsley
   or 1 teaspoon dried
½ teaspoon dried thyme
½ teaspoon dried rosemary
1 large yam or sweet potato, cut into
   2-inch cubes
2 cups fresh or frozen whole green beans

BASIC BALANCER
4 servings
40 minutes

In a large nonstick skillet over medium-high heat, cook chicken 5–6 minutes on each side until browned. Add broth, herbs, potato and beans. Bring to a boil. Reduce heat, cover and simmer 20 minutes, or until chicken is cooked through and vegetables are tender.

Meatballs

1 pound ground chicken, white meat
1½ cups sprouted bread crumbs
2 tablespoons kefir cheese
1 clove garlic, minced
1 tablespoon dried parsley
⅛ teaspoon pepper
3 large eggs
1 tablespoon olive oil

BASIC BALANCER

4 servings

30 minutes

Place all ingredients in a large bowl and mix until blended. In a large sauté pan or skillet, heat oil over medium-high heat. Shape meat mixture into 2-inch balls and sauté in heated pan. Roll balls in pan occasionally to sear and cook all sides. Sauté balls until cooked through, about 12–15 minutes.

✑ *Meatballs may be placed in heated tomato or red sauce and served over cooked corn or quinoa pasta. Double recipe and freeze half for future use.*

Oven Fried Chicken

3 cups sprouted bread crumbs
1½ tablespoons fresh thyme leaves, finely
    chopped (or 1¼ teaspoons dried)
1½ tablespoons fresh rosemary, finely
    chopped (or 1¼ teaspoons dried)
1 teaspoon salt
1 teaspoon pepper
3 cups yogurt
4 pounds chicken pieces

BASIC BALANCER

8 servings

1 hour 20 minutes

Preheat oven to 400 degrees. In a medium bowl, toss the bread crumbs, thyme, rosemary, salt and pepper. Put the yogurt into a second bowl. Dip the chicken pieces in the yogurt and then coat with the seasoned crumbs. Arrange the chicken on two large baking sheets and bake for 45 minutes–1 hour, or until golden and cooked throughout. Serve hot or at room temperature.

✑ *Phase Four diet may substitute buttermilk for yogurt.*

Stir-Fry Chicken

2 tablespoons arrowroot
1 can chicken broth (14½ ounce or 1¾ cups)
1 tablespoon tamari sauce
1 pound boneless chicken breasts, cut into strips
¼ teaspoon ground ginger
⅛ teaspoon garlic powder
5 cups vegetables, such as carrots, peppers,
    green onions, water chestnuts, and/or celery
2 cups cooked quinoa

BASIC BALANCER
4 servings
30 minutes

In a small bowl, mix arrowroot, 1 cup of broth, and tamari sauce. Set aside. In a nonstick skillet, stir fry chicken over medium heat until browned. Set aside. Coarsely chop or julienne vegetables. Heat the same skillet over medium heat, add remaining broth, ginger, garlic, and vegetables. Cover and cook 5 minutes, until vegetables are crisp-tender. Add arrowroot mixture. Cook until mixture boils and thickens, stirring constantly. Return chicken to the pan and heat through. Serve over quinoa.

Rosemary Lemon Chicken

1 small onion, peeled and halved
1 tablespoon dried rosemary,
    or 2 tablespoons fresh
2 cloves garlic (optional)
¼ cup water
2 drops lemon extract (or to taste)
2 tablespoons maple syrup
⅓ cup chicken broth
6 skinless chicken breasts, cleaned

BASIC BALANCER
6 servings
1 hour 20 minutes

Preheat oven to 375 degrees. In a food processor, purée rosemary, onion, garlic, water, lemon extract, syrup and chicken broth. Pour marinade into large glass bowl, add the chicken and coat with the marinade. Marinate for 30 minutes – 4 hours in the refrigerator. Remove chicken from marinade and place in baking pan sprayed with cooking oil. Cover and bake for 30 minutes. Remove cover and bake for another 15 minutes, until chicken is cooked in center. Baste occasionally with marinade during cooking.

Quick Italian Chicken

4 pounds boneless, skinless chicken breasts
   (about 1½–2 pounds)
1 can stewed Italian tomatoes (28 ounce can),
   including juice
2 tablespoons minced onions or chopped
   green onions
½ cup vegetable broth
¼ teaspoon pepper

BASIC BALANCER
4 servings
55 minutes

Preheat oven to 350 degrees. Place chicken in a 2 quart covered casserole dish greased with cooking spray.
In a small bowl, combine remaining ingredients and pour oven chicken. Cover and bake 30 minutes.
Uncover and continue baking an additional 15 minutes, or until chicken is cooked.

Tandoori Chicken

1 medium onion, coarsely chopped
1 clove garlic, coarsely chopped (optional)
2 drops lemon extract
¾ cup yogurt
2 tablespoons tandoori spice blend
½ teaspoon salt
1 tablespoon olive oil (optional)
¼ teaspoon black pepper
6 split chicken breasts

BASIC BALANCER
6 servings
Overnight

In a food processor or blender process onions, garlic and lemon extract until a smooth paste is formed.
Add yogurt and tandoori spice blend, oil, salt and pepper. Clean and skin chicken breasts and pat dry.
With a sharp knife, make three diagonal slashes on each piece of chicken. Place chicken in pan and cover
with marinade, turning to coat. Refrigerate 3–24 hours. Preheat oven to 475 degrees. Place chicken on
nonstick or foil-lined pan, bake 20–25 minutes. Great served with quinoa grain.

 *Tandoori spice blend can be found in the spice section of the grocery store. It is a combination of corian-
 der, ginger, cumin, cloves, nutmeg, cinnamon, turmeric, cayenne pepper, cardamom and paprika. Boneless breast of chicken or chicken tenders may be substituted for chicken breasts.*

Tandoori Chicken Shish-Ka-Bob

4 boneless breasts of chicken,
   uncooked and cubed
1 tablespoon tandoori spice blend
2 cups yogurt
Use all or a combination of the following:
   1 medium onion, cubed
   8 cherry tomatoes
   8 medium whole mushrooms
   8 chunks green pepper
   8 chunks zucchini

BASIC BALANCER
4 servings
6–11 hours

Marinate cubed chicken breasts in tandoori spice and yogurt for 5–10 hours. Cube vegetables as close to the same size as possible. Alternate vegetables with chicken on skewers and broil until done, turning once to prevent burning.

℮ *Tandoori spice blend can be found in the spice section of most grocery stores.*

Dehydrated Foods

Dehydrating foods is a great way to preserve and store your food supply. Dried foods cut down on space consumption and can maintain their quality for years if properly prepared and sealed.

Store dried foods in clean jars with tightly sealed lids. Plastic containers and bags allow moisture from the air to penetrate the food. Even indirect sunlight can quickly deteriorate dried foods, so keep containers in a dark place. Make sure jars are labeled clearly. Remember to use quality foods when dehydrating. Poor quality foods will not improve with drying.

When dehydrated foods are reconstituted, they return to their original volume. For, example, a quart of sliced carrots dries to about ½ cup. When reconstituted with water or broth, they return to their original volume of one quart. If foods get over dried and too hard to eat, just add a few drops of water, shake in a jar, and let stand for 30–60 minutes. This will make the food soft and pliable again. Conversely, if dried foods absorb moisture, simply place them back in the dehydrator to dry.

Each dehydrator comes with an instruction booklet that includes the cooking times for various foods. Circulating air, not heat, dries the foods. Most foods can be dried at 90 degrees. Thicker foods like fruit leathers and sauces should be dried at around 110–115 degrees, just high enough to retard mold growth. Although higher temperatures dry foods faster, lower temperatures maximize the preservation of enzymes. Drying time for foods varies due to the inherent differences in fruits and vegetables. In order to allow the air to circulate properly, distribute food pieces so they do not touch each other on the drying trays.

I prefer the Excalibur dehydrator because of its size, temperature range, ease of cleaning, and nonstick drying sheets for wet foods. Small, round, on-the-counter dehydrators can be used, but make sure they have a fan and temperature control. If the heat cannot be adjusted, the trays have to be rotated every 1–2 hours or the food on the bottom will cook and sometimes burn.

To dry loose herbs, such as mint, comfrey, or uva ursi, place them in the bottom of a large paper bag and hang in a dark place, like a closet. Shake the bag daily to change the position of the overlapped leaves. Herbs can also be bundled with twist ties, string, or rubber bands and hung in a dark place to dry. Dry and store herbs in whole leaf form because the flavor and volatile oils escape as soon as herb leaves are crushed. Stored properly, whole leaves retain their quality for many years.

Solar dehydrators and sun-drying methods deteriorate the nutritional value and destroy the color of foods. It is not recommended unless there is no other choice for dehydrating.

Almost any food can be dehydrated. Dried fruits and vegetables make great snacks. Cutting fruits and vegetables into bite-size pieces makes them easy to use. Also the uniform shape provides reconstitution within the same cooking time.

Slice foods on the thick side, especially for watery foods like cucumbers, tomatoes, melons and peaches. Thin pieces will become brittle and hard to remove from the trays. Cut cherry tomatoes in half and lay cut side down on the trays to prevent curling. A medium peach can be cut into 12–16 wedges. Melons should be cut into 1-inch squares. When drying green beans or any food with a seed, make sure they are thoroughly dried.

Spice powders, dried soup or stew, rose petals, and applesauce are some simple dried foods. For spice powders, separately dry radishes, garlic, or paprika peppers. When they are completely dry, grind into powders, sift and use in sauces, salad dressings, and sprinkle on sandwiches and in quesadillas.

Extra soups or stews can be dehydrated for later use or on the next camping trip. When drying wet foods like soups or sauces, place chopsticks or pencils under the four sides of the nonstick sheets to keep the food from running over.

Dry fragrant rose petals for tea. Just remove all the petals and lay them on the drying trays. Place a loose screen on top to prevent them from blowing around inside the dehydrator.

Whole blueberries and cranberries dehydrate into hard balls. They come back to life when reconstituted for pancakes, dessert breads, cookies and muffins. They can also be crumbled dry and used in batter.

Commercial mushrooms can be dehydrated sliced or whole. Crumble dried mushrooms and add them to foods.

Make applesauce by adding water to dried apple slices and simmering for about 15 minutes. Sprinkle with cinnamon and maple sugar.

Experiment with the recipes in this section. Have fun exploring the realm of dehydrated foods.

Banana Chips

4 ripe bananas

DEEP CLEANSER
4 servings
14 hours

Slice bananas crosswise, ¼-inch thick. Lay on mesh dehydrator trays. Dehydrate 7–14 hours at 125–140 degrees, until completely dry. Store in glass jars with tight lids.

ℰ *For dried banana sticks, follow recipe for Banana Chips. Instead of slicing bananas into chips, cut in half lengthwise and then cut each piece in half crosswise. Bake at 135–145 degrees.*

Beet Chips

4 beets

DEEP CLEANSER
4 servings
10 hours

Remove beet tops and clean beet bulbs. Slice ⅛-inch thick by hand or with a food processor. Lay slices on a mesh dehydrator tray. Dehydrate 6–10 hours at 115–125 degrees, or until completely dry and crisp. Store in a glass jar with a tight lid.

ℰ *Beware, this snack will turn your tongue red!*

Cashew Yogurt

1 cup raw cashews
1 cup water

PHASE FOUR
6 servings
8 hours

Purée cashews and water in a blender. Add more water if needed to make consistency of heavy cream. Pour into glass jar and cover with cheesecloth, towel, or napkin. Set jar in dehydrator for 6–8 hours at 90–100 degrees, until it tastes tart and sour. Yields about 2 cups. Jar may also be wrapped in a blanket or down jacket and put in a warm place. The process will take longer as the temperature will be lower.

✑ *Almonds may be substituted, but they need to be soaked overnight first.*

Dehydrated Tomato Sauce

Basil Tomato Sauce or Quick Red Sauce

DEEP CLEANSER
4 servings
12 hours

Double or triple the sauce recipe. Add extra spices as the herbs and spice flavors diminish in the drying process. Sauce can be puréed in the blender or run through a juicer for a smoother texture. Place in dehydrator on 85–90 degree setting, until completely dry, 10–12 hours. To prevent sauce from running off dehydrator trays, place chopsticks or pencils under the four edges of nonstick sheets. Each tray holds about 2 cups of sauce. To reconstitute, put in a saucepan and cover with water. Simmer 10–15 minutes, checking occasionally in case more water is needed.

✑ *Dehydrated fresh, cooked tomato sauce preserves more nutrients than simmering for hours. For tomato paste, reconstitute tomato sauce with less water. For a tomato broth, use more water to reconstitute than for sauce. Drying tomato sauce adds a sun-dried tomato flavor.*

Fruit Leather

Although personal preference will dictate your choice of fruit, here are some suggestions:

apricot, banana, peach, rhubarb with rose hips,
bananas with hazelnut butter, or strawberry
(Remember not to mix fruits)

Wash and cut fruit, removing any bruises and blemishes. Fruit leather can be made with either raw or cooked fruits. To cook fruits, place in a sauce pan with a little water and cook, stirring occasionally. If the fruit is bland, simply add a sweetener, extract or other flavoring when cooking to enhance the taste. Using a food processor, blend raw or cooked fruit and add sweetener and/or herbs. Spread 2–3 cups of this fruit purée on nonstick sheets, making about a 13-inch square. Dehydrate 10–15 hours at 125–135 degrees, or until completely dry. Flip the square ⅔ through to speed up the drying process. Once dry, cut the square with a scissors or knife into 2 × 2-inch or 3 × 3-inch squares. Roll up each square, wrapping individually in plastic wrap and then in a plastic bag. Or, rolls can be stored in a small, wide jar with a tight lid.

℮ *Fruit leathers are a great on-the-go snack.*

Maple Taffy

32 ounces yogurt
1 cup maple syrup

SUPER CLEANSER
12 servings
24 hours

In a medium bowl, blend ingredients together. Pour mixture onto dehydrating trays covered with plastic wrap and spread into rectangles ⅛-inch thick at the center and ¼-inch thick at the edges. Dehydrate until mixture is pliable like leather, about 4–6 hours. Cut rectangles in half and roll up from long side. Cut logs into pieces with scissors. Place pieces back into dehydrator for an hour to dry edges. Store in airtight container.

℮ *For Pumpkin Maple Taffy, add ½ cup pumpkin, 1 teaspoon cinnamon, and ½ teaspoon pumpkin pie spice. Other flavors can be made by adding puréed fruit or extracts.*

Tomato Leather

4 ripe tomatoes

DEEP CLEANSER

4 servings

10 minutes

Cut tomatoes and purée in blender or food processor until smooth. Pour onto a nonstick solid dehydrator tray. Spread evenly about ¼-inch thick. Dehydrate 6–10 hours at 115–125. Cut into strips or squares and make rolls. Store in airtight glass jars or plastic bags. This vegetable snack can't be beat!

How thick the spread is on the trays determines the consistency. The thicker the spread, the chewier the leather. For a spicy snack, add ¼ teaspoon garlic powder, 1 tablespoon onion powder, and a dash of cayenne pepper. For herbed tomato leather, add 1 teaspoon each of dried oregano, thyme, and basil.

Zucchini Chips

2 medium zucchini, sliced crosswise ¼-inch thick
3 tablespoons tamari sauce or miso, diluted
  with water
½ teaspoon garlic powder
½ teaspoon onion powder
dash of cayenne pepper

DEEP CLEANSER

4 servings

8 hours

In a small bowl, combine tamari, and spices. Place zucchini slices on mesh dehydrator trays and brush the tamari/miso mixture over the top. Dehydrate 5–8 hours at 115–125 degrees, until completely dried.

Zucchini slices can also be dehydrated plain, without spices.

Cakes and Sweets

These recipes introduce a wide variety of cakes and sweets from Carob Pound Cake to Baked Bananas.

In the Basic Diets, maple syrup is the primary sweetener used since it's the easiest to digest. As you progress through the levels of the diet, other natural sweeteners may be substituted.

Many baking recipes call for melted butter. An easy way to melt butter without using a microwave is to put it in a small ovenproof dish and toast on the light setting in the toaster oven.

Treat your body to an easily prepared, tasty, and safe snack.

Apricot Cake

½ cup chopped dried apricots
4 tablespoons water
2½ cups sprouted spelt flour
1 teaspoon baking powder
½ teaspoon baking soda
¼ teaspoon salt
½ cup butter, at room temperature
1¼ cups maple sugar
3 large eggs
1 teaspoon vanilla extract
1 cup Yogurt Cheese, at room temperature

DEEP CLEANSER
8 servings
1 hour

Preheat oven to 325 degrees. In a small bowl, soak apricots in the water. Grease and flour an 8 cup bundt pan. In a small bowl, combine flour, baking powder, baking soda, and salt; set aside. Using an electric mixer, beat the butter at medium speed until creamy, about 30 seconds. Add the sugar and beat until light and fluffy, about 5 minutes, stopping the mixer to scrape the sides occasionally. Add eggs, vanilla, Yogurt Cheese, and dry ingredients, one at a time, mixing each just until blended. Gently fold in apricots and water mixture. Spread batter evenly in the pan. Bake 35–40 minutes or until cake springs back when lightly touched. Cool in the pan for 10 minutes, then invert cake onto rack and cool completely. Cut and serve.

Cake may be topped with Maple Frosting or garnished with Yogurt Cheese Whipping Cream. Recipe can also be baked in a mini bundt pan that makes 8 individual cakes; bake for 30 minutes. Basic Balancers may substitute sour cream for Yogurt Cheese.

Apricot Yogurt Parfait

2¼ cups yogurt
4 tablespoons maple syrup
6 apricots

SUPER CLEANSER
4 servings
10 minutes

Wash, cut in half, remove pits and chop apricots. Combine all the ingredients and divide between 4 individual glasses. Chill until ready to serve.

Baked Bananas

1½ teaspoons butter
2 bananas
2 teaspoons 100% cranberry juice
4 teaspoons maple sugar
¼ teaspoon cinnamon

DEEP CLEANSER
2 servings
20 minutes

Heat oven to 400 degrees. In a baking dish, melt butter in the heated oven for about 5 minutes, until butter melts. Slice the bananas in half lengthwise and crosswise and turn the quarters in the butter so they are coated. Sprinkle the bananas with the cranberry juice, sugar, and cinnamon. Bake about 10 minutes. Serve with vanilla yogurt if desired.

Banana Cheesecake

CRUST:
    1 Sprouted Graham Cracker pie crust

FILLING:
    2 cups Yogurt Cheese
    ½ cup maple sugar
    2 mashed bananas
    1 tablespoon vanilla extract
    4 large eggs (or 6 egg whites)

TOPPING:
    1½ cups yogurt
    1 tablespoon maple sugar
    1 tablespoon vanilla extract

DEEP CLEANSER
8 servings
4 hours

Preheat oven to 350 degrees. For the crust: Make Sprouted Graham Cracker Crust and press crumbs up side and bottom of 9-inch spring form pan. For the filling: Blend bananas, sugar, and vanilla in a food processor. Add eggs one at a time. Add Yogurt Cheese, blend and pour into crust. Bake 30 minutes. For the topping: Mix topping ingredients in a small bowl. Remove cheesecake from oven and spread on the topping. Return to oven for 5 minutes. Cool, then chill.

Banana Cream Parfait

2 cups Yogurt Cheese
3 tablespoons maple syrup
3 teaspoons vanilla extract
2 ripe bananas, thinly sliced

DEEP CLEANSER
4 servings
5 minutes

Mix all ingredients in a medium bowl. Spoon into tall glasses or dessert bowls. Serve chilled.

Caramel Corn

1½ cups maple syrup
⅛ teaspoon cream of tartar
1 tablespoon butter
2 quarts popped corn

BASIC BALANCER
8 servings
35 minutes

Place popped corn in a large bowl. In a large saucepan, whisk the cream of tartar into the syrup and bring to a boil. Continue boiling at about 265 degrees, stirring occasionally, until syrup thickens and caramelizes, for 10–12 minutes. Grease a baking sheet with cooking spray. Remove thickened syrup from heat, mix in butter and pour over popped corn. Working quickly, coat corn with caramel and turn out on prepared sheet. Pat into one layer. Let cool. Break into pieces and serve. Store in airtight container.

Carob Fudge

1 tablespoon softened butter
½ teaspoon vanilla extract
½ cup carob powder
¼ cup maple syrup
¼ cup toasted quinoa flakes (optional)

SUPER CLEANSER
12 servings
10 minutes

Mix butter, vanilla, carob and maple syrup into a smooth stiff dough. Add toasted quinoa flakes for a crunchy texture. Spread in a pan or roll into twelve 1-inch balls. Chill.

Carob Fudge Nut Balls

1 cup hazelnut butter
1 cup maple syrup
1 cup carob powder
1 teaspoon vanilla extract
½ cup dried unsweetened coconut

PHASE TWO
12 servings
20 minutes

Mix all ingredients except coconut in a medium bowl. Chill for 15 minutes. Form into teaspoon-size balls and roll in dried coconut. Serve or keep refrigerated.

Carob Pound Cake

6 tablespoons butter, at room temperature
1¼ cups maple sugar
1 cup sprouted spelt flour plus 2 tablespoons
6 tablespoons carob powder
½ teaspoon baking soda
¼ teaspoon baking powder
¼ teaspoon salt
1 large egg
2 large egg whites
6 tablespoons yogurt
1 teaspoon vanilla
2 tablespoons water

DEEP CLEANSER
12 servings
1 hour 15 minutes

Preheat oven to 350 degrees. Spray 6 to 8 cup bundt pan with cooking spray. In medium bowl, combine flour, carob, baking soda, baking powder and salt. In small bowl, whisk egg and egg whites until blended. Combine yogurt, vanilla, and water in a separate bowl. Using electric mixer, beat butter and sugar until blended, about 3 minutes. Gradually add egg mixture, beat until smooth, about 3 minutes. At low speed, add flour mixture alternately with yogurt mixture in 3 additions. Beat until combined. Transfer to prepared pan. Bake 35–40 minutes, until tester inserted in center comes out clean. Cool in pan on rack 10 minutes. Turn out cake onto rack, cool completely.

Can be made 3 days ahead. Cover tightly and let stand at room temperature. Serve with Maple Frosting drizzled on top if desired.

Carob Sour Cream Cake

1 large egg
1 cup maple sugar
¼ teaspoon salt
½ cup sour cream
1 ½ cups sprouted spelt flour
1 teaspoon baking soda
1 teaspoon vanilla
½ cup boiling water
4 tablespoons carob powder

Preheat oven to 350 degrees. In a medium mixing bowl, beat the egg and add the sugar and salt. In a separate bowl, mix the sour cream, flour, soda and vanilla. Add this mixture to the egg mixture and stir until smooth. In a small bowl, mix carob powder and boiling water by stirring with a fork; mix into batter and evenly distribute in a 9-inch cake pan. Bake 20–25 minutes, or until done.

ᴄ *Can be frosted with Maple Sugar Icing.*

Crunch Parfait

2 cups crushed corn flakes
¼ cup coconut, shredded (optional)
¼ cup maple sugar
2 tablespoons melted butter
½ teaspoon vanilla extract
1 cup Cranberry Spread
1 cup Yogurt Cheese
¼ cup maple syrup

BASIC BALANCER
4 servings
20 minutes

Put corn flakes in a plastic bag and use rolling pin to crush. Place corn flakes and coconut in medium bowl. Add sugar, butter, and vanilla and mix. In a small bowl mix Yogurt Cheese and maple syrup. Layer ½ of the crumb mixture, Cranberry Spread, and yogurt mixture, in 4 glasses. Repeat layers with remaining ½ crumbs, Cranberry Spread and yogurt mixture. Chill and serve.

Carrot Cake

⅓ cup soft butter
2 cups maple syrup
½ cup Yogurt Cheese
2 large eggs
2 large egg whites
1 teaspoon vanilla extract
2 cups quinoa flour
2 teaspoons cinnamon
2 teaspoons baking powder
1 teaspoon baking soda
½ teaspoon salt
2 cups grated carrots

SUPER CLEANSER

8 servings

1 hour

Preheat oven to 350 degrees. In a large bowl, cream butter and syrup. Beat in Yogurt Cheese, eggs, egg whites and vanilla. Combine flour, cinnamon, baking powder, baking soda, salt and add to creamed mixture; mix well. Let batter stand for 5 minutes. Stir in grated carrots. For a layer cake, turn batter into two greased and floured 8 or 9-inch baking pans. Bake 35–40 minutes. Or use a 9 × 13-inch pan and bake 45–50 minutes. Cool for 10 minutes and turn onto wire racks. Let cool and top with Yogurt Cheese Frosting or Cream Cheese Frosting.

⤳ *Basic Balancers may substitute 1 cup of corn flour for 1 cup of quinoa flour.*

Creamy Maple Yogurt

1 cup Yogurt Cheese
¼ cup maple syrup

SUPER CLEANSER

2 servings

10 minutes

Whisk ingredients until smooth. Serve over fruit or enjoy as custard.

Fruit Cobbler with Maple Topping

6 cups fresh or frozen apricots (2 pounds),
    sliced ½-inch thick
¼ cup maple sugar
1 tablespoon arrowroot
¾ cup quinoa flour
¼ cup quinoa flakes
⅔ cup maple sugar
½ cup butter

SUPER CLEANSER
6 servings
45 minutes

Preheat oven to 375 degrees. Grease a 10-inch baking pan and arrange apricots in bottom. Fold in ¼ cup sugar and arrowroot into apricots. In a large bowl, mix flour, flakes, and ⅔ cup sugar. Using a pastry knife, cut in butter until mixture is crumbly and well combined. Sprinkle the crumb mixture topping evenly over the fruit. Bake 25–30 minutes, until the topping is light brown.

  Deep Cleaners and beyond may substitute 1 cup sprouted or 1 cup corn flour for quinoa flour. Other fruits may be substituted as they come back into the diet.

Gingerbread

1½ cups maple syrup
1 tablespoon butter
1 cup Yogurt Cheese
2 large eggs
2 cups quinoa flour
1 tablespoon ground ginger
1 teaspoon baking powder
1 teaspoon cinnamon
½ teaspoon nutmeg
½ teaspoon salt

SUPER CLEANSER
9 servings
45 minutes

Preheat oven to 350 degrees. In a mixing bowl, cream syrup and butter. Beat in eggs and Yogurt Cheese, mix until smooth. Add remaining ingredients and mix well. Spread in an 9 × 9-inch greased and floured baking pan. Bake 25–30 minutes, until toothpick inserted in the center comes out clean.

  Deep Cleansers and beyond may substitute quinoa flour with sprouted wheat flour. Phase Four may substitute ¾ cup honey or molasses for ¾ cup maple syrup.

Layered Cheesecake

1 Corn Flake Crust

BOTTOM LAYER:
8 ounces Yogurt Cheese (kefir or cream cheese),
   at room temperature
½ cup maple syrup
2 large eggs
½ teaspoon vanilla extract

TOP LAYER:
1 cup Yogurt Cheese (sour cream),
   at room temperature
1 cup water
¼ cup maple syrup (or to taste)
½ teaspoon vanilla extract
⅛ teaspoon cinnamon

BASIC BALANCER
8 servings
1 hour

Preheat oven to 325 degrees. For the bottom layer: Blend Yogurt Cheese and syrup in a medium bowl. Add eggs and vanilla. Pour into Corn Flake Crust. Bake for 25–30 minutes or until firm. For the top layer: Blend Yogurt Cheese, water, syrup, vanilla and cinnamon. Spread over baked layer and return to the oven for an additional 5 minutes. Cool, then chill.

༄ *Deep Cleansers and Basic Balancers may use ingredients listed in the parenthesis when appropriate.*

Maple Bundt Cake

1 large egg
1 cup maple syrup
1 teaspoon vanilla
2 tablespoons melted butter
2 tablespoons Yogurt Cheese
¼ cup water
1½ cups sprouted spelt flour
1½ teaspoons baking powder
¼ teaspoon salt

DEEP CLEANSER
8 servings
55 minutes

Preheat oven to 350 degrees. Beat the egg thoroughly, add syrup, vanilla, butter, Yogurt Cheese, water, and dry ingredients. Bake for 40–45 minutes in a greased six cup bundt pan or loaf pan.

Maple Layer Cake

⅔ cup softened butter
2 cups sprouted spelt flour
1 cup maple sugar
2½ teaspoons baking powder
½ cup maple syrup
¼ cup yogurt
½ teaspoon vanilla extract
2 large eggs

DEEP CLEANSER
8 servings
45 minutes

Preheat oven to 350 degrees. Cream butter and sugar. Add the flour, salt, baking powder, and liquid ingredients. Mix. Pour into a greased and floured 9-inch pan. Bake for 30–35 minutes.

Angel Food Cake

½ cup sprouted spelt flour
½ cup sprouted seed flour
1½ cups maple sugar
1½ cups egg whites (10–12 large eggs)
1 teaspoon cream of tartar
1 teaspoon vanilla extract
¼ teaspoon almond extract (optional)
¼ teaspoon salt (optional)

DEEP CLEANSER
10 servings
1 hour

Preheat oven to 350 degrees. In a medium bowl combine flours, and ¾ cup maple sugar. In a separate bowl whip egg whites and cream of tartar with electric beater until foamy. Gradually beat in the remaining ¾ cups sugar. Add the extracts and salt. Beat just until stiff peaks form. Do not overbeat. With a large whisk or spatula fold the flour mixture by thirds into the egg whites. Place the batter in an ungreased 10-inch tube pan. Bake for 25–30 minutes or until the cake is golden brown and springs back when touched. Invert the cake until cool. Remove it from the pan and serve.

∽ *Serve cake plain or drizzle Maple Caramel Frosting over the top.*

Marbeled Pumpkin Cheesecake

1 Corn Flake Crust
2 packages cream cheese (8 ounces each)
¾ cup maple sugar
2 large eggs
1½ teaspoons pumpkin pie spice
1 pound canned pumpkin

PHASE TWO
10 servings
1 hour 30 minutes

Preheat oven to 325 degrees. With an electric mixer, beat together the cheese and maple sugar until blended. Add eggs one at a time, beating well after each addition. Remove ½ cup of the cheese mixture and set it aside. Stir in pie spice and the pumpkin into the remaining mixture until they are well blended. Pour pumpkin mixture into prepared crust. Drop teaspoons of the reserved cheese mixture randomly over the pumpkin mixture. With a knife or metal spatula, swirl the blade through the white and orange mixtures to marble.

Bake about 50 minutes, until the center barely jiggles when the cake is gently shaken. Cool on a rack. Cover and chill until cold, at least 2½ hours or up to one day. If using a spring form pan, run a knife around the edge before removing pan sides.

Vanilla Custard

2 cups Yogurt Cheese
½ cup water
½ cup maple sugar
2 large eggs
1 teaspoon vanilla
cinnamon

SUPER CLEANSER
6 servings
2 hours

Preheat oven to 325 degrees. In a small saucepan, mix Yogurt Cheese and water, stir in sugar. Over low heat without letting it boil, stir to dissolve sugar. Beat the eggs in a medium bowl. Add vanilla extract. Gradually whisk the hot yogurt into egg mixture. Pour custard into 6 individual custard cups. Dust with cinnamon. Place custard cups in baking pan and add warm water, at least 1-inch up the sides. Bake 35–40 minutes. Remove custard cups from water and chill.

༄ *Deep Cleansers may substitute 1 cup of kefir cheese for Yogurt Cheese. Basic Balancers may substitute with sour cream, or any combination of sour cream, Yogurt Cheese and kefir cheese to make 2 cups.*

No Bake Pudding

1 package Mori-Nu Mates, Vanilla
   or Lemon Pudding Mix (4 ounces)
1½ cups Yogurt Cheese
3 tablespoons water

CORE DIET
4 servings
30 minutes

Place Yogurt Cheese in a blender, pulse until smooth. Add water and blend until creamy. Add pudding powder and blend again. Stop machine and scrape down sides. Continue blending 2 minutes until pudding is light and creamy. Scoop into pudding cups. Chill and serve. Store in refrigerator.

⌒ ½ cup sour cream or kefir cheese can be substituted for ½ cup Yogurt Cheese.

Poppy Seed Pound Cake

3 cups sprouted spelt flour
⅓ cup poppy seeds
1½ teaspoons baking powder
¾ teaspoon salt
1 cup butter, at room temperature
1⅔ cups maple sugar
6 large egg whites
½ cup yogurt
2 drops lemon extract

DEEP CLEANSER
12 servings
1 hour 20 minutes

Preheat oven to 350 degrees. Grease and flour a 12 cup bundt pan. In a medium bowl, whisk together flour, poppy seeds, baking powder, and salt. Set aside. In a large bowl, cream butter and sugar until the mixture is fluffy. Beat in egg whites one at a time, beating well after each addition. Beat in yogurt and lemon extract. In three additions, beat in flour mixture, scraping down sides of bowl occasionally. Spoon the batter evenly into the prepared pan and bake until the cake is lightly browned and a toothpick inserted into the center comes out clean, about 35–40 minutes. Let cool in pan 10 minutes. Invert onto wire rack and cool completely.

⌒ Poppy seeds digest as a vegetable!

Brownie Sheet Cake

4 cups sprouted spelt flour
2 cups maple sugar
2 teaspoons baking soda
1 teaspoon cinnamon
¼ teaspoon salt
1 cup water
½ cup butter
¼ cup carob powder
¼ cup Yogurt Cheese
2 large eggs
1 teaspoon vanilla extract
Maple Frosting or maple cream

DEEP CLEANSER
24 servings
25 minutes

Preheat oven 375 degrees. Grease a 15 × 10-inch jelly roll pan with ghee or butter. Combine flour, sugar, baking soda, cinnamon and salt in a large bowl. Place butter, water and carob powder in a small saucepan; heat until butter is melted, stirring frequently. Remove from heat and add to flour mixture. Beat until well blended. Add Yogurt Cheese, eggs and vanilla extract, beat well. Pour batter into prepared pan. Bake 17 minutes or until toothpick comes out clean. Top with Maple Frosting or maple cream.

Pumpkin Cake

3 cups quinoa flour
2 teaspoons baking powder
2 teaspoons baking soda
1 tablespoon ground allspice
1 tablespoon ground cloves
1 tablespoon ground cinnamon
1 tablespoon ground ginger
¼ cup softened butter
2 cups maple sugar
4 large eggs
3 cups pumpkin, fresh or canned
1 teaspoon vanilla extract

SUPER CLEANSER
12 servings
1 hour 30 minutes

Preheat oven to 350 degrees. Grease 12 cup bundt pan. Sift first 7 ingredients into medium bowl. Using electric mixer, beat butter and 2 cups of maple sugar in large bowl to blend. Add eggs one at a time, beating well after each addition. Add pumpkin and vanilla and beat until combined. Stir in dry ingredients. Transfer batter to prepared pan. Bake until tester inserted near center comes out clean, about an hour. Cool cake in pan on rack 20 minutes. Turn out cake onto rack and cool completely.

~ *4 teaspoons pumpkin pie spice can be substituted for individual spices.*

Pumpkin Chiffon Pie

1 Sprouted Pie Crust
1½ cups canned pumpkin
  (or fresh cooked, puréed)
1 large egg yolk, lightly beaten
1 cup yogurt
1 tablespoon arrowroot
½ cup maple syrup
2 tablespoons melted butter
1 teaspoon cinnamon
½ teaspoon ginger
¼ teaspoon salt
¼ teaspoon nutmeg
¼ teaspoon cloves
3 large egg whites

DEEP CLEANSER
8 servings
1 hour

Preheat oven to 450 degrees. In a large bowl, mix pumpkin, egg yolk, yogurt, arrowroot, maple syrup, butter, spices, and salt until smooth. In another bowl, beat egg whites until stiff peaks form. Fold egg whites into pumpkin mixture. Pour into prepared Sprouted Pie Crust or in a greased pan without a crust. Bake for 10 minutes at 450 degrees. Reduce heat to 350 degrees for 30–35 minutes or until knife inserted in the center comes out clean. Cool.

Pan-Fried Apricots

1 tablespoon butter
8 fresh apricots, halved
2 tablespoons maple syrup

SUPER CLEANSER
4 servings
10 minutes

Melt butter in skillet over medium heat. Wash apricots, cut in half and remove pits. Add apricots to skillet and cook for 1 minute. Drizzle syrup over apricots and cook 2–3 minutes longer until apricots are slightly browned but still keep their shape.

Pumpkin Spice Cake

3 cups sprouted spelt flour
2 teaspoons baking powder
2 teaspoons baking soda
2 teaspoons pumpkin pie spice
2 teaspoons cinnamon
½ cup butter, softened
2¼ cups maple sugar
4 egg whites
½ cup yogurt
½ cup water
2 cups canned pumpkin
1 teaspoon vanilla

DEEP CLEANSER
12 servings
1 hour 20 minutes

Preheat oven to 350 degrees. Spray 12 cup bundt pan with cooking spray. Put first six ingredients in medium bowl. Using electric mixer, beat butter and maple sugar in large bowl to blend. Add egg whites one at a time, beating well after each addition. Add yogurt, water, pumpkin, and vanilla, beat until combined. Stir in dry ingredients. Transfer to prepared pan. Bake until tester inserted comes out clean, about 45 minutes. Cool cake in pan on rack 20 minutes. Turn out cake onto rack and cool completely.

Yogurt Sundae

1 cup yogurt
2 tablespoons maple syrup
2 tablespoons Granola
2 ripe bananas, sliced

DEEP CLEANSER
2 servings
5 minutes

Blend maple syrup into yogurt and divide between two dessert bowls. Top with banana slices and Granola.

Upside-Down Apricot Cake

CARAMEL:
- ½ cup maple sugar
- 3 tablespoons water

CAKE:
- 4 medium ripe apricots, pit and cut each
  into four wedges
- 2 cups sprouted spelt flour
- 1 ½ teaspoons baking powder
- ¼ teaspoon cinnamon
- ¼ teaspoon salt
- ½ cup softened butter
- 1 ¼ cup maple sugar
- ½ teaspoon vanilla extract
- 3 large egg whites
- ¼ cup Yogurt Cheese
- ½ cup water

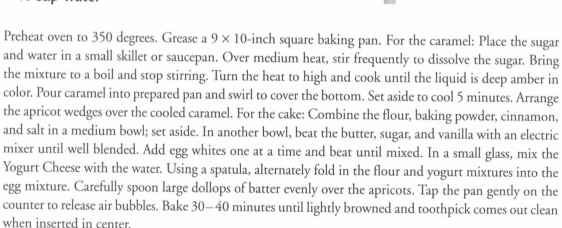

Preheat oven to 350 degrees. Grease a 9 × 10-inch square baking pan. For the caramel: Place the sugar and water in a small skillet or saucepan. Over medium heat, stir frequently to dissolve the sugar. Bring the mixture to a boil and stop stirring. Turn the heat to high and cook until the liquid is deep amber in color. Pour caramel into prepared pan and swirl to cover the bottom. Set aside to cool 5 minutes. Arrange the apricot wedges over the cooled caramel. For the cake: Combine the flour, baking powder, cinnamon, and salt in a medium bowl; set aside. In another bowl, beat the butter, sugar, and vanilla with an electric mixer until well blended. Add egg whites one at a time and beat until mixed. In a small glass, mix the Yogurt Cheese with the water. Using a spatula, alternately fold in the flour and yogurt mixtures into the egg mixture. Carefully spoon large dollops of batter evenly over the apricots. Tap the pan gently on the counter to release air bubbles. Bake 30–40 minutes until lightly browned and toothpick comes out clean when inserted in center.

Remove pan from oven and run a knife around the edge of the cake. Put a plate or cutting board on top of the pan. Invert but do not remove the pan for 5 minutes to let the caramel and fruit cool slightly. Remove pan and serve warm or at room temperature.

Frostings and Toppings

Cream Cheese Frosting

1 cup softened cream cheese
½ cup maple syrup

PHASE TWO
8 servings
10 minutes

In a medium bowl, whip ingredients, or use an electric mixer. Spread over cake. Thin with maple syrup to drizzle over cake. Yields about 1½ cups frosting.

Hazelnut Butter Topping

1 cup hazelnut butter
½ cup maple syrup

PHASE TWO
4 servings
5 minutes

Blend ingredients until smooth. Make desired consistency by adjusting syrup amount. Great served over French Vanilla Frozen Yogurt.

Maple Caramel Frosting

1 cup maple syrup
5 tablespoons yogurt

SUPER CLEANSER
8 servings
10 minutes

In a 10 × 12-inch heavy frying pan, over medium heat, slowly pour in maple syrup until it just covers the bottom. Adjust amount based on the size of the pan. When it is warm to the touch, add 5 tablespoons of yogurt. Stir constantly until it thickens. Immediately spread it on top of cake as a quick glaze. It is not intended to cover the cake entirely.

Maple Crumb Cobbler Topping

¾ cup quinoa flour
¼ cup quinoa flakes
⅔ cup maple sugar
½ cup butter

SUPER CLEANSER
6 servings
45 minutes

In a small bowl, combine flour, flakes, and sugar. Using a pastry knife or fork, cut in butter until mixture is crumbly and well combined.

↪ *Place 1–2 pounds of fruit mixed with ¼ cup maple sugar in a 10-inch baking pan. Sprinkle crumb topping over fruit. Bake 25–30 minutes at 375 degrees, until topping is golden brown. Deep Cleansers and beyond may substitute 1 cup of sprouted or corn flour for quinoa flour.*

Maple Frosting

3 cups maple sugar
½ cup softened butter
3 tablespoons Yogurt Cheese
¼ cup maple syrup
½ teaspoon vanilla extract

SUPER CLEANSER
8 servings
15 minutes

Cream sugar and butter in a large bowl. Add Yogurt Cheese, syrup, and vanilla. Beat on high until frosting reaches spreading consistency. Yields about 2 cups.

Maple Sugar Icing

1 cup maple sugar
1 cup sour cream

BASIC BALANCER
8 servings
15 minutes

In a small saucepan, bring ingredients to a boil and cook, stirring over medium-low heat 15 minutes, until the frosting thickens. Cool slightly and spread over 9-inch single layer cake.

↪ *Try frosting over Carob Sour Cream Cake.*

Yogurt Cheese Frosting

1 cup Yogurt Cheese
6 tablespoons maple syrup
¼ cup melted butter
1 ½ teaspoons vanilla
2 drops lemon or orange extract or to taste

SUPER CLEANSER
4 servings
5 minutes

Mix all ingredients until smooth.

⌐ *For carob frosting add ¼ cup carob powder and omit extract. For a fruit frosting, add ½ cup additional Yogurt Cheese, then add puréed dates or apricots or other fruit to taste.*

Yogurt Cheese Whipping Cream

1 cup slightly thinned Yogurt Cheese
   (to consistency of sour cream)
4 tablespoons maple syrup or maple sugar
¼ teaspoon vanilla

SUPER CLEANSER
4 servings
2 minutes

With a whisk, beat until fluffy. When using maple syrup instead of maple sugar, it is not necessary to thin Yogurt Cheese as much since the syrup is a liquid. Use more sweetener for a sweeter taste.

Frozen Desserts

Making frozen desserts is not the long process it once was. With a frozen dessert maker you can be enjoying Tangerine Sorbet within thirty minutes. (See Cooking Equipment in Chapter Two)

In lieu of a frozen dessert maker, ice cube trays may be used for these recipes.

Frozen dessert are the best when they are eaten just after freezing in the machine. The consistency is like soft ice cream. Store frozen desserts in single serving size containers as they need to thaw slightly to soften. Recycle small yogurt containers to freeze extra servings. Although, in my kitchen, there is rarely any left over to freeze.

Banana Frozen Yogurt

2 cups Yogurt Cheese
¼ cup maple syrup (or more to taste)
¼ cup kefir cheese
¼ cup water
2 medium bananas

DEEP CLEANSER
4 servings
Overnight

Purée all ingredients in a blender. Pour into ice cube trays, freeze or chill mixture overnight or process in ice cream maker according to directions.

⤷ *Krups "La Glaciere" (See Equipment) freezes the mixture in 15 minutes after it has been chilled overnight. For variation, add ¼ cup carob powder.*

French Vanilla Frozen Yogurt

3 large eggs
½ cup kefir cheese
1 ½ cups water
1 cup maple sugar
2 cups Yogurt Cheese
1 tablespoon vanilla

DEEP CLEANSER
8 servings
Overnight

Beat eggs, kefir and water together in a large saucepan. Add sugar and cook over low to medium-low heat, stirring constantly, until thickened, about 10 minutes. Do not boil. Mixture should coat the spoon. Cool, then add Yogurt Cheese and vanilla. Refrigerate overnight or process in ice cream maker or frozen dessert maker according to directions.

⤷ *Substitute cashew milk for water when cashews come back into the diet.*

Cranberry Frozen Yogurt

1 cup Yogurt Cheese
1 cup Cranberry Spread
½ cup kefir cheese
½ cup maple syrup
½ cup Cranberry Juice

DEEP CLEANSER
6 servings
Overnight

Purée all ingredients in a blender. Pour into ice cube trays, freeze or chill overnight or process in an ice cream maker.

❧ *Krups "La Glaciere" (See Equipment) freezes the mixture in 15 minutes.*

Apricot Sorbet

⅓ cup packed, dried apricots, about 15 halves
2 cups water
⅓ cup maple sugar

SUPER CLEANSER
6 servings
Overnight

Combine apricots and water in a saucepan and bring to a boil over medium-high heat. Reduce heat and simmer 30 minutes. Pour into a blender or food processor and purée. Add enough water to apricot mixture to make 4 cups. Stir in sugar. Chill thoroughly or overnight. Yields about 1 quart.

Tangerine Sorbet

2½ cups tangerine juice, fresh or frozen
1 cup maple sugar

PHASE THREE
8 servings
40 minutes

Purée juice and sugar in a blender until smooth. Pour into ice cube trays, freeze or process mixture in ice cream or frozen dessert maker.

❧ *Super Cleansers may substitute 100% apricot nectar. Frozen tangerine juice is sold in most health food stores in 10 ounce containers. This recipe uses two containers.*

Cookies, Crackers, and Bars

Thanks to essential cooking, the cookie jar can be filled! These easy recipes offer a variety of treats that can be enjoyed at home or on the run.

Granola Bars and Quinoa Flake Cookies are a lunch box delight. Using the continuous kitchen philosophy, make a double batch and freeze half.

Apricot Bars

1 ½ quinoa flour
2 tablespoons maple syrup
½ cup room temperature butter
6 fresh apricots or 1 cup finely diced
   dried apricots

SUPER CLEANSER
8 servings
25 minutes

Preheat oven to 350 degrees. In a medium bowl, mix flour, syrup and butter until coarse crumbs form. Press into a 9 × 9-inch pan. Bake 15 minutes. Cool. If using fresh apricots, slice and spread evenly on top of baked dough. If using dried apricots, soak in 1 cup of boiling water until softened. They are easier to spread if puréed in blender or food processor with soaking liquid. Spread jam-like mixture on baked crust. Cut and serve.

Carob Brownies

½ cup melted butter
2 large eggs
1 cup maple syrup
1 teaspoon vanilla extract
½ cup carob powder
1 cup quinoa flour
2 teaspoons baking powder

SUPER CLEANSER
9 servings
50 minutes

Preheat oven to 350 degrees. In a medium bowl, beat together butter, eggs, syrup, and vanilla. Add carob powder and mix well. Add flour and baking powder, mix until blended. Spread batter into an 8 × 8-inch greased baking pan. Bake for 40 minutes or until toothpick comes out clean. Let cool in the pan and cut into squares.

   Deep Cleansers may substitute sprouted seed flour for quinoa flour and Basic Balancers may substitute corn flour or a combination of the flours. Make a double batch in a 9 × 13-inch pan and bake 40 minutes. Freeze extras.

Butterscotch Brownies

1 cup maple sugar
1 large egg
¼ teaspoon salt
1 teaspoon baking powder
1 cup sprouted spelt flour
1 teaspoon vanilla extract
⅓ cup butter

DEEP CLEANSER
9 servings
30 minutes

Preheat oven to 350 degrees. In a large bowl, mix all ingredients together, except butter. Melt butter and add to mixture. Spread in an 8 × 8-inch baking pan. Bake 15 minutes, or until done.

℮ *For a larger batch of brownies, triple recipe and use a jelly roll pan (approximately 11 × 17 inches).*

Carob Cake Brownies

¼ cup melted butter
½ cup maple syrup
1 teaspoon vanilla extract
¼ cup yogurt
2 large eggs
½ cup carob powder
1 teaspoon baking powder
1 cup quinoa flour

SUPER CLEANSER
9 servings
50 minutes

Preheat oven to 350 degrees. In a large bowl, mix butter, syrup, vanilla, yogurt and eggs. Add carob, baking powder and quinoa flour. Blend. Pour batter into 8 × 8-inch greased baking pan. Bake 30–35 minutes or until knife inserted in middle comes out clean. Serve with yogurt.

℮ *Deep Cleansers may substitute quinoa flour with sprouted spelt flour and Basic Balancers may use corn flour, and serve with toasted coconut. Make a double batch in a 9 × 13-inch pan. Bake 40 minutes. Extra brownies may be frozen.*

Carob Cookies

½ cup melted butter
1 cup maple syrup
3 large eggs
2 teaspoons vanilla extract
2 cups quinoa flour
2 cups corn flour
½ cup carob powder
½ cup unsweetened shredded coconut (optional)

BASIC BALANCER
20 servings
1 hour

Preheat oven to 350 degrees. In a large bowl, whisk butter, syrup, eggs, and vanilla. In a separate bowl, combine flours and carob powder. Add to butter mixture and mix well. Add coconut if desired. Drop in tablespoonfuls onto a greased cookie sheet. Bake 8–10 minutes. Cool on wire racks and store in airtight container. Yields 5 dozen.

Cheese Crackers

½ cup softened butter
½ cup kefir cheese
1¼ cups sprouted wheat flour
1 teaspoon salt
1 teaspoon onion powder, cayenne, garlic
  powder, or green chili flakes

BASIC BALANCER
12 servings
1 hour

Using a mixer or food processor, cream butter and cheese. Add the flour, salt, and seasoning. Dough will start to form a ball as it is mixed. Divide dough into two and roll each section into a roll about 6-inches long by 1½-inches in diameter. Wrap in wax paper and chill until firm. Dough may also be frozen for later use. Preheat oven to 400 degrees. Cut dough into ⅛-inch slices and place on ungreased baking sheet. Bake 8–10 minutes, or until crisp and slightly browned. Yields 4 dozen.

Coconut Icebox Cookies

2 cups maple sugar
⅔ cup butter
2 large eggs
1 teaspoon vanilla
1 teaspoon baking soda dissolved
   in 1 tablespoon water
3 cups sprouted spelt flour
1 teaspoon cream of tartar
¼ teaspoon salt
2 cups shredded coconut

BASIC BALANCER
12 servings
4–12 hours

In an electric mixer, cream sugar and butter. Add eggs, vanilla and baking soda dissolved in water; mix well. Add flour, cream of tartar, salt and coconut; mix until blended. Divide batter in half and form each half into a roll 12-inch long. Wrap in wax paper and refrigerate 4 hours or overnight. Preheat oven to 375 degrees. Remove cookie rolls from the refrigerator and slice each roll into 24 pieces. Put on an ungreased cookie sheet and bake 8–10 minutes. Makes 4 dozen cookies.

Cranberry Cookies

½ cup butter (1 stick)
1¼ cups packed maple sugar
1 large egg, at room temperature
1 teaspoon vanilla extract
½ teaspoon baking soda
½ teaspoon cream of tartar
½ teaspoon salt
2½ cups sprouted spelt flour
½ cup coarsely chopped cranberries
24 whole cranberries, sliced in half

DEEP CLEANSER
20 servings
4 hours

Using an electric mixer, beat butter and sugar in a large bowl at medium speed until fluffy. Beat in egg, vanilla, baking soda, cream of tartar and salt. With mixer on low, beat in flour until blended. Stir in remaining ingredients except cranberries. Divide batter in half. Shape each half into an 8-inch long log. Wrap and chill until hard, about 3 hours. Heat oven to 350 degrees. With a serrated knife, cut 1 roll (keep other refrigerated) into 24 slices, about ¼-inch thick. Place 1-inch apart on a greased cookie sheet(s). Press a cranberry half on each. Bake 10 minutes until edges are golden brown. Cool on a wire rack. Yields about 4 dozen cookies.

Coconut Macaroons

5 large egg whites
⅔ cup maple sugar
6 tablespoons sprouted spelt flour
1 teaspoon vanilla extract
3 cups shredded dried coconut, unsweetened

BASIC BALANCER
10 servings
30 minutes

Preheat oven to 325 degrees. In a large mixing bowl, beat egg whites until soft peaks form. Add sugar and flour one tablespoon at a time, beating after each addition. Add vanilla and fold in coconut. Drop teaspoonfuls onto cookie sheets coated with cooking spray. Bake 10–12 minutes until edges are lightly browned. Makes about 3 dozen cookies.

Date Bars

1½ cups dried dates (8 ounces),
   pitted and finely chopped
1 teaspoon baking soda
1 cup hot water
½ cup maple sugar
4 tablespoons softened butter
1 large egg
1 large egg white
¼ teaspoon salt
1 teaspoon vanilla
1¼ cups quinoa flour

SUPER CLEANSER
9 servings
45 minutes

Heat oven to 350 degrees. Place dates in a small bowl, add baking soda and hot water. Mix and set aside to cool, about 10 minutes. In a large bowl, blend sugar and butter until crumb like. Add egg and egg white. Mix well. Add the date mixture, salt, vanilla, and flour. Mix. If using nuts, add at this time. Spoon batter into a greased 8 × 8-inch pan. Bake 25–30 minutes.

To make it easier, put dates in a food processor and pulse to finely chop. Deep Cleansers and beyond may substitute 1½ cups sprouted flour for quinoa flour. Phase Two Diet may add ½ cups chopped hazelnuts.

Date Squares

2 cups, pitted and chopped dates
1½ cups quinoa flour
1½ cups quinoa flakes
1 cup maple sugar, firmly packed
½ teaspoon baking soda
½ cup butter (1 stick)

SUPER CLEANSER
16 servings
40 minutes

Preheat oven to 350 degrees. Coat an 8-inch square baking pan with cooking spray. Place dates in a small saucepan with 1 cup water. Cook over medium heat until soft, about 12 minutes. Remove from heat and let cool. In a large bowl, combine flours, flakes, sugar, and baking soda. Add butter and blend with pastry knife or fingers until mixture resembles coarse crumbs. Spoon two-thirds of the dough into prepared pan, and press into bottom and up sides. Spread top with date mixture. Cover with remaining dough. Press lightly. Bake for 25 minutes or until edges are golden brown. Cool pan completely on a wire rack. Cut into 2-inch squares. Store in an airtight container for up to a week.

Deep Cleansers and beyond may substitute sprouted spelt flour for quinoa flour.

Fudgey Carob Brownies

1 cup carob powder
½ cup maple syrup
⅔ cup melted butter
4 large eggs
5 tablespoons quinoa flour
2 teaspoons vanilla extract

SUPER CLEANSER
12 servings
40 minutes

Preheat oven to 350 degrees. In a medium bowl, mix carob, syrup, and butter until blended. In another bowl, beat eggs until light. Add eggs to carob mixture. Stir in flour and vanilla. Spread evenly into a greased 9 × 9-inch baking pan. Bake for 25 minutes or until the surface is firm. Let cool in pan before cutting.

Deep Cleansers may substitute sprouted spelt flour for quinoa flour and Basic Balancers may substitute with corn flour. Make a double batch in a 9 × 13-inch pan, bake for 40 minutes and freeze extras.

Gingersnaps

1 ½ cups sprouted spelt flour
½ teaspoon baking soda
1 teaspoon ground cinnamon
1 teaspoon ground ginger
¼ teaspoon ground cloves
¼ cup maple sugar
¼ cup softened butter
¼ cup dark molasses
2 large egg whites
½ teaspoon salt (optional)

PHASE THREE
3 dozen cookies
45 minutes

Preheat oven to 300 degrees. Lightly grease 2 baking sheets with cooking spray. In a large bowl, combine flour, baking soda, cinnamon, ginger, and cloves. Whisk to mix. In the bowl of an electric mixer, combine sugar, butter, molasses, egg whites, and salt. Beat until smooth and creamy. Drop teaspoonfuls of dough about 1½-inch apart on baking sheets. Bake 10 minutes, until lightly browned. Remove cookies from baking sheet to cool.

Granola Bars

2 cups quinoa flakes
¼ cup maple syrup
2 teaspoons vanilla or almond extract
½ cup maple sugar
2 tablespoons melted butter
2 large egg whites, lightly beaten
¼ cup chopped dates or apricots (optional)
2 teaspoons cinnamon

SUPER CLEANSER
8 servings
1 hour 20 minutes

Preheat oven to 250 degrees. In a medium bowl, mix the ingredients, except cinnamon, in the order listed. Mix well. Place mixture in a 8 or 9-inch square nonstick or greased baking pan. Using the back of a fork or slightly moistened finger tips, press mixture evenly into a flat surface. Sprinkle the top with cinnamon. Bake 45 minutes. Remove pan from oven and while warm, cut into bars. Cool in pan. Makes 8 bars.

To make 24 bars, triple recipe and use jelly roll pan (approximately 11 × 17-inches). For variation, Basic Balancers may substitute ½ cup dried shredded coconut. Coconut extract may be used instead of vanilla.

Hazelnut Butter Cookies

½ cup hazelnut butter
½ cup softened butter
½ cup maple sugar
½ cup maple syrup
1 large egg (or two egg whites)
2 cups sprouted spelt flour
½ teaspoon baking soda
½ teaspoon baking powder
¼ teaspoon salt (optional)

PHASE TWO
5 dozen cookies
24 hours

In a large bowl, mix the hazelnut butter and butter, blend in sugar and syrup. Add the egg and beat well. In a medium bowl, mix flour, baking soda, baking powder and salt. Add to butter mixture and mix thoroughly. Chill dough 4 hours or overnight. Preheat oven to 350 degrees. Drop cookie dough by teaspoonfuls onto ungreased baking sheets, 1½-inches apart. Bake 7–8 minutes.

Chopped hazelnuts may be sprinkled on the top prior to baking if desired.

Maple Cookies

3 tablespoons butter
½ cup maple syrup
1 large egg, lightly beaten
2 tablespoons yogurt
½ teaspoon baking soda
1 cup quinoa flour
1 teaspoon cream of tartar

SUPER CLEANSER
12 servings
25 minutes

Preheat oven to 350 degrees. In a small bowl add melted butter, maple syrup, egg and yogurt. Blend well. Add flour, soda and cream of tartar into maple mixture and mix thoroughly. Drop by tablespoonfuls onto greased cookie sheet and bake 8–10 minutes, or until lightly brown. Yields 2 dozen cookies.

Deep Cleansers may substitute sprouted spelt flour for quinoa flour.

Meringue Cookies

4 large room temperature egg whites
½ cup maple sugar

SUPER CLEANSER
12 servings
1 hour 30 minutes

Preheat oven to 225 degrees. In a mixing bowl, beat egg whites until stiff, add sugar 1 tablespoon at a time, continuing to beat until sugar dissolves and soft peaks form when beaters are lifted. Lay parchment on cooking sheet. Put spoonfuls of meringue on parchment paper. Bake for 20 minutes until edges are slightly browned. Turn off oven, leave door closed and let cookies remain in oven until hardened, about 6 hours. Yield about 3 dozen cookies.

✑ *These cookies can be baked in the evening and left in the turned off oven overnight. For a carob meringue cookie, add 4 tablespoons carob powder after blending sugar. For a nut cookie, fold in ½ cup chopped nuts after blending sugar.*

Quinoa Cranberry Crisps

2 cups softened butter
3 cups maple sugar
2 teaspoons vanilla extract
2 large eggs
3 cups sprouted spelt flour
2 teaspoons baking soda
2 teaspoons cinnamon
3 cups quinoa flakes
2 cups chopped dried cranberries

DEEP CLEANSER
24 servings
45 minutes

Preheat oven 350 degrees. In a large bowl, cream butter, sugar and vanilla until light and fluffy. Add eggs one at a time, beating well with each addition. In a separate bowl, combine flour, baking soda, and cinnamon. Gradually stir into sugar mixture. Then fold in quinoa flakes and cranberries. Drop rounded spoonfuls onto greased cookie sheet and bake 10–12 minutes. Yields about 4 dozen.

Poppy Seed Crackers

¼ cup poppy seeds
1½ cups sprouted spelt flour
½ teaspoon salt
½ teaspoon baking powder
4 tablespoons butter
1½ tablespoons Yogurt Cheese or kefir cheese,
  plus water to dilute cheese

DEEP CLEANSER
4 servings
40 minutes

Preheat oven to 350 degrees. Put seeds, flour, salt and baking powder in the bowl of a stand-up mixer. Cut the butter into pieces and add to the bowl. Mix on low until the butter resembles coarse meal. In a glass measuring cup, add the Yogurt Cheese and enough water to make ½ cup. Add the yogurt mixture to the flour and mix until the dough is formed. Wrap the dough in plastic wrap and refrigerate 10 minutes. Divide the dough in half. On a lightly floured surface, roll out one piece of dough to a ⅟₁₆-inch thick rectangle. The shape will be slightly irregular. Transfer the dough to an ungreased baking sheet. Repeat with the second piece of dough. Bake until crisp and golden, about 20 minutes. Let cool and break into pieces.

> *Semi-Final Phase may substitute flax seeds for poppy seeds.*

Pumpkin Cookies

⅓ cup butter
1 cup maple sugar
½ cup canned pumpkin (or fresh cooked)
2 large egg whites
2 tablespoons water
½ teaspoon vanilla extract
1¼ cups quinoa flour
½ teaspoon baking powder
½ teaspoon cinnamon
¼ teaspoon salt
¼ teaspoon allspice or pumpkin pie spice

SUPER CLEANSER
12 servings
40 minutes

Preheat oven to 350 degrees. In a mixer bowl, cream butter and sugar. Add pumpkin, egg whites, water and vanilla; mix well. In a separate bowl, mix flour, baking powder, salt, cinnamon, and allspice; add to pumpkin mixture. Drop cookies by tablespoonfuls onto a well-greased cookie sheet and bake about 10–12 minutes. Yields about 3 dozen cookies.

> *Phase Two Diet and beyond may add ½ cup of raisins to batter.*

Quinoa Flake Cookies

6 tablespoons softened butter
2 cups maple syrup
1 large egg
2 large egg whites
2 teaspoons vanilla
4 cups quinoa flour
1 cup quinoa flakes
1 cup chopped dates (optional)

SUPER CLEANSER

18 servings

1 hour 20 minutes

Preheat oven to 325 degrees. Cream together butter and syrup. Beat in the egg, egg whites, and vanilla. Then add the flour and flakes. Mix in the dates. Drop in small spoonfuls onto greased cookie sheet, flatten with a fork. Bake 18–20 minutes.

↶ *Recipe makes approximately 6 dozen 2-inch cookies. Cookies can be frozen. Apricots can be substituted for dates.*

Quinoa "Oatmeal" Cookies

½ cup softened butter
1 cup maple sugar
1 large egg
1 teaspoon vanilla extract
1 tablespoon water
¾ cup quinoa flour
1 cup quinoa flakes
½ teaspoon baking soda
½ teaspoon baking powder
¼ teaspoon salt
½ cup dried cranberries

SUPER CLEANSER

12 servings

30 minutes

Preheat oven to 350 degrees. Using an electric mixer, cream butter and sugar. Add egg, vanilla, and water, mix well. In a separate bowl, combine flour, flakes, soda, powder, and salt. Add flour mixture to sugar and beat until combined. Mix in cranberries. Drop by tablespoonfuls onto greased cookie sheet and bake 10 minutes or until lightly browned. Yields about 2 dozen.

↶ *Deep Cleansers and beyond may substitute 1 cup sprouted spelt flour for quinoa flour. Phase Two may use raisins instead of cranberries.*

Quinoa Cookies

2 large eggs, at room temperature
3 large egg whites, at room temperature
1 teaspoon vanilla extract
1 teaspoon ground cinnamon
½ teaspoon salt
1 teaspoon baking powder
1 cup maple sugar
2¾ cup quinoa flakes
⅓ cup quinoa flour

SUPER CLEANSER
3 dozen cookies
40 minutes

Preheat oven to 350 degrees. Lightly grease two baking sheets. Combine the eggs, egg whites, vanilla, cinnamon, salt, baking powder, and sugar in the bowl of an electric mixer. Beat at high speed until doubled in volume. Using a spatula, fold in the flakes and flour. Drop by tablespoonfuls onto baking sheets 1-inch apart. Bake 8–10 minutes until lightly browned. Immediately remove cookies from baking sheets, cool and serve.

Wheat Thin Crackers

1½ cups sprouted wheat flour
½ cup sprouted spelt flour
½ teaspoon salt
1½ teaspoons onion or garlic powder
½ cup butter
paprika

DEEP CLEANSER
12 servings
1 hour

Preheat oven to 425 degrees. In a medium bowl, combine flours, salt, and seasoning. Cut in the butter with a pastry cutter or two knives until mixture resembles coarse crumbs. Add 6–8 tablespoons of water, or more as needed until dough sticks together when pressed. Divide dough in two and place between two sheets of waxed paper. Roll each piece of dough out as thin as possible, about ⅛-inch thick. Remove the top layer of wax paper and flip dough onto baking sheet. Cut into 1 × 1-inch squares and prick with tines of a fork. Lightly salt the tops and dust with paprika if desired. Bake 8–10 minutes, or until lightly browned, removing crackers around the edge if they brown too fast. Cool and serve. Store in air tight container.

↩ *For variation, add cayenne pepper, thyme, dill, green chili flakes or a combination of seasonings.*

Sprouted Graham Crackers

2 cups sprouted wheat flour
1 cup quinoa flour
1 teaspoon arrowroot
½ teaspoon salt
1 rounded teaspoon cinnamon
2½ teaspoons baking powder
¾ cup softened butter
¼ cup maple syrup
1 cup maple sugar
1 teaspoon vanilla extract
⅛–¼ cup water

DEEP CLEANSER
12 servings
1 hour 45 minutes

In a medium bowl, combine flours, arrowroot, salt, cinnamon, and baking powder. In a large bowl, mix butter, syrup, sugar, and vanilla. Add the dry ingredients alternately with the water, using just enough moisture to form the batter into a dough ball. Cover with plastic wrap and refrigerate for at least 1 hour. Preheat oven to 325 degrees. Lightly grease two cookie sheets. Divide dough in half, putting each half between two sheets of waxed paper. Roll out to rectangle about ⅛-inch thick. Remove the top layer of waxed paper and transfer dough to prepared cookie sheet by turning dough side down. If needed, the dough can still be rolled on the cookie sheet before removing the waxed paper. If crackers are being used for crumbs, edges can be left jagged. For a square cracker, cut rolled dough into 3-inch squares and repeat rolling out process with trimmings. Repeat with other half of dough. Prick each square with a fork 6 times to create 3 lines across each cracker. Bake 25–30 minutes. Remove the crackers around the edge if they get too brown. Yields twenty-four 3-inch square crackers.

Chapter 7

Sources

The variety of sources assembled here will assist in your discovery of natural foods. A natural foods retail store is the ideal source for obtaining items for the diet. The staff is usually experienced and familiar with the products and willing to special order items for their customers.

Hopefully, these sources will serve as a springboard for obtaining more information about natural products. Inquire about retail stores, co-ops, and farmers markets that exist in your immediate area or surrounding region.

For your convenience, make a copy of the Shopping List for the week of menus you are about to begin and take it along to the store. Even though you might not buy all the ingredients at that time, it is good to start locating them.

Always read the labels and ask questions about the food source and growing methods of the products you buy. Check the expiration date on packages and consider the shelf life of a product and *how long* it has been sitting on the shelf!

There are sources listed for foods such as maple syrup, honey, meats and fruits, but it is always better to purchase these items from a local grower when possible. Remember, the source of the river is the beginning of its course. May your journey to discover natural foods and their benefits be an enlightened one.

Just a reminder that the telephone numbers starting with the prefix 800, 888 and 877 are toll-free calls.

The following sources are listed in order of the food categories outlined in the diet.

PRODUCTS

FRUITS

ALBERTS ORGANICS
Box 624, 200 Eagle Court, Bridgeport, NJ 08014
609 241-9090 / Fax 609 241-9676
Organic produce which varies with the seasons

ORGANIC VALLEY/CROPP COOPERATIVE
507 W. Main Street, La Farge, WI 54639
608 625-2602 / Fax 608 625-2666
E-MAIL: organicvalley@mwt.net /
   www.organicvalley.com
Organic produce which varies with the seasons

■ Both of these sources are excellent companies, but the best organic produce would be those picked fresh or bought at a local market.

DRIED FRUITS

GENESEE NATURAL FOODS
290 Gold Road, Genesee, PA 16923
814 228-3200 / Fax 814 228-3638
Full line of organic and unsulphured dried fruit

NOW FOODS
550 Mitchell Road, Glendale Heights, IL 60139-2581
800 999-8069 or 630 545-9000 /
   Fax 800 886-1945 or 630 545-9075
E-MAIL: nowvitamin@aol.com /
   www.nowvitamins.com
Unsulphured, dried apples, unsweetened apricots, banana chips, unsweetened coconut and raisins

TIMBER CREST FARMS
4791 Dry Creek Road, Heraldsburg, CA 95448
707 433-8251 / Fax 707 433-8255
Full line of unshulphured, dried fruit; Sonoma brand dried tomatoes

LAKEWOOD PRODUCTS
Miami, FL 33242-0708
305 324-5900
Pure cranberry juice and black cherry juice

FROZEN FRUITS

CASCADIAN FARMS
719 Metcalf Street, Sedro Woolley, WA 98284-1456
800 869-7105 or 360 855-0100 / Fax 360 855-0444
E-MAIL: danl@cfarm.com / www.cfarm.com
Organic fruits: blackberries, blueberries, raspberries, and strawberries

TREE OF LIFE MIDWEST
225 Daniels Way, Bloomington, IN 47404-9772
800 999-4200 / Fax 800 603-1881
www.treeoflife.com
Organic frozen fruits: blueberries, raspberries, and strawberries

JUICES

AFTER THE FALL PRODUCTS, INC.
1700 Clark road, Havre De Grace, MD 21078
800 544-9857 or 410 939-1403 / Fax 410 939-6263
Organic apple juice

KNUDSEN & SONS, INC.
Box 369, Chico, CA 95927-0369
916 899-5000 / Fax 916 891-6397
Pure cranberry juice and black cherry juice

SANTA CRUZ ORGANICS
Speedway Avenue, Chico, CA 95927
530 899-5000 / Fax 530 891-6397
Organic apricot nectar

VEGETABLES

ALBERTS ORGANICS
Box 624, 200 Eagle Court, Bridgeport, NJ 08014
609 241-9090 / Fax 609 241-9676
Organic produce which varies with the seasons

ARROWHEAD MILLS
Box 2059, Hereford, TX 79045
806 364-0730 / Fax 806 364-8242
Corn flakes, puffed corn, white and yellow corn grits, cornmeal (blue, hi-lysine, yellow, and white)

BARBARA'S BAKERY, INC.
3900 Cypress Drive, Petaluma, CA 94954
707 765-2273 / Fax 707 765-2929
Barbara's Amazing Bakes (corn/quinoa baked corn chips): Lightly Salted, Blue Corn, and Quinoa

CASCADIAN FARMS
719 Metcalf Street, Sedro Woolley, WA 98284-1456
800 869-7105 or 360 855-0100 / Fax 360 855-0444
E-MAIL: danl@cfarm.com/
www.cfarm.com
Organic frozen vegetables: sweet corn, green beans, peas, peas and carrots, potatoes, spinach, and winter squash

EREWHON (U.S. MILLS)
200 Reservoir Street, Needham, MA 02194-3146
800 422-1125 or 781 444-0440 / Fax 781 444-3411
Organic corn flakes and organic kamut flakes

GARDEN OF EATIN'

5300 Santa Monica Blvd., Los Angeles, CA 90029
800 333-5244 / Fax 213 462-3268
California Bakes (baked corn chips) and blue and yellow tortillas

GRAINFIELD'S (WEETABIX CO.)

20 Cameron Street, Clinton, MA 01510
800 334-5809
Corn flakes (corn and malt syrup) and toasted oats. Raisin Bran and Crispy Rice for later in the diet

GREY OWL FOODS

510 SE 11th Street, Grand Rapids, MN 55744-3951
800 527-0172 or 218 327-2281 / Fax 218 327-2283
E-MAIL: gofgr@uslink.net
Organic wild rice and organic Canadian wild rice

INDIAN HARVEST

Box 428, Beemidji, MN 56619-0428
800 752-8588
http://www.indiaharvest.com
Wild rice

MRS. LEEPER'S PASTA

12455 Kerran Street, #200, Poway, CA 92064
619 486-1101 / Fax 619 486-5115
Corn pasta

ORGANIC VALLEY/CROPP COOPERATIVE

507 W. Main Street, La Farge, WI 54639
608 625-2602 / Fax 608 625-2666
E-MAIL: organicvalley@mwt.net /
   www.organicvalley.com
Organic produce which varies with the seasons

MODERN PRODUCTS/FEARN NATURAL FOODS

6425 W. Executive Drive, Thiensville, WI 53092
800 877-8935 or 414 352-3333 / Fax 414 352-4478
All natural vegetable broth

PACIFIC GRAIN PRODUCTS

PO Box 2060, Woodland, CA 95776
800 333-0110 / Fax 209 276-2936
Nutty corn cereal (corn and honey)

SANTA CRUZ CHIPS COMPANY

PO Box 1153, Boulder Creek, CA 95006
530 899-5000 / Fax 530 891-6397
Baked blue corn chips

TREE OF LIFE MIDWEST

225 Daniels Way, Bloomington, IN 47404-9772
800 999-4200 / Fax 800 603-1881
www.treeoflife.com
Organic frozen vegetables: corn, green beans, spinach, French fries, and peas

DAIRY PRODUCTS

ALTA DENA CERTIFIED DAIRY

17637 E. Valley, City of Industry, CA 91744
800 535-1369 ext. 404 / Fax 626 854-4287
Yogurt and kefir cheese

BODY ECOLOGY

1266 W. Paces Ferry Road #505, Atlanta, GA 30327
800 478-3842 or 404 266-2156
Kefir and kefir cheese

BROWN COW WEST CORPORATION

3810 Delta Fair Blvd., Antioch, CA 94509-4008
510 757-9209 / Fax 510 757-9160/
E-MAIL: jenniferw@browncowfarm.com /
   www.browncowfarm.com
Yogurt

CABOT CREAMERY COOPERATIVE, INC.

Box 128, Cabot Vermont 05647-0128
800 639-4301 ext. 160 or 802 563-2231 /
   Fax 802 563-2604 /
E-MAIL: cabot@plainfieldbypass.com /
   www.cabotcheese.com
Butter

HAWTHORNE VALLEY FARM

327 Rt. 21C, Ghent, NY 12075
518 672-4465 / Fax 518 672-4887
Organic bio-dynamic yogurt (plain and vanilla)

HORIZON ORGANIC DAIRY
7490 Clubhouse Road, Suite 103, Boulder, CO
    80301-3720
888 494-3020 or 303 530-2711 / Fax 303 530-2714
E-MAIL: markr@horizon.com /
    www.horizonorganic.com
Yogurt, organic sour cream, organic butter, organic
cottage cheese, organic cream cheese, and eggs

LIFEWAY FOODS, INC
7625 Austin Avenue, Skokie, IL 60077-2602
847 967-1010 / Fax 847 967-6558
Lowfat and fat-free kefir

ORGANIC VALLEY
159 E. Main Street, La Farge, WI 54639-8677
608 625-2602 or 503 285-8279 /
    Fax 608 625-2600 or 503 289-4179
E-MAIL: pacgreen@teleport.com
Organic butter and organic cottage cheese

THE ORGANIC COW OF VERMONT
Box 55, Tunbridge, VT 05077-0055
802 685-3123, ext. 110 / Fax 802 685-4332
Organic butter, organic cottage cheese, and organic
sour cream

PURITY FARMS GHEE
14635 Westcreek Road, Sedalia, OH 80135-9605
800 568-4433 or 303 647-2368 / Fax 303 647-9875
Ghee

STONEYFIELD FARM YOGURT
10 Burton Drive, Londonerry, NH 03053
603 437-4040 / Fax 603 437-7594
Organic yogurt

WHITE WAVE INC.
1990 N. 57 Court, Boulder, CO 80301
800 488-9283 or 303 443-3470 / Fax 303 443-3952
www.whitewave.com
Baked tofu, organic tofu, and tempeh

YO'GOURMET (VMC CORP)
Box 3195, Weehawken, NJ 07087-8152
800 863-5606 / Fax 201 863-3137
E-MAIL: vmc.corp@mciinternet.com
Yogurt starter

MEATS

ORGANIC VALLEY/CROPP COOPERATIVE
507 W. Main Street, La Farge, WI 54639
608 625-2602 / Fax 608 625-2666
E-MAIL: organicvalley@mwt.net /
    www.organicvalley.com
Organic poultry

SHELTON'S POULTRY, INC.
204 Loranne Ave., Pomona Ca. 91767-5798
800 5411833 or 909 623-4361 / Fax 909 623-0634
E-MAIL: turkbaron@sheltons.com
Chicken and turkey franks, whole turkeys, and turkey
patties

NUTS AND SEEDS

ARROWHEAD MILLS
110 South Lawton Street, Hereford, TX 79045
800 740-0730 or 806 364-0730 / Fax 806 364-8242
Organic amaranth, organic pearl barley, organic toasted
buckwheat, organic flaxseeds, organic millet, organic
quinoa, whole organic rye, and organic sesame seeds

ONCE AGAIN NUT BUTTER, INC.
12 South State Street, Nunda, NY 14517-0429
888 800-8075 or 716 468-2535 / Fax 716 468-5995
E-MAIL: oanb@servtech.com
Hazelnut butter

BOB'S RED MILL NATURAL FOODS
5209 SE International Way
Milwaukie, OR 97222
800 553-2258 or 503 654-3215 / Fax, 503 653 1339
E-MAIL: dennis@bobsredmill/
www.bobsredmill.com
Flax seed and meal, corn flour

INDIAN HARVEST
Box 428, Beemidji, MN 56619-0428
800 752-8588
http://www.indiaharvest.com
Seeds and beans

MARANATHA NATURAL FOODS
The Nut Butter Company
PO Box 1046, Ashland, OR 97520
800 299-0048 / Fax 541 488-3369
Almond and cashew butter

NEW ENGLAND NATURAL BAKERS
203 Long Plain Road
South Deerfield, MA 01373-9640
800 910-2884 or 413 665-8599 / 508 422-6981 /
    Fax 413 665-8416
E-MAIL: nenbi@aol.com
Whole almonds, tamari almonds, and sunflower seeds

NOW FOODS
800 999-8069 / Fax, 800 886-1045
E-MAIL: nowvitamins@aol.com /
    www.nowvitamins.com
*Sprouting seeds: alfalfa, red clover, five bean mix
(azuki, lentils, red and green mung and soybeans),
fenugreek seeds, mung beans, radish seeds, and sprout
mix (clover, alfalfa, fenugreek and radish)*
    *Nuts and seeds: almonds, cashews, pecans, pine nuts,
pistachios, pumpkin seeds, sesame, sunflower, and
walnuts*

SPROUTED BREAD, FLOUR, AND PASTA

ESSENTIAL EATING SPROUTED FLOUR COMPANY
P.O. Box 125, Torreon, NM 87061
877 384-0337 / Fax 866 870-0776
E-MAIL: foodproducts@creatingheaven.net /
    www.creatingheaven.net
*Certified organic—sprouted spelt flour, Sprouted
Cream of Spelt Cereal, sprouted wheat flour,
sprouted rye flour, and quinoa flour*

ALVARADO STREET BAKERY
500 Martin Avenue, Rohnert Park, CA 94928-2047
707 585-3293 / Fax 707 585-8954
E-MAIL: alvaradost@aol.com
*Sprouted sourdough bread, sprouted whole wheat
bread, and sprouted rye bread*

ARROWHEAD MILLS
10 South Lawton Street, Hereford, TX 79045
800 749-0730 or 806 364-0730 / Fax 806 364-8242
*Flours: hi-lysine, blue and yellow organic cornmeal,
organic barley, organic oats, organic whole rye, organic
spelt, and vital wheat gluten*

THE BAKER'S CATALOG
P.O. Box 876, Norwich, VT 05055-0876
800 827-6836
Lora Brody's Bread Dough Enhancer and tapioca flour

BERLIN NATURAL BAKERY
PO Box 311, Berlin, OH 44610-0311
800 837-5334 or 330 893-2734 / Fax 800 837-5334
Sprouted spelt bread

CASADOS FARMS
Box 852, San Juan Pueblo, NM 87566
505 852-2433 or 505 753-8180
Sprouted wheat flour (panocha flour)

ENER-G FOODS, INC.
Box 84487, Seattle, WA 98124-5787
800 331-5222 or 206 767-6660 / Fax 206 764-3398
Tapioca flour

FOOD FOR LIFE BAKING CO., INC.
2991 Doherty Street, Corona, CA 91719-5811
800 797-5090 / Fax 909 279-1784
E-MAIL: info@food-for-life.com /
  www.food-for-life.com
*Breads: Ezekiel 4:9 Sprouted (regular, low-sodium,
and sesame), 7 Grain Sprouted, Cinnamon Raisin,
California Raisin, Organic Ezekeil 4:9 Cinnamon
Raisin, and Sprouted Whole Wheat*

LORA BRODY'S
302 Highland Avenue, West Newton, MA 02165
617 262-6212 or 617 928-1005 /
  Fax 617 266-3997 or 617 558-5383
E-MAIL: blanche007@aol.com
Bread Dough Enhancer and Sourdough Enhancer

NATURE BAKE
1170 NE 63rd Street, Portland, OR 97213
503 335-8077 / Fax 503 335-0677
*Organic Honey Sprouted Bread, Buttermilk
Multigrain Bread
    These breads are available at all Wild Oats/
Natures Fresh stores, Food Front, Peoples Co-op, and
Fred Meyer Nutrition Centers in Oregon, Southern
Washington, and Alaska*

NATURE'S PATH AND MANNA
7453 Progress Way, Delta, B.C. V4G 1E8 Canada
604 940-0505 / Fax 604 940-0522
*Sprouted 9-Grain Bread, and Sprouted 9-Grain
Sesame Bread
    Manna bread varieties: Carrot Raisin, Sunseed,
Carrot Raisin Rye, Whole Rye, Fruit and Nut, Whole
Wheat, Millet Rice, Sunspelt, and Multi Grain Oat Bran*

NOW FOODS
550 Mitchell Road, Glendale Heights, IL
  60139-2581
800 999-8069 or 630 545-9000 /
  Fax 800 886-1945 or 630 545-9075
E-MAIL: nowvitamin@aol.com /
  www.nowvitamins.com
*Corn flour, tapioca flour, corn grits, flax seed and meal,
quinoa grain and flour*

OASIS BREADS
440 Venture Street, Escondido, CA 92029
760 747-7390 / www.oasisbreads.com
*Sprouted 7 Grain Bread, Sprouted Wheat Bread,
Flourless Sprouted Rye Bread, Sunflower Seed,
California Fruit Loaf, Oat Bran, Raisin Oat Bran,
Salt Free 7 Grain, and Sprouted Kashi*

QUINOA CORPORATION
24248 Crenshaw Blvd. #220, Torrance, CA
  90505-5340
310 530-8666 / Fax 310 530-8764
E-MAIL: quinoacorp@aol.com
*Pastas: Elbows, Rotelle, Rotini, Pagoda (red pepper and
dried spinach), Spaghetti, and Veggie Curls*

SHILOH FARMS
Box 97, Sulphur Springs, AR 72768
800 362-6832 or 501 298-3297 / Fax 501 298-3359
E-MAIL: shilohf@nwark.com / www.users.nwark.com
Corn flour

QUINOA PRODUCTS

ARROWHEAD MILLS
10 South Lawton Street, Hereford, TX 79045
800 749-0730 or 806 364-0730 / Fax 806 364-8242
Whole grain quinoa and quinoa flour

EDEN FOODS
701 Tecumseh Road, Clenton, MI 49236
800 248-0320 or 517 456-7424 /
  Fax 517 456-6075
Whole quinoa grain

QUINOA CORPORATION
24248 Crenshaw Blvd. #220, Torrance, CA
  90505-5340
310 530-8666 / Fax 310 530-8764
E-MAIL: quinoacorp@aol.com
*Ancient Harvest: organic quinoa grain, organic quinoa
flour and organic quinoa flakes, polenta pasta*

NATURAL GRAINS

PACIFIC GRAIN PRODUCTS
PO Box 2060, Woodland, CA 95576
800 333-0110 / 916 662-6074
Nutty corn cereal, puffs, and crackers available in several flavors

PURITY FOODS, INC.
2871 W. Jolly Road, Okemos, MI 48864
800 437-5539 or 517 351-9231 /
   Fax 517 351-9391 /
E-MAIL: purityfood@voyager.net /
   www.elm-intl.com/purity.htm
Spelt flour products, Delta Fiber Flakes (made from sugar beet fiber), and white and whole spelt flours

RUDOLPH'S SPECIALTY BAKERIES, LTD.
390 Alliance Avenue, Toronto, ON. Canada
   M6N2H8
416 763-4315
E-MAIL: rudolph@rudolphsbreads.com /
   www.rudolphsbreads.com
100% organic rye bread

RYVITA
Shaffer, Clarke and Co.
3 Parkland Drive, Damien, CT 06820-3639
800 431-2959 or 203 655-3555
Ryvita crackers (rye flour crackers): Tasty Dark Rye and Tasty Light Rye

SWEETENERS

Maple Syrup Products

AMERICAN SPOON FOODS
PO Box 566, Petosky, Michigan 49770
888 735-6700 / Fax 800 647-2512
www.spoon.com
Maple Cream and Pumpkin Butter made with maple sugar; Catalog and Stores

BASCOM MAPLE FARMS, INC.
Box 137, Alstead, NH 03602
800 835-6361
Maple syrup, maple cream, maple sugar and maple powder

CALENDARS SUGAR HOUSE
RD #2 Box 174, Thompson, PA 18465-9666
570 727-2982
Maple syrup, maple cream, maple candies, and granulated maple sugar
   This is my supplier. They have the best maple syrup and sugar!

COOMBS VERMONT GOURMET
Box 186, Jacksonville, VT 05342-0186
888 266-6271 or 802 368-2513 / Fax 802 368-2516
E-MAIL: vtmaple@sover.net
Maple syrup, honey, maple candies, organic molasses, and organic cane sugar

LOCH'S MAPLE
RR#1 Box 177A,
Springville, PA 18844
570 965-2679
E-MAIL: maple4u@epix.net / www.lochsmaple.com

UPCOUNTRY NATURALS OF VERMONT
167 Portland Street, St. Johnsbury, VT 05819-2047
800 241-1039 or 802 748-5141 / Fax 802 748-9647
Maple syrup

VOLKER FAMILY APIARY
R. R. #3 Box 25, Wyalusing, PA 18853
570 746-3152
Maple syrup

Natural Sweeteners and Sweet Alternatives

ARROWHEAD MILLS
10 South Lawton Street, Hereford, TX 79045
800 749-0730 or 806 364-0730 / Fax 806 364-8242
Sorghum molasses

BODY ECOLOGY
1266 W. Paces Ferry Road #505, Atlanta, GA 30327
800 478-3842 or 404 266-2156
White stevia powder (considered a dietary supplement by the FDA)

FRUITSOURCE PRODUCTS/SUNSPIRE
2114 Adams Avenue, San Leandro, CA 94577-1010
510 569-9731 or 510 568-4948
Brown rice syrup

LUNDBURG FAMILY FARMS
Box 369, Richvale, CA 95974-0369
530 882-4551 / Fax 530 882-4500
www.lundberg.com
Organic brown rice syrup

NOW FOODS
550 Mitchell Road, Glendale Heights, IL
    60139-2581
800 999-8069 or 630 545-9000 /
    Fax 800 886-1945 or 630 545-9075
E-MAIL: nowvitamin@aol.com /
    www.nowvitamins.com
Barley malt powder, date sugar, maple sugar, sucanat, cane juice powder, comb honey and stevia (considered a dietary supplement by the FDA)

PLANTATION MOLASSES
Allied Old English
100 Markley Street, Port Reading, NJ 07064-1897
800 225-0122 or 732 636-2060 / Fax 732 636-2538
Blackstrap molasses

REALLY RAW HONEY, INC.
1301 S. Baylis Street, Ste. 225, Baltimore, MD
    21224-5237
800 732-5729 or 410 675-7233 / Fax 410 675-7411
www.reallyrawhoney.com
Raw honey

SILVER FOREST NATURAL FOODS
RR #2 Box 105-A, Genessee, PA 16923-9802
814 228-3205 / Fax 814 228-3638
Blackstrap molasses, malt syrups, sorghum molasses, and brown rice syrup

SUZANNE'S SPECIALTIES
PO Box 5179, Somerset, NJ 08875
800 762-2135
Barley malt syrup, rice syrup and cane juice

T AND A GOURMET
Box 5179, Somerset, NJ 08875
800 762-2135 / Fax 732 545-4226
Rice syrup, fruit jams, and syrups

WHOLESOME FOODS
Box 2860, Daytona Beach, FL 32120-4708
904 258-4708 / Fax 904 947-4708
E-MAIL: info@wholesomefoods.com /
    www.holesomefoods.com
Organic molasses, organic cane syrup, sucanat, and cane juice syrup

OILS

THE HAIN FOOD GROUP
50 Charles Lindgergh Blvd., Uniondale, NY 11553
800 434-4246 or 516 237-6200 / Fax 516 237-6240
Extra virgin olive oil

LIFESTAR INTERNATIONAL, INC.
301 Vermont Street, San Francisco, CA 94103
800 858-7477
Salute Sante' grape seed oil

SIGGS
Importd by Atlantique
140 Sylvan Avenue, Englewood Cliffs, NJ
    07632-2502
201m947-1000 / Fax 201 947-7667
Grape seed oil

SPECTRUM NATURALS, INC.
133 Copeland Street, Petaluma, CA 94952-3181
800 995-2705 or 707 778-8900 / Fax 707 765-1026
E-MAIL: spectrumnaturals@netdex.com
Organic extra virgin olive oil

SOY PRODUCTS

EDEN FOODS
701 Tecumseh Road, Clinton, MI 49236
800 248-0320 or 517 456-7424 / Fax 517 456-6075
Organic tamari and organic miso

FEARN NATURAL FOODS
Division of Modern Products, Inc
Mequon, WI 53092
800 877-8935
Soy powder and liquid lecithin

HERBS AND SPICES

FRONTIER COOPERATIVE HERBS
Box 299, Norway, IA 52318-0299
800 669-3275 or 319 227-7996 / Fax 319 227-7966
E-MAIL: info@frontierherb.com /
    www.frontierherb.com
Herbs, spices, organic coffee, and green/black teas

REAL SALT
Redmond Minerals, Inc.
Redmond, UT 84562
800 367-7258
Real salt (shaker)

DESOUZA'S INTERNATIONAL, INC.
Box 395, Beaumont, CA 92223-0395
800 373-5171 or 909 849-5172 / Fax 909 849-1348
www.desouzas.com
Solar sea salt

PENZEYS, LTD.
P. O. Box 933, Muskego, Wisconsin 53150
414 679-7207 / Fax 414 679-7878
Over 250 spices and seasonings; Catalog

THE BAKER'S CATALOG
P. O. Box 876, Norwich, Vermont 05055-0876
800 827-6836
Herbs, yeast, Lora Brody's Bread Dough Enhancer, sea salt, and vanilla

SPECIAL ITEMS

ALVITA HERBAL TEAS, A TWINLAB DIVISION
600 Quality Ddrive #E, American Fork, UT
    84003-3302
800 258-4828 or 801 756-9700 / Fax 801 763-0789
Large variety of medicinal teas in both bags and bulk, including Herbal Remeteas

CAFE ALTURA ORGANIC COMPANY
760 E. Santa Maria Street, Santa Paula, CA
    93060-3634
800 526-8328 or 805 933-3027 / Fax 805 933-9367
E-MAIL: cafealtura@worldnet.att.net /
    www.cafealtura.com
Organic coffee

DISTANT LANDS COFFEE ROASTER
13081 State Hwy. 64 West, Tyler, TX 75704-9493
800 346-5459
Organic coffee

EDEN FOODS
701 Tecumseh Road, Clinton, MI 49236
800 248-0320 or 517 456-7424 / Fax 517 456-6075
Kudzu root, sea salt (with and without iodine), and Japanese teas

FIRST COLONY COFFEE & TEA COMPANY, INC.
Box 11005, Norfolk, VA 23517
800 446-8555 / Fax 717 623-2391
Organic coffee

FOLLOW YOUR HEART
Earth Island
7848 Alabama Avenue, Canoga park, CA 91304
818 347-9946
Vegenaise (mayonnaise made with grape seed oil)

UNIVERSAL FOOD CORPORATION
Red Star Yeast & Products
433 E. Michigan Street, Milwaukee, WI 53202
800 558-9892 or 414 347-3832 /
   Fax 414 347-4789
Active dry, baking, and nutritional yeast

KAL
1500 Kearns Blvd., Suite B-200, Park City, UT
   84068
435 655-6000 / Fax 435 655-9820
Nutritional yeast

TRADITIONAL MEDICINALS
4515 Ross Road, Sebastopol, CA 95472
707 823-8911 / Fax 707 823-1599
Offers a large variety of herbal remedial teas

VINEGAR-FREE SALSA

GARDEN OF EATIN', INC.
5300 Santa Monica Blvd. Los Angeles, CA 90029
800 333-5244 / Fax 213 462-3268
Great Garlic and Hot Habanero

GARDEN VALLEY NATURALS
Organic Food Products, Inc.
1333 Marsten Rd, Burlingame, CA 94010
800 579-5569 or 415 579-5565
Vinegar-free salsa

MUIR GLEN ORGANIC TOMATO PRODUCTS
424 N. 7th Street, Sacramento, CA 95814-0210
800 832-6345 or 916 557-0900 / Fax 916 557-0903
www.muirglen.com
Vinegar-free salsa

ESSENTIAL EATING BAKERIES

SIMPLE KNEADS BAKERY
227 B. South Elm Street, Greensboro NC 27401
336 370-4446
E-MAIL: simple_kneads@msn.com
Specializing in muffins, cookies and breads made with Essential Eating organic sprouted flours. Call or e-mail for brochure. Mail order available.

VISION'S SOWN
2530 W. Finch Street, 3rd Floor, Chicago IL 60645
773 973-2261
E-MAIL: visionsownabc@yahoo.com
Specializing in sprouted baked goods made with Essential Eating organic sprouted flours. Call or e-mail for product and price list. Mail order available. Custom orders welcome.

EQUIPMENT

THE BAKER'S CATALOG
P. O. Box 876, Norwich, VT 05055-0876.
800 827-6836
Baking equipment, bread machines, grain mills, and Donvier Wave Yogurt Strainer; Catalog

CHAMPION JUICER
Nutritional Resources, Inc.
302 E. Winona Avenue, Warsaw, IN 46580
800 867-7353 / Fax 219 267-2614
www.nutritionalresources.com
Champion Juicer

COOKING.COM
800 663-8810
Donvier Wave Yogurt Strainers, Item #110326

EXCALIBUR PRODUCTS
A Division of KBI
6083 Power Inn Road, Sacramento, CA 95824
916 381-4254
www.excaliburdehydrator.com
Excellent food dehydrator

HEALTHWISE
13659 Victory Blvd., Van Nuys, CA 91401
800 942-3262
Juicers, dehydrators, yogurt makers, bread machines, grain mills, steamers, and sprouters

INNER BALANCE
360 Interlocken Blvd., Suite 300, Broomfield, CO
   80021-3440
800 482-3608 / Fax 800 456-1139
Yogurt maker and vegetable steamer

JOHNNY'S SELECTED SEEDS
Foss Hill Road, Albion Maine 04910
207 437-4357 /
   Fax 800 437-4290 or 207 437-2165
"Bioset" Seed Sprouter; Catalog of seeds for sprouting

KRUPS NORTH AMERICA, INC.
P. O. Box 3900
Peoria, IL 61612
800 526-5377
La Glaciere ice cream and frozen dessert maker

MIRACLE EXCLUSIVES, INC.
64 Seaview Blvd., Port Washington, NY 11050
800 645-6360
E-MAIL: miracle-exc@juno.com
Juicers

OMEGA PRODUCTS
Harrisburg, PA 17111-4523
717 561-1105 / Fax 717 561-1298
E-MAIL: omegaus@aol.com
Juicers

QUALITY HEALTH PRODUCTS, INC.
922-A Black Diamond Way, Lodi, CA 95240
800 826-4148 (outside CA) 800 521-5455 (in CA)
Excalibur dehydrators, yogurt makers, and bread machines

SPROUTAMO CORP.
Box 17, Lake Mills, WI 53551
920 648-3853 / Fax 920 648-2115
Easysprout sprouter

THE SPROUT HOUSE
17267 Sundance Drive, Romona, CA 92065
800 777-6887 / Fax 760 788-7979
www.sprouthouse.com
Sproutman's Sprout Bag

WILLIAM-SONOMA
Box 7456, San Francisco, CA 94120-7456
800 541-2233
Food processors, yogurt makers and ice cream makers (for frozen treats); Catalog

SUPPLEMENTS

This book expresses the importance of supplements in todays diet, but does not explain which supplements to take, the dosage, or length of time required to restore health. For an excellent source, description and explanation for the supplements to complement *Essential Eating, A Cookbook* refer to *Creating Heaven Through Your Plate* By Shelley Summers, Warm Snow Publishing. 800 235-6570. *www.2gohealth.com/creatingheaven.htm.*

FOOD MARKETS

When shopping for healthful food, patronize your local health food stores, natural food markets, farmers markets and co-ops. Three great food chains are listed below. Check for stores in your area.

WEGMANS

1500 Brooks Avenue, Rochester, NY 14603
800 934-6267 (800-wegmans)
For information and online shopping:
    www.wegmans.com

Stores are located in New York, New Jersey, and Pennsylvania.

In their full-service grocery stores they feature organic produce and a Nature's Marketplace section stocked with natural, healthful foods including beverages, frozen foods, and nutritional supplements.

WHOLE FOODS MARKET, INC.

601 North Lamar, Suite 300 Austin, TX 78703
512 477-4455 / Fax 512 477-1069
For information and online shopping:
    www.wholepeople.com

Stores are operated under the following names: Whole Foods Market, Bread And Circus, Fresh Fields, Wellspring Grocery, Nature's Heartland.

They offer a full-service, whole foods grocery store with an extensive selection of natural and organic foods. Stores also feature bakery and deli sections.

WILD OATS MARKETS, INC.

3375 Mitchell Lane, Boulder, CO 80301
303 440-5220
E-MAIL: info @wildoats.com
For information and online shopping:
    www.wildoats.com

Stores are operated under a family of trade names including Wild Oats Community Markets, Alfalfa's Markets, Capers Markets, Oasis Fine Foods, Sunshine Grocery, Uptown Whole Foods, Beans, Grains And Things, Henry's Marketplace, Ideal Market, Food For Thought, Nature's Northwest, Sun Harvest, and Vitamin Expo. 110 stores in 22 states and British Columbia, Canada.

An extensive selection of natural and gourmet food products featuring organic and locally grown produce, chemical and preservative free groceries, hormone and antibiotic-free meats, cruelty-free body care and eco-household products.

FRESHLIFE

Whole Foods Supermarket
2300 East Third Street, Williamsport, PA 17701
888 371-LIFE (5433)/570 322-8280
www.freshlife.com
E-MAIL: *barb@freshlife.com*

Your one stop mail order location for the products listed in Essential Eating. They offer an extensive selection of organic produce, quinoa products, sprouted flours and maple products available for mail order.

Appendix

Food Categories

Foods fall into different digestive categories. The following foods are grouped based on how they digest in the body.

FRUITS

Fruits can be fresh, dried, cooked, canned or juiced. They digest by fermenting in the intestines; this process is accelerated by enzymes that speed up the fermenting.

apples
apricots
avocados
bananas
berries:
   blackberries
   blueberries
   gooseberries
   raspberries
   strawberries
cherries

citrus:
   grapefruits
   lemons
   limes
   oranges
   pineapples
   tangelos
   tangerines
coconuts
cold-pressed
   coffee extract
currants

dates
figs
grapes
guavas
kiwis
mangoes
melons:
   cantaloupes
   crenshaws
   honeydews
   muskmelons
   watermelons

nectarines
papaya
peaches
pears
persimmons
plums
quinoa
   can combine with fruit
rhubarb

VEGETABLES

Like fruits, vegetables basically ferment in the intestines, a process accelerated by additional enzymes.

agar-agar
arrowroot
artichokes
asparagus
beans:
   green
   lima
   sprouted
beets
broccoli
brussel sprouts
bok choy
cabbage
capers
carrots

cauliflower
celeriac
celery
chard
chives
collards
corn
cornmeal
cranberries
cucumbers
edamame
eggplant
endive
fennel
garlic

greens:
   arugula
   beet greens
   chicory
   corn salad
   dandelion
   escarole
   radicchio
   turnip greens
   watercress
horseradish
Jerusalem
  artichoke
jicama
kale
kohlrabi

leeks
lettuce
mushrooms
mustard greens
okra
olives
parsnip
peas:
   green
   snap
   snow
peppers:
   chili
   green/red/
   yellow/
   jalapeno

poppy seeds
potatoes:
  white
  colored
  sweet
pumpkins
radishes
rutabaga
salisfy
scallions

seaweeds
shallots
sorrel
spinach
onions
sprouted:
  beans
  grains
  legumes

squash, summer:
  crookneck
  patty pan
  zucchini
squash, winter:
  acorn
  banana
  butternut
  delicata
  hubbard
  spaghetti

tapioca
tomatillo
tomatoes
turnips
wild rice
yams

HERBS, SPICES, EXTRACTS AND TEAS

Cooking Herbs

anise
basil
bay leaves
caraway
cardamom
cayenne
celery seed
chervil
chili powder

chives
cilantro
cream of tartar
cumin
curry powder
dill
fennel
garlic powder
lovage

marjoram
mint
mustards:
  powdered
  seed
onion powder
oregano
paprika
parsley

pepper
rosemary
sage
salt
savory
sorrel
tarragon
thyme
turmeric

Spices

allspice
cinnamon
cloves
coriander
ginger
mace
nutmeg

Old Bay
  Seasoning
pumpkin pie
  spice
saffron
tandoori
wasabi powder

Extracts

almond
anise
coconut
lemon

orange
peppermint
root beer
vanilla

Teas

black teas
catnip
chamomile
green teas

lavender
lemon balm
peppermint
spearmint

These foods need hydrochloric acid in the stomach to digest properly.

Meats

bear	elk	organ meats	rabbit
beef	goat	pheasant	turkey
buffalo	goose	pork	veal (beef)
chicken	lamb	quail	venison
duck	moose		

Fish

cod	maui-maui	trout
hailbut	salmon	tuna
orange roughy	sole	

Dairy

buttermilk	eggs	milk:	sour cream
cheeses:	goat cheese	*cow*	yogurt
hard	kefir	*goat*	yogurt cheese
soft	kefir cheese		
cottage cheese			
cream cheese			

Nuts and Seeds

almonds	filberts	peanuts	pumpkin seeds
black walnuts	hazelnuts	pecans	sesame seeds
Brazil nuts	hickory	pine nuts	sunflower seeds
cashews	macadamia	pistachios	walnuts
chestnuts			

Miscellaneous

brewer's yeast
carob powder
nutritional yeast

STARCHES

Starches are foods that need pancreatic enzymes to properly digest. Carbohydrates, unlike starches, are foods that quickly turn into digestible sugars, so they include fruits, vegetables and starches. Because of the "don't combine starches with proteins" rule, it is important to differentiate between carbohydrates and starches.

amaranth	oats	teff	triticale
barley	rice	tempeh	unsprouted beans and legumes
buckwheat	rye	tofu	
couscous	soy cheeses	textured vegetable products (TVP)	
kamut	soy powders		wheat
millet	spelt		

SWEETENERS

These are all the natural sugars.

Blackstrap molasses	date sugar	malt syrup	rice syrup
cane syrups:	fructose	barley malt syrup	rice bran syrup
granulated cane juice sucanat	sorghum molasses	honey	stevia (an additive)
	maple syrup	maple sugar	

OILS

Oils and fats require bile, a soap-like substance, from the liver and gallbladder to digest properly.

almond oil	grape seed oil	peanut oil	soybean oil
butter	mayonnaise	safflower oil	soy margarine
canola oil	olive oil	sesame oil	sunflower oil
corn oil			

SPECIAL FOODS

alcohol	brewer's yeast	coffee	nutritional yeast
baking powder	carob powder	gluten	vinegar
baking soda	chocolate	mayonnaise	yeast

Foods containing vinegar:

catsup	mayonnaise	pickles	Worcestershire sauce
chutneys	mustard	salsa	
horseradish		Tabasco sauce	

FOOD DIGESTION CHART:
EASIEST TO HARDEST

FOOD CATEGORY	FOODS (EASIEST TO DIGEST→ → → → → → HARDEST TO DIGEST)
FRUITS:	dates (easiest), apricots, avocados, bananas, figs, coconut, persimmons, berries, cherries, currants, grapes, peaches, nectarines, melons, plums, rhubarb, citrus, pineapple, kiwi, papaya, guava, mangoes, apples and pears, "cold-pressed" coffee (hardest)
VEGETABLES:	Vegetables on the Super Cleanser YES Foods list (easiest), all other vegetables, and then: potatoes, corn, cabbage family: broccoli, cauliflower, cabbages, Brussel sprouts, kale, collard greens and kohlrabi (hardest)
DAIRY PRODUCTS:	yogurt (easiest), eggs, kefir, kefir cheese, sour cream, cream cheese, cottage cheese, buttermilk, cheese, milk (hardest)
MEATS:	fish (easiest), chicken, turkey, other poultry, lamb, rabbit, all beef, pork, bear, buffalo, elk, goat, moose, veal, venison, shellfish (clams, conch, crabs, langoustines, lobster, mussels, shrimp) (hardest)
NUTS AND SEEDS:	hazelnuts (easiest), almonds, cashews, pecans, macadamia, pistachios, Brazil nuts, all other nuts and seeds (hardest)
GRAINS:	quinoa (easiest), 100% sprouted sourdough bread, 100% sprouted grains and their flours and pastas, panocha, oats, millet, rice, rye, amaranth, barley, buckwheat, couscous, teff, triticale, kamut, spelt, wheat (hardest)
SWEETENERS:	100% maple syrup and granulated maple sugar (easiest), stevia, malt syrups, rice and bran syrups, blackstrap molasses, sorghum molasses, cane and date sugars, fructose, honey, all other sweeteners (hardest)
OILS:	butter (easiest), olive oil, grape seed oil, corn oil, safflower oil, soybean oil, other oils, vegetable shortening, margarine (hardest)
SOY PRODUCTS:	miso (easiest), tamari, tempeh, tofu, all other soy products, soy powder (hardest)
BEANS AND LEGUMES:	sprouted beans and legumes (easiest), unsprouted beans and legumes (hardest)
HERBS AND SPICES:	cooking herbs and spices (easiest), medicinal herbs and spices (excluding goldenseal), herbal teas, green and black teas (hardest)
SPECIAL ITEMS:	carob powder (easiest), vinegar, most condiments, coffee, tequila, brewer's and nutritional yeast, other alcohols, mayonnaise, chocolate (hardest)

Refer to the YES/NO Foods lists to see how this chart applies to each phase of the diet.

FRUIT AND VEGETABLE SEASONS

Listed below are the growing locations and harvest seasons for various produce. The particular fruits and vegetables listed are available at most grocery stores. Refer to this harvest season guide for availability when purchasing produce locally. Remember, fresh is best.

FRUITS	HARVEST SEASON
APPLES	September through November but available almost year round due to cold storage
APRICOTS	Mid-May through August for domestic crop; December through January for New Zealand and Chilean fruit
AVOCADOS	All year; best prices April through August
BANANAS	All year; sporadic for specialty bananas
BERRIES:	
BLACKBERRIES	Different varieties from late May through mid-September from California and Oregon
BLUEBERRIES	Mid-April through September from different parts of the United States and Canada
RASPBERRIES	Different varieties from California, Oregon, and Washington mid-May through December
RED CURRANTS	Early July to early August mostly from Oregon
STRAWBERRIES	January through July in California; November through January from Florida, Mexico, and New Zealand
CHERRIES	Mid-May through July; peak in June from Washington and New York; Mid-November through January from New Zealand
CITRUS:	
GRAPEFRUIT	All year; peak January through June from California and Florida
ORANGES	Different varieties all year from California, Florida, and Arizona
DATES	All year; best selection November through March
FIGS	August through early September from California
GRAPES	All year; June through December from California; January through June from Mexico and Chile
GUAVAS	August through October
KIWI	November through April from California; March through October from New Zealand
MANGOES	Sporadically January through August; peak in June
MELONS	Different varieties all year; peak August through September from California, Mexico, New Zealand, and Chile

NECTARINES	Mid-June through mid-September; peak in July
PAPAYA	May through July and October through November mostly from Hawaii
PASSION FRUIT	March through September
PEACHES	Mid-May through mid-October; peak in August
PEARS	All year; peak August through December
PERSIMMONS	September through mid-December; peak mid-October through November
PINEAPPLES	All year; peak April through June from Hawaii, Honduras, Mexico, the Dominican Republic, and Costa Rica
PLUMS	Mid-May through mid-October; peak in August
POMEGRANATES	September through December; peak in October from California
PRICKLY PEARS	August through December from Washington, Oregon, and Arizona
QUINCES	September through November; peak in October
RHUBARB	February through June from Washington, Michigan, and California

VEGETABLES	HARVEST SEASON
ARTICHOKES	Peak season March through mid-May from California
ASPARAGUS	Peak season March through June
BEANS:	
SNAP	Peak season May through August
FRESH SHELLED	April through June for fava beans; July through September for lima beans; August through October for cranberry beans
BEETS	Peak season June through October
BROCCOLI	Peak season October through April
BRUSSEL SPROUTS	Peak season September through February mostly from California
CABBAGE	All year
CARROTS	All year
CAULIFLOWER	Peak season late autumn through spring
CELERY	All year
CELERY ROOT	October through April
CRANBERRIES	September through November

CORN	May through September
CUCUMBERS	All year; peak season June through September
EGGPLANT	Peak season July through October
FENNEL	October through April
GARLIC	All year; largest harvest July through September
GREENS	January through April for collards, dandelion greens, kale, and mustard greens; June through October for beet greens; October through March for turnip greens; July through October for chard; salad greens are available year round; September through May for Belgian endive; August through December for chicory and escarole
JICAMA	Peak season October through June
LEEKS	October through May
MUSHROOMS	All year; seasonal availability for specialty mushrooms
OKRA	Peak season June through August
ONIONS	All year (chives, greens onions or scallions, and shallots)
PARSNIPS	November through March
PEAS	April through August for green and shell peas; February through June for edible-pod peas
PEPPERS	All year for some varieties; peak July through October for most types
POTATOES	All year
RADISHES	All year
RUTABAGAS	Peak season October through March
SORREL	July through October
SPINACH	All year
SPROUTS	All year
SQUASH:	
SUMMER	Peak season July through September
WINTER	Peak season September through March for most kinds
SPAGHETTI	August through February
SUNCHOKES	October through April
SWEET POTATOES	All year; peak October through March
TOMATOES	Peak season July through September
TURNIPS	October through March
YAMS	All year; peak October through March

Bibliography

The nutritional philosophies of this book are expanded upon
and reflected on in the following publication:

Creating Heaven Through Your Plate, by Shelley Summers,
1999, 2000 (Warm Snow Publishers, P. O. Box 75, Torreon,
NM 87061) To order this book call 800-235-6570 or visit
www.2gohealth.com/creatingheaven.htm.

For those interested in information and locations for Essential Eating Cooking Classes™ or Essential Eating™ food
products visit essentialeating.com or creatingheaven.net.

Glossary

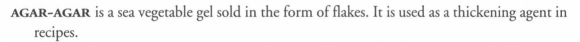

AGAR-AGAR is a sea vegetable gel sold in the form of flakes. It is used as a thickening agent in recipes.

AMARANTH is a grain that is sweet and peppery in taste and crunchy in texture. It is a good source of iron and calcium. It is reintroduced in the Semi-Final Phase of the diet.

ARAME is sea vegetable high in vitamins and minerals. It has a sweet and mild sun-dried flavor.

ARROWROOT is obtained from the root of a West Indian plant. It is sold in powder form and can be exchanged measure for measure for cornstarch as a thickening agent in recipes.

ARUGULA is also known as rocket salad. The young leaves have a tangy spiciness. The leaves are added to salads and sauces, or steamed.

AVOCADO is a fruit with a green skin and a soft lighter green flesh interior. When selecting an avocado, they must be firm but ripe. Too soft and they are overripe and too hard and they are immature. If possible, buy them firm and let them ripen at home. Place in a paper bag on the counter to ripen faster. Hass avocado has a rough dark skin and is the most popular.

BARLEY is a grain. When the outer hull, which is not easily digestible, is removed the grain is called pearled barley.

BARLEY MALT SYRUP is a highly concentrated sweetener. 'Malt' or 'malted' indicates a grain that has been sprouted. Malt, short for maltose, is the sugar in grains. Barley malt is boiled until it achieves a dark color and a strong sweet taste. Malt syrups vary in color and sweetness. It is added back into the diet in Phase Two.

BLACKSTRAP MOLASSES is a sweetener. It has a high content of minerals and iron and is easily assimilated. This molasses comes from sugar cane. In Phase Three when backstrap molasses is added to the diet, any cane juice or granulated cane juice is also included.

BRAN SYRUP (see rice bran syrup)

BREWER'S YEAST is the yeast by-product of brewing beer. It comes in powder, flakes, or tablets. It is a great source of B vitamins, among other nutrients, and it digests like a protein.

BROTH is the water in which vegetables, fish, or chicken have been boiled. Another word for broth is stock. Homemade broth is preferred, but canned organic is permissible.

BUCKWHEAT is a grain but not a member of the wheat family. It is used in the form of kasha or buckwheat groats.

CANE SUGAR or table sugar is also known as sucrose or turbinado. For a healthier choice see 100% evaporated cane juice or sucanat. Nutritionally, there is a vast difference between eating refined sucrose in desserts and eating natural sugar in fruits and vegetables. Foods made with refined sucrose often contain little more than sugar, whereas fruits and vegetables provide fiber, vitamins and minerals in addition to sucrose.

CARBOHYDRATES are foods that quickly turn into digestible sugars. They include fruits, vegetables, and starches. For a list of carbohydrates refer to the Appendix.

CAROB POWDER is ground dried carob bean pods. Carob beans come from the pod of an evergreen tree that grows in the Mediterranean. The beans are finely ground into a powder. Roasted and raw carob powders are available. Raw carob powder tastes sweeter and lighter than the roasted variety, but it is harder to find.

CELERIAC or celery root is an old-fashioned vegetable with an ugly-duckling appearance and a wonderful swan flavor. It varies in size from as small as an apple to as large as a small cantaloupe. It has a brownish, bumpy exterior and a taste between fresh celery and parsley. Enjoy it in season from fall to early spring.

CELERY ROOT (see celeriac)

CHARD is a leafy vegetable available in both red and green varieties, although both taste the same. It is from the beet family and is delicious in salads.

CHICORY, also known as French endive, is a leafy vegetable. It is wonderful in salads and its root can be roasted. Its root is used as a coffee substitute without the caffeine.

COCONUT can be purchased dried and shredded or fresh. When splitting a whole fresh coconut, hold the shell in your hand, not a hard surface, then tap with a hammer until the shell cracks open. Remove the white meat from the brown shell, cut into chunks and refrigerate. Fresh coconut may also be shredded and dried. See Raw Coconut under Recipes.

COLD-PRESSED COFFEE is the most wonderful coffee you will ever taste. A coffee extract is made from coffee beans. Coffee made this way is digested as a fruit by the body, since coffee beans are the fruit of a tree. See the recipe for Cold-Pressed Coffee in Chapter 6.

COLD-PRESSED OILS are those that are not subjected to temperatures higher than 110 degrees. Most oils are extracted from foods using high heat which destroys most of the nutrients in them. Use only "cold-pressed" oils in these recipes.

CONCENTRATED OILS require a lot of handling and processing to make, and therefore, are not in their natural form. The more you process any food, the more difficult it becomes to digest and utilize. See Olive Oil, Grape seed Oil, Corn Oil, Safflower Oil and, Soybean Oil.

CORN FLOUR is corn ground into flour.

CORN PASTA is made from corn flour. It is available in spaghetti and elbow styles. See Sources.

CORNMEAL can be white, yellow or blue in color due to the different varieties of corn. Cornmeal varies in texture from brand to brand. For these recipes, use a slightly finer ground cornmeal.

CORN SALAD is a green leafy vegetable.

COUSCOUS is a finer ground version of bulgur (wheat.) This tiny pasta which originates in North Africa is versatile and cooks in a few minutes.

DANDELION is an herb. The greens are often added to salads or steamed for a few minutes. It has cleansing properties and aids digestion.

DATE SUGAR is made from granulated, dehydrated dates. It is sweeter than white sugar and contains more nutrients, especially iron. Two-thirds cup of date sugar can be substituted for one cup of white sugar.

DIGESTIVE ENZYMES are enzymes in the stomach that aid in the digestion of proteins, carbohydrates, and fats.

DULSE is a red colored sea vegetable that grows off the coast of Maine, Canada, Oregon and Alaska. It has a soft and chewy texture with a salty seafood taste. It can be eaten out of the bag or soaked in water for a few minutes to soften. Dulse is high in iron, protein, A and B vitamins. Dulse can also be dried in a dehydrator and crumbled on quinoa, soups, pasta or popcorn.

EGGS refer to large chicken eggs, preferably from free-range flocks that are not given hormones or chemicals. Such eggs are available from natural health food stores. Eggs are one of the easiest proteins to digest.

ENDIVE (see chicory)

ESCAROLE is a vegetable that is similar to leaf lettuce and is related to endive. It is popular as a salad addition.

EVAPORATED CANE JUICE is a sweetener made from 100% evaporated sugar cane juice that is organically grown. It is naturally brown in color and possesses all the nutrients from the sugar cane. See sucanat.

FENNEL is a light green vegetable with a bulb-like base, celery-shaped stalks and feathery dill-like tops. Fennel has a delicate, anise-like flavor. It is in season from fall through spring.

FRUCTOSE is a semi-processed sugar made from fruit. It is used as a sweetener in baking and cooking. It returns to the diet in the Semi-Final Phase.

GLUTEN is the vegetable protein of grains that will stretch and hold air bubbles. It is derived from wheat flour with the starch removed. Because of its ability to stretch and hold air bubbles, wheat gluten, or vital wheat gluten, is often added to bread recipes to enhance their texture and consistency. Lora Brody's Bread Dough Enhancer is sold in the bakery section of grocery stores and may be substituted for gluten in recipes. See Sources.

GOLDENSEAL is a root herb that acts like a natural antibiotic. The problem with goldenseal according to Shelley Summers, *Creating Heaven Through Your Plate,* Warm Snow Publishing, is that besides its terrible taste, it also acts as natural insulin in the body, thereby lowering blood sugar levels. Because of the high levels of hypoglycemia seen in bodies, she suggests avoiding the use of goldenseal. Instead use bee propolis, a product that bees gather from plants, which also acts as a natural antibiotic. Bee propolis is also used as an antiviral, antifungal, antimicrobial and antibacterial. Propolis is resinous, which makes it hard for the body to digest; so take it in extract or tincture form.

GRAPE SEED OIL is a flavorful, natural oil made from grape seeds. This oil has a pale, leafy color and a slightly nutty flavor. Two benefits of using grape seed oil is the substantial amount of vitamin E it contains and its ability to withstand high temperatures without burning.

GRITS are sometimes called corn grits or hominy grits. Yellow or white in color, they are forms of ground corn. Grits are milled from corn that has been soaked with lime to soften the skins.

HAZELNUTS are often called filberts. They contain high levels of potassium, sulfur, and calcium. They are sold shelled, unshelled or ground into nut butter.

HAZELNUT BUTTER is hazelnuts that have been ground into a nut butter. It is available at most natural foods stores.

HIJIKI is a sea vegetable high in vitamins and minerals. It is tough in the raw state, but softens when cooked.

HONEY, a natural sweetener, is sold in over 300 varieties in the United States alone. Buy locally harvested honey. The floral source determines a honey's taste, which can range from very mild to intense.

HYDROCLORIC ACID or HCL is an enzyme that is vital in breaking down proteins. HCL works most efficiently when used with pepsin, also a stomach secretion. Both are required for the proper absorption of minerals and digestion of proteins.

JERUSALEM ARTICHOKE is a tuber (bulbous, fleshy, underground stem) also known as "sun chokes." This vegetable can be scrubbed, sliced, and stir-fried and does not have to be peeled. It is available October through June.

JICAMA, pronounced hee-keh-maa, is brown and thin-skinned, ranging in size from less than a pound to six pounds. It has a mild and faintly sweet flavor and its texture is crisp and juicy. Peel jicama prior to eating raw or cooked.

KAMUT is a grain similar to durum wheat. It has a higher protein content than conventional wheat. Kamut has a rich buttery taste and is used to make pasta.

KEFIR is an acidophilus culture, and like yogurt is easy to digest. Kefir has the consistency of thick milk.

KEFIR CHEESE is an acidophilus culture, and like yogurt it is easy to digest. Kefir cheese is similar to the consistency of cream cheese with more of a "tangy" taste.

KUDZU ROOT may be used in recipes requiring a thickener.

LECITHIN is found in the body and in certain plants and helps break down cholesterol. Liquid lecithin is thick and sticky until heated. It is an excellent emulsifier. Lecithin adds the thickness and creaminess to recipes that is usually provided by an egg. Liquid lecithin can be used in any of the Basic Diets.

MALT SYRUP is a natural sweetener. 'Malt' or 'malted' indicates a grain that has been sprouted. Malt, short for maltose, is the sugar in grains. Barley malt syrup is a malt syrup. Malt syrups vary in color and sweetness.

MAPLE CANDY is 100% maple syrup cooked and formed into hard candy.

MAPLE CREAM is 100% maple syrup that is cooked into a thick spread that needs to be kept refrigerated to keep its consistency.

MAPLE SUGAR is 100% maple syrup boiled down to a sugar consistency. It is often called granulated maple sugar.

MAPLE SYRUP is a sweet syrup made from the sap of the sugar maple tree.

MILLET is a grain. It is the oldest and one of the most complete proteins, used most often as a tasty cereal. It is reintroduced into the diet in Phase Three.

MISO is fermented soybean paste. The mashed soybeans are aged and cured like cheese. It is used primarily as a seasoning and in the preparation of sauces. Miso paste comes in a variety of flavors and colors, from Blonde to Hatcho. Barley miso is also a wonderful addition to many recipes.

MUSTARD GREENS are a leafy vegetable that is quite pungent. They are often used in salads and have a strong taste.

NORI is a sea vegetable high in vitamins and minerals. Nori grows wild off the coast of Maine and California. It is a good source of protein, B vitamins, vitamin C and E. It is a thin, purplish-black sheet of pressed seaweed, most commonly used in sushi rolls.

NUTRITIONAL YEAST is a yeast grown mostly on molasses. The flavor can vary depending on the growing medium. It is a great source of B vitamins among other nutrients. It digests like a protein.

OLIVE OIL is a concentrated oil made from olives. It is the easiest concentrated oil to digest. The key to good olive oil lies in it's color and aroma. Use organic, extra-virgin olive oil. See "cold-pressed" oils.

OKRA is a vegetable. It is a green colored pod. The smaller pods are the most tender.

PANOCHA is another word for sprouted wheat flour.

POLENTA, either white or yellow in color, is essentially another name for grits or coarse cornmeal.

PORTOBELLO MUSHROOM is a giant-sized mushroom that is a mature crimini mushroom. It has a smooth cap and a dark brown underside. A cousin of the white button mushroom, portobello has a much earthier flavor. Cook portobello whole or slice and grill as a meat replacement. Cooking brings out its hearty flavor.

PROTEINS are foods that need hydrochloric acid in the stomach for proper digestion. They are foods such as dairy, eggs, fish, meats, nuts, and seeds. Yeasts and carob powder also are considered proteins. Proteins are added back into the diet in the Semi-Final Phase. Do not combine proteins with starches as it causes major digestive problems. When proteins and starches are mixed, many toxins are created in the system because one of the foods does not break down. For a complete list of proteins see the Appendix.

QUINOA, pronounced keen-wa, is a small grain that resembles millet (or bird seed) but comes from a herb similar to lambs quarters. It behaves like a grain but digests like a fruit. It cooks in about 15 minutes just like rice. Quinoa also comes in flour and flake form. Quinoa that is too alkaline may cause indigestion—this is easily remedied. To raise the acidity level, cook it in water with a grated lemon rind or a teaspoon of lemon extract. This helps to balance the pH which makes quinoa easily digestible for everyone. Quinoa can be combined with a fruit because it is an herb.

QUINOA FLAKES are another form of quinoa used in place of oatmeal in many of the recipes.

QUINOA FLOUR is quinoa ground into flour.

QUINOA PASTA is made from quinoa flour. It is available in spaghetti, elbow and veggie curls. See Sources.

RADICCHIO is a variety of chicory, having red or red-spotted leaves, that form round or elongated heads. The leaves are often added to salads, but they can also be steamed or seared.

RICE is a grain and digests as a starch. It is reintroduced in Phase Four of the diet.

RICE BRAN SYRUP is a sweetener. The rice is fermented and then boiled until its consistency reaches a thick syrup, much like honey. It is added back into the diet in Phase Two.

RICE MILK is made from rice. Rice Dream is a popular brand name. Remember, rice milk is a starch so you can't use it with protein foods. Try rice milk on oatmeal or to make White Gravy for a rice and vegetable dish.

RICE SYRUP (see rice bran syrup)

RYE is a grain reintroduced in Phase Four of the diet. Make sure to read the label on rye products. Usually, wheat flour is added to rye breads to make them rise as rye doesn't contain any natural gluten. Two great rye products are 100% Rye Bread made by Rudolph's and Tasty Light Rye Crisp Bread made by Ryvita. See Sources.

SAFFLOWER OIL is a concentrated oil high in polyunsaturated fats. Concentrated oils are not natural and are very difficult to digest. It is rich in vitamin C as long as it is a "cold-pressed" oil. It returns to the diet in the Semi-Final Phase.

SHELLFISH is an aquatic animal that has a shell. Lobster, shrimp, clams, mussels, and crabs are all shellfish. The protein structure in shellfish is very hard for the body to break down—hence the many allergies to shellfish.

SORGHUM MOLASSES is a sweetener. Unlike blackstrap molasses it does not come from cane sugar, but from a plant that is related to cane. Its chemical structure is different from cane juice and is more difficult to digest.

SORREL is a green leafy vegetable that is excellent in salads or as a seasoning. Its taste is best described as lightly sour with a lemon flavor.

SOYBEAN OIL is a concentrated oil that is extracted from soybeans. Remember, concentrated oils are not natural and they are difficult to digest. Soy products digest like starches.

SOY CHEESE is cheese made from soybeans. It is lactose free, high in proteins, and is available in the same varieties as regular cheese such as American, Swiss, and many more. Soy cheese digests as a starch and is reintroduced to the diet in the Semi-Final Phase.

SOY FLOUR is made from the soy bean and digests like a starch. The protein content is high and it adds lecithin and B vitamins to foods. It is used in baking and also added to cereals, soups, or stews. Soy products are reintroduced to the diet in the Semi-Final Phase.

SOY MILK is a liquid which is extracted from soybeans and made to taste like milk. It is high in protein and comes in a variety of flavors. Soy products are digested like starches and reintroduced to the diet in the Semi-Final Phase.

SOY POWDER is made by first cooking the soybeans and then grinding them. The consistency is much finer than soy flour because the hulls, which are not a good source of nutrition, are removed. Because of the high processing of soy powders, they take the highest levels of enzymes to break down. For this reason soy powder is always an embellishment to the diet.

SPELT is a grain that contains more B vitamins than any other of the wheat grains. Sprouted spelt flour is recommended as one of the sprouted flours used in these recipes.

SPROUTED CREAM OF SPELT CEREAL is a courser grind of sprouted spelt flour ideally suited for cereal.

SPROUTED BEANS are a simple way to make beans and legumes digestible and delicious. Unsprouted beans and legumes are indigestible. Beans, legumes, lentils and dried peas are notorious gas producers because the human body simply does not have the enzymes needed to digest them. When you sprout beans and legumes, you reverse the vegetable sugars-to-starch process. As the sprouts grow, the starches are converted back into vegetable sugars. Once this process is complete, the body can digest them as a vegetable. See Sprouting Beans in the Recipe Chapter.

SPROUTED FLOUR is made from sprouted grain. Most bodies recognize sprouted flour as a vegetable rather than a starch which requires pancreatic enzymes to digest. Therefore, eating sprouted grains does not stress the pancreas. Sprouted spelt flour, sprouted wheat flour, and sprouted rye flour is available from the Essential Eating Sprouted Flour Company. See Sources.

SPROUTED SOURDOUGH BREAD is bread that is made with sprouted grains. The grains are ground coarsely and used as you would use flour. This bread is easy to digest and tastes great. Available at natural health food stores.

SPROUTED WHEAT FLOUR or panocha (see sprouted flour)

SPROUTED RYE FLOUR (see sprouted flour)

STARCHES are foods that need pancreatic enzymes to digest properly. Carbohydrates, unlike starches, are foods that quickly turn into digestible sugars, such as fruits, vegetables, and starches. When starches are added back into the diet in the Semi-Final Phase they cannot be mixed with proteins. Mixing starches and proteins create toxins in the system because one of the foods does not break down. For a list of starches refer to the Appendix.

STEVIA is a herb that grows in Peru, China, and Brazil. It comes in an extract or white powder form. Considered a food additive by the FDA, stevia extract is extremely sweet and tastes a little like molasses. A drop or two is equal to a spoonful of other sweeteners, yet it will not cause sugar reactions in the bloodstream.

STOCK is water in which vegetables, fish, or chicken is boiled to make a broth. Broth is another word for stock. Homemade stock is preferred but canned organic is permissible.

SUCANAT is a popular brand of granulated cane juice. Sucanat may be used in recipes, in equal measurements, for white refined or brown sugar. It is reintroduced in the Core Diet.

SUPPLEMENTS are comprised of vitamins, nutrients, and herbs. There are many health assets and benefits offered by supplements and their forms are as varied, from capsules to liquids to powders. Their potencies vary thereby affecting their dosages. Supplements compensate for deficiencies in our bodies due to genetics or improper diet. One of the best sources for learning what supplements to take is *Creating Heaven Through Your Plate,* By Shelley Summers, Warm Snow Publishing. See Sources under Supplements.

TAMARI is a natural soy sauce. It is the liquid that results from making miso, a fermented soybean paste. Tamari is fermented to the point that most bodies do not recognize it as a starch. It is one of the easiest soy products to digest.

TAPIOCA is extracted and dried from the root of the cavassa plant in South America. Based on its digestive characteristics, it digests like a vegetable.

TAPIOCA FLOUR is a powdered form of tapioca most often used in dessert recipes. Based on its digestive characteristics, it digests like a vegetable.

TEMPEH, pronounced tem-pay, is a soy product. It is produced by fermenting presoaked and cooked soybeans.

TEFF is a miniscule African grain and is best used as a cereal or mixed with other grains. It is reintroduced into the diet in the Semi-Final Phase.

TEQUILA is an alcohol made from a cactus. Tequila is the easiest alcohol for the body to digest. If and when you do add alcohol to your system, take extra vitamins and minerals to compensate for the nutrients it requires to flush alcohol from the body. Tequila can be added to any of the fruit juices.

TOFU, or bean curd, is made by curdling soybean milk and pressing it into a cake. It has a high protein content and is easily digested. Tofu has no flavor of its own—it assumes the flavor of whatever you cook it with. It is very versatile as a substitute for meat, cheese, and spreads, to name a few. Tofu digests as a starch, so remember to eat it only with other starches, fruits, vegetables, sweeteners, and oils.

TRITICALE is a grain and digests as a starch. It is a cross between rye and wheat and is very high in protein. It is reintroduced in the Semi-Final Phase of the diet.

VEGENAISE is a mayonnaise-like dressing without eggs, dairy products, refined sugars, fillers, or preservatives. Vegenaise can be added to the diet in Phase Three since its main ingredient is grape seed oil.

YOGURT is called "predigested" because the milk molecule is so thoroughly broken down that low levels of HCL and lactose enzymes easily complete the process. Plain yogurt can be used as a milk substitute in many recipes by diluting it to the consistency of milk. To make one cup, spoon three or four tablespoons (depending on the desired thickness) of yogurt into a measuring container and add water to make one cup. Most store brands have sugar (fructose) and starch emulsifiers added, so be sure to read the labels.

YOGURT CHEESE is yogurt that has been drained of most of its liquid. The liquid or whey is discarded producing a cheese with the consistency of cream cheese. Used in dips, salads, and baked goods, yogurt cheese does not overpower a recipe because the strong tasting whey has been strained off.

YOGURT CHEESE STRAINER is a container that strains the whey or liquid out of yogurt leaving Yogurt Cheese. Cheesecloth may also be used, but the yogurt strainer is a wonderful convenience. See Sources.

WASABI is a powdered horseradish that is sold in health food stores and some grocery stores. Just mix it with water to form a paste.

WHEAT GLUTEN (see gluten)

WHOLE FOODS are not processed in any way. They maintain their nutritional properties because they are not separated mechanically or chemically in any way. The natural state is the whole, not parts that are altered for convenience or taste. Whole food maintains its integrity by remaining intact.

WHOLISTIC EATING means conscientiously ingesting whole foods in order to support and discourage disease. It involves making food choices that nourish a person's well-being. Eating wholistically is a philosophy of self-love.

Epilogue

Converting to essential eating can be interesting both physically and mentally. Do what you can and enjoy the process. Remember, no meal is the "last supper," for tomorrow is another eating opportunity. Do not place guilt or shame on yourself for what you eat. Just start over right now making better food choices. Your body is ready. Love yourself. It's easy and you're worth it.

As an experienced Pathwhacker (someone who whacks the often rocky and overgrown path allowing the light to shine the way), I applaud those that have chosen to whack the path toward eating essentially. Collectively, the Essential Eating Pathwhackers are making a difference for themselves and the results are benefiting us all.

Index

G

nut butters, in sandwiches, 123
nut milk, 70, 71
nutritional rules, 28
nutritional value:
  of dehydrated food, 8
  of whole foods, 1, 2
nutritional yeast, 38
  in diet phases, 19–26
nuts:
  in Basic Balancer Diet, 21
  in Core Diet, 27
  in Deep Cleanser Diet, 20
  digestibility of, 27, 32–33, 35
  in Phase Four Diet, 24
  in Phase Three Diet, 23
  in Phase Two Diet, 22
  in Semi-Final Diet, 25
  in Super Cleanser Diet, 19
  see also specific kinds of nuts

O

oats, 33
  wheat flakes as substitute for, 77
oils, 35
  alternatives to, 61
  in Basic Balancer Diet, 21
  in Core Diet, 27
  in Deep Cleanser Diet, 20
  digestibility of, 35
  in Phase Four Diet, 24
  in Phase Three Diet, 23
  in Phase Two Diet, 22
  in Semi-Final Diet, 25
  in Super Cleanser Diet, 19
olives, black, 30
  in Caponata, 175
  Green Bean and Olive Salad, 114
  Olive Rosemary Bread, 96
  Pasta with Olive Mushroom Sauce, 170
  in Tuna Pasta Nicoise, 216
omelets:
  Hash Brown Omelet, 176
  Italian Omelet, 176
  Vegetable Omelet, 186
onions:
  dehydrating, 8
  Eggplant, Tomato and Onion Gratin, 192
  Potato, Onion and Kefir Cheese Frittata, 179
  Roasted Celery Root, Onions and Mushrooms, 198
  in Roasted Root Vegetables, 199
  in Tandoori Chicken Shish-Ka-Bob, 228
orange juice, in Sunrise Shake, 85

oregano, in Lemon Oregano Sea Bass, 216
organic foods, 6
overeating, 3
oyster mushrooms, in Miso Soup, 134

P

pancakes, 109
  Cornmeal Pancakes, 106
  Potato Pancakes, 197
  Pumpkin Pancakes, 110
  Zucchini Pancakes, 205
pancreas:
  and digesting grains, 33
  and fruit eating, 28
panocha flour, 33, 78, 91, 92
parfait:
  Apricot Yogurt Parfait, 236
  Banana Cream Parfait, 238
  Crunch Parfait, 240
parsnips:
  in Roasted Root Vegetables, 199
  in Sweet Root Vegetable Soup, 139
pasta:
  Buttered Noodles, 167
  Pasta Primavera, 172
  Pasta with Olive Mushroom Sauce, 170
  Pasta with Quick Red Sauce, 170
  in Quick Chicken Noodle Soup, 132
  in Tuna Casserole, 217
  Tuna Pasta Nicoise, 216
patties:
  Potato Vegetable Patties, 180
  Veggie Patties, 186
peaches:
  drying, 230
  Peach Juice, 84
pears, and blood sugar level, 29
peas, dried:
  digestibility of, 27, 36
  in Sprouted Pea Soup, 153
  in Sprouted Pea Stew, 154
  sprouting, 147–148
peas, green:
  Curried Quinoa with Zucchini and Peas, 169
  Green Pea Soup, 133
  Green Pea and Quinoa Soup, 133
  in Herbed Mixed Peas, 194
peppers:
  in Caponata, 175
  dehydrating, 8
  prepared ahead of use, 42
  in Quick Gazpacho, 137
  Quinoa Stuffed Peppers, 181
  in Shelley's Chili, 151

RECIPE INDEX

QUICK ORDER FORM

—〰—

To purchase additional copies of Essential Eating, A Cookbook:

INTERNET ORDERS: www.essentialeating.com. Click on Order.

FAX ORDERS: Toll free (888) 267-0605. Fill out and fax this form.

TELEPHONE ORDERS: Call toll free (877) 771-1216.

POSTAL ORDERS: Azure Moon Publishing, P.O. Box 771-10, Waverly, PA 18471, USA.
Telephone: (570) 586-1557. Fill out and send this form.

NAME: _____

ADDRESS: _____

CITY, STATE, ZIP: _____

TELEPHONE: _____

E-MAIL ADDRESS: _____

TITLE	QUANTITY	PRICE
ESSENTIAL EATING, A COOKBOOK	___ × $29.95 US/$44.95 CAN	
PA SALES TAX: Please add 6% for books shipped to Pennsylvania addresses (1.80 per book).		
U.S. SHIPPING AND HANDLING: $5.00 for the first book and $3 for each additional book.		
TOTAL		

PAYMENT IN U.S. FUNDS: ☐ Cheque enclosed, payable to *Azure Moon Publishing*

☐ VISA   ☐ MasterCard

CARD NUMBER: _____

NAME ON CARD: _____ EXP. DATE: ____ /____

Thank you for your order.